W9-BMG-677

JERRY D. SMITH

AN INTRODUCTION TO SCHEME

An Introduction to Scheme

JERRY D. SMITH

University of Tennessee at Chattanooga

PRENTICE HALL
Englewood Cliffs, NJ 07632

Library of Congress Cataloging-in-Publication Data

SMITH, JERRY D.
An introduction to Scheme / Jerry D. Smith,
p. cm.
Bibliography: p.
Includes index.
ISBN 0-13-496712-7
1. SCHEME (Computer program language) I. Title.
QA76.73.S34S65 1988 88-4178
005.13'3–dc19 CIP

Editorial/production supervision: Colleen Brosnan
Cover design: Bruce Kenselaar
Cover photograph: Reginald Wickham
Manufacturing buyer: Mary Noonan

Printed in the United States of America
10 9 8 7 6 5 4 3 2 1

ISBN 0-13-496712-7

Prentice-Hall International (UK) Limited, *London*
Prentice-Hall of Australia Pty. Limited, *Sydney*
Prentice-Hall Canada Inc., *Toronto*
Prentice-Hall Hispanoamericana, S.A., *Mexico*
Prentice-Hall of India Private Limited, *New Delhi*
Prentice-Hall of Japan, Inc., *Tokyo*
Simon & Schuster Asia Pte. Ltd., *Singapore*
Editora Prentice-Hall do Brasil, Ltda., *Rio de Janeiro*

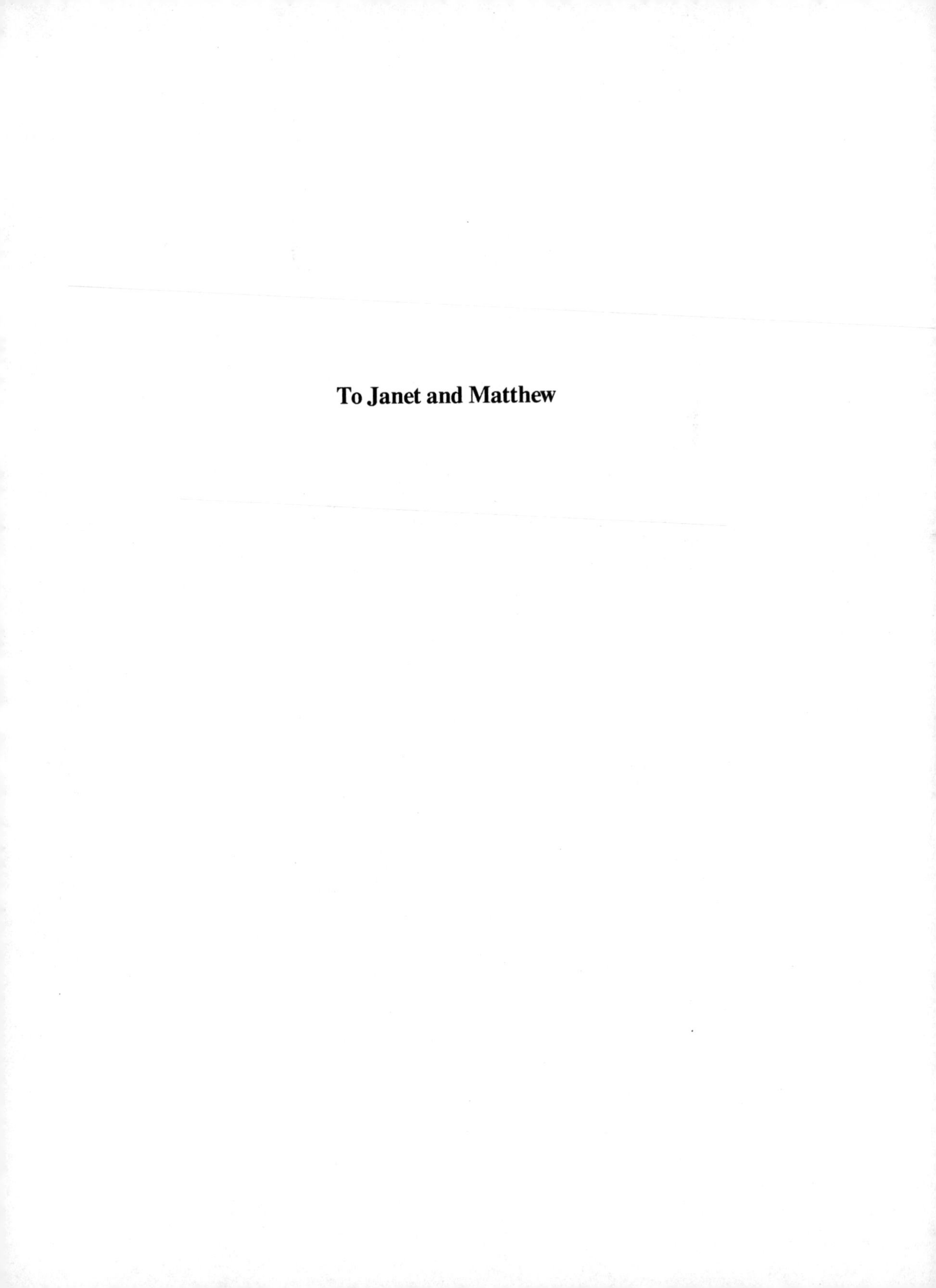

To Janet and Matthew

Contents

Preface

The purpose of this book is to provide an introduction to the Scheme dialect of LISP, a programming language typically used in artificial intelligence (AI) research. The central theme of this text is that Scheme is one of the most versatile programming languages available today, useful for a variety of programming projects. In particular, Scheme's utility is not limited to AI programming projects. Thus, the focus of the text is Scheme programming, and not AI programming. This point is emphasized throughout the text by presenting programming examples derived from traditional computer science applications. The final chapter presents a database application that can be extended to AI, systems software, or file processing applications.

Scheme provides several powerful features that make it an ideal language for systems programming applications. In particular, its provision for control of process continuation and its support for lazy evaluation make Scheme ideal for operating system (OS) development – especially classroom modeling of OS operations. Also, Scheme is an ideal language for prototyping interpreters and compilers. The next to last chapter suggests an interpreter construction project.

A considerable number of Scheme programming examples are presented in this text. Some are very brief and designed to emphasize one aspect of Scheme programming. Others are of moderate length and of two types:

1. utilities/library functions
2. specific implementations of some application

For the first kind of examples, several functions are provided in standard Scheme which, in effect, extend the standard; e.g., functions for string insertion and deletion operations, formatted output, console input, etc. Regarding the second, the final chapter focuses on a mini-database, or file processing, application; another chapter presents a four-function calculator; and the next to last chapter provides a simple version of

Common LISP's **format** function that supports column-formatted, left- or right-justified output, something that is not provided by the Scheme standard.

Implementations of Scheme typically depart radically from the Scheme standard proposed in Rees and Clinger (1986) – primarily in the area of language extensions. In this text we focus on standard Scheme, providing a few of our own extensions – each extension coded in standard Scheme – as mentioned above. This approach should make the text and example programs compatible with most Scheme implementations.

The restriction of discussion primarily to standard Scheme allows us to focus on Scheme and Scheme programming, avoiding potential side discussions of a host of language extensions. Moreover, this enhances the applicability of the text. We feel that this text is most suitable for the following situations:

1. as a text for a one semester course in Scheme (LISP)
2. as a supplement to an AI course
3. as a supplement to an advanced systems programming course
4. as a self-study text on Scheme

This text is not suitable as an introduction to programming. In particular, it assumes that the reader is experienced with at least one high-level programming language. In terms of a computer science curriculum, students should have programming experience in a language such as Pascal, Modula-2, or C, and at least a CS2-level background; i.e., students should have had an introduction to data structures and algorithms, including linked lists, binary trees, and the bubble sort.

Acknowledgments

First, I would like to thank the reviewers for their valuable comments and suggestions.

Next, I would like to recognize the people at Prentice-Hall for their efforts in the development of this text, in particular, my editors Valerie Ashton and Colleen Brosnan.

There are many individuals who have contributed to the development of the Scheme programming language, including Sussman and Steele (1975) and Rees and Clinger (1986); Scheme is an enormous contribution to computer science.

Finally, I would like to acknowledge all of the individuals at Texas Instruments who contributed to the development of TI Scheme and the PC Scheme implementation.

Chapter 1

Overview of Scheme

1.1 Introduction

This chapter provides a brief introduction to and overview of Scheme. Selected aspects of LISP dialects, in general, and Scheme, in particular, are introduced with occasional comparisons to more traditional programming languages. This brief overview of some of Scheme's features should set the stage for later chapters where a more thorough discussion is presented.

In general, each language has advantages and disadvantages with respect to other languages. In our opinion, Scheme is one of the most interesting and most elegant computer programming languages available and is ideal for a variety of applications. Although the intention here is not to present a biased view of one language, Scheme, it is quite difficult to hide our enthusiasm. Moreover, since Scheme is the primary focus of this text, it is only natural to present its most interesting and powerful features.

1.2 Scheme and LISP

LISP is one of the oldest computer programming languages. LISP, which stands for LISt Processing, was developed by Professor John McCarthy in the late 1950s. Although LISP evolved primarily as a support tool for artificial intelligence (AI) research and applications, it is becoming increasingly popular among non-AI programmers. LISP, as a result of this trend and an overall increased interest in AI, is becoming one of the most popular computing languages.

Both LISP and FORTRAN were developed early in the history of computing, yet remain popular for current computing applications. Over the years LISP has been the primary language for symbolic processing, as has FORTRAN for numeric processing.

Although LISP and FORTRAN share this longevity, they have little else in common. FORTRAN has remained popular because of the huge software base (written in FORTRAN) for scientific programming. For example, there are numerous scientific subroutine packages available in FORTRAN that facilitate numeric processing. Ironically, the widespread adoption of FORTRAN for scientific computing has prevented its evolution; it has essentially remained static, with little support for modern programming constructs and techniques.

On the other hand, LISP has enjoyed a dynamic and exciting evolution, chiefly due to its adoption by the academic and research communities. LISP has been used to tackle many difficult programming tasks in AI. As a result, a variety of LISP dialects have been developed and discarded in support of various programming needs. The instability of LISP dialects that would have prevented its commercial adoption in the past has led to the development of modern LISP dialects which incorporate many modern programming constructs, e.g., object-oriented programming, lexical scoping, and so on. Modern LISP programming systems are well acknowledged for their software development support, regardless of the application – data processing, numeric processing, or symbolic processing.

The two most popular LISP dialects to emerge in recent years are Common LISP (Steele, 1984) and Scheme (Sussman and Steele, 1975; Steele and Sussman, 1978; Rees and Clinger, 1986). Common LISP has emerged out of the need for AI researchers to work in a common language, that is, in order to share software. The Common LISP dialect has been very much influenced by previous LISP dialects, and in a sense, is simply a union of various competing LISP dialects, including Scheme. Consequently, it has evolved as a very large language with little personality of its own.

Scheme, on the other hand, while retaining the most popular and enduring features of LISP, was designed as "its own language." As a result, it has evolved as a smaller and more modern dialect of LISP. This size reduction is not a sign of weakness; Scheme offers some of the most powerful programming features available today, such as continuations, engines, proper tail recursion, etc.

There are several benefits that have resulted from Scheme's trimmer physique and support for modern language constructs. One of the most important is its suitability for microcomputer implementation. The number of language primitives described in the language standard (Rees and Clinger, 1986) is significantly less than for Common LISP. Thus, Scheme, like C and Pascal, is an ideal language for modern computing environments where the trend is toward microcomputers and workstations.

1.3 Scheme Programming Environments

In not-so-modern times, programming languages were chiefly categorized as being either interpreter- or compiler-based. BASIC is the classic example of an interpretive language; FORTRAN is a good example of a traditional compiler language. Past approaches to software development have led to certain misconceptions about languages, in particular LISP dialects, that must be addressed here.

In general, an interpreter-based system is one for which there is minimal modification or distillation of the source code prior to execution. That is, each time a program is executed the source code must be re-interpreted before execution. Moreover, this typically means that each time a program loop is executed at least some code interpretation is required prior to a statement's execution. We can view source code along a continuum:

	original source code		intermediate (distilled) code		executable machine code	
———		———		———		———

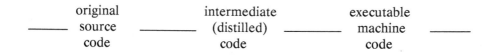

In this case, the original source code may be distilled to some intermediate form, say, when the file of source code is first processed by the interpreter. In order to execute the program, however, the distilled code must continually be converted to the machine code for the host computer.

An extreme case is one where an interpreter uses the original source code as the intermediate code, i.e., performs no transformation to an intermediate form. (This is typically the kind of interpreter written as a programming project in a systems programming course.)

A compiler-based system is one for which there is significantly more transformation of the source code, in some cases, all the way to assembly, object, or executable code for the host computer. Obviously, the latter is appropriate and required for the final stage(s) of software development, in order to produce stand-alone software. Modern compiler-based systems perform code optimization, designed to optimize either space utilization or execution time of the resulting executable code. It is the optimization phase of code compilation that is somewhat a problem during software development, especially during program debugging. Software development is hindered by the time required for each compilation of the source code, and by the dissimilarity between the code written by the programmer and that produced by the compiler.

In the old days, FORTRAN was a compiled language and LISP was an interpreted language. LISP programmers focused primarily on software development for difficult applications, as opposed to producing commercial software. For all of the above reasons, early LISP systems executed slowly compared to those that employed FORTRAN. Moreover, LISP supported (and continues to support) run-time checking of data types, which can slow down an interpreter. There are many circumstances where run-time type checking is especially convenient, and therefore well worth any accompanying slowdown at execution time. There is, however, no inherent reason why LISP code cannot execute efficiently, given a good LISP compiler.

In the traditional sense, an ideal situation is to do program development with an interactive, interpretive system and to produce the final software with a compiler. Some software development systems combine these functions into a single product. In other cases, the programmer must purchase both the interpreter and the compiler separately for a given language, but this may not be a disadvantage.

There is a trend toward (modern) software development systems that provide interactive editing, debugging, and execution of source code. The optimization phase of compilation conflicts with the debugging component of this software, in the sense that the LISP system must either undo the optimization to reconstruct the original source code or inhibit optimization during a debug phase. Regardless of the language, COBOL, C, Scheme, or whatever, systems that support interactive program development have become popular. In this sense, it is inaccurate to think of BASIC as an interpreter language and FORTRAN as a compiler language, even though that has been the tradition.

Traditionally, interactive program development has been most appropriately supported by interpretive development systems. The programmer needs to cycle quickly through editing, debugging, and running the program. Conversion of source code to an interpreted form is quicker than compilation to object code. Again, it is easier for the system to support debugging operations against intermediate code than compiled, object code, for a variety of reasons that are beyond the scope of this text. However, code that must be further interpreted before and during execution will execute more slowly than compiled, executable code.

More recently, in order to strike a balance between ease of program development and program execution speed, software vendors have provided interactive development systems in which the distinction between interpreter and compiler is less clear-cut. Typically, an interactive Scheme system will incorporate a compiler of sorts that can distill, even optimize, the source code as it is provided by the user, significantly enhancing execution speed during program development.

Today's programmers recognize the advantages of systems that support interactive editing and debugging of software. The recent availability of C interpreters and compilers for microcomputers is a good example of this phenomenon. To a large extent, LISP programming systems have provided the impetus for the resurgence of interest in interpreter-like systems.

Throughout this text, interpretive or interpreter-based systems include the latter, more modern systems which incorporate code compilation; typically, the compilation is transparent. The extent to which C, LISP, and PROLOG systems can be labeled as interpreter- or compiler-based is a matter of point of view and terminology, in the sense that source code is typically "compiled" to some "distilled" form and must be "interpreted" in order to execute.

Most of the recent LISP and Scheme implementations support this modern approach to programming. For example, in this text we use PC Scheme from Texas Instruments (Texas Instruments, 1987) for all our programming examples, and we use terminology such as "Scheme does this..." instead of "The interpreter does this..." or "The compiler does that...."

1.4 Standard Scheme

In this text the terminology "standard Scheme" is used, for the sake of convenience, to mean the most recent revision to Scheme, e.g., Rees and Clinger (1986). As the language standard may incorporate minor changes in the future, our "s" in "standard" remains lowercase. In general, there are two approaches to a text such as this: (1) pick a Scheme implementation and use it to its fullest or (2) stay with the language standard mentioned above. This text takes the latter approach overall, with some attention given to the PC Scheme implementation.

We mentioned that Scheme is a relatively small language. Although there are many advantages to small languages, there are some minor disadvantages. For example, standard Scheme provides no built-in functions for reading a line of text from the terminal, and no built-in functions for formatted output. (This can only be considered a disadvantage in the narrowest sense, that is, we have to build our own.) Possibly the most interesting and enjoyable aspect of Scheme programming is that it's so easy to provide these utilities – Scheme is a very extensible language.

1.5 Functions versus Subroutines

One of the greatest strengths of Scheme, its functional nature, can be the most confusing for programmers who are used to traditional languages such as FORTRAN, Pascal, and PL/I. The latter languages support the development of modular programs through the use of two types of subprograms: functions and subroutines. In these languages functions typically return some scalar value, and may be used anywhere that an expression is valid. Subroutines are quite different in that they are treated like a program statement, and data passage (in particular, "output" from the subroutine) occurs through an argument/parameter list. For example, a subroutine parameter can be set up to return the result of multiplying each element of an array by some scalar value – the result/output of the subroutine may be a composite data structure, such as an array. This type of data passage requires support for *call by address* argument/parameter passing.

Scheme, on the other hand, is a "functional" language in the sense that it supports functions only – subroutines are not necessary, or even desirable. Also, Scheme is a list processing (LISP) language; the list data structure is central to Scheme. In the event that multiple data values are to be returned by a Scheme function, the proper technique is to collect them in the form of a list, and then return the list. Scheme always passes arguments to functions using *call by value*. That is, a copy of each argument's value is passed, as opposed to its address in memory. With this technique, there is no danger of inadvertent corruption of variable values in the calling function. The ability to return composite output values in the form of a list makes this approach to argument passing very convenient.

More formally, a function call in Scheme has the structure

```
(<function_name> <argument>...)
```

where **<function_name>** can be either a built-in function (Scheme primitive) or a user-defined function, and **<argument>...** represents zero or more arguments. In general, we stay away from formal specifications in this textbook. See Dybvig (1987) for a more formal and reference-like approach. Also, the latest Scheme language revision (Rees and Clinger, 1986) is a helpful supplement to this text.

Some programmers who are used to subroutine-supporting languages have an initial misconception about LISP because of this provision for functions only. The ability to embed a function call almost anywhere in a program is a powerful feature. The functional nature of Scheme is one of its most distinguishing characteristics. Functions are also addressed later.

1.6 List Processing

Another distinguishing feature of Scheme (LISP) is its facility for list processing. Whereas languages such as C and Pascal require the programmer to write a library of routines for linked list manipulation, Scheme provides a host of language primitives for list processing. In general, the Scheme programmer uses the list as an abstract data type, whereas the Pascal programmer must build such structures and accompanying routines with pointer variables and pointer manipulators.

As mentioned, the list data structure is central to Scheme. A list is formed by enclosing any number of items within matching left and right parentheses. For example, the following are two Scheme lists:

```
(+ 2 34)
(a b c)
```

The first is composed of three items: a plus sign, the number 2, and the number 34. The most likely interpretation of this list is as a function call to the addition operator with two arguments, in which case the value 36 would be returned. Note that Scheme is a *prefix* language, that is, the operator is specified before the operands. There are several advantages to this, most of which are associated with language and programming flexibility. For example, a varying number of arguments is easily accommodated. That is, only one addition operator is needed to sum four numbers:

```
(+ 1 2 3 4)
```

whereas in an infix-based language, such as Pascal, multiple addition operators are required.

All we know about the second list, **(a b c)**, out of context, is that it is composed of three items. But Scheme allows us to define additional mnemonics for primitives. Although it has little mnemonic value, the "a" could represent the primitive "add", that is, the addition operator. In this case, "b" and "c" would most likely represent variables.

1.7 Function Syntax

A Scheme program is composed of one or more functions, and each function is composed of lists (possibly nested). Typically, lists contain either data, variables, or the names of other functions. For example, the following Scheme code defines a function that squares a number:

```
(define (square n) (* n n))
```

The first item is **define**, which is a Scheme keyword that signals the definition of new identifiers, in this case, a function. Scheme syntax prescribes a prefix-like specification. The second item, a list, names the new function and specifies its parameters—in this case, one parameter, **n**. Subsequent items constitute the function body. In this case, **square** is defined to be the multiplication of a number, the argument/parameter, **n**, by itself.

In the previous function there is no need to specify which function is the "main" function and which functions are subordinate; this issue is resolved at execution time. That is, whether or not **square** will be used by itself, or called by some other function, is immaterial at the time of its creation. In this sense, all functions are created equal. Thus, the programmer is free to think about a function's function, and is less burdened by syntax. In contrast, interacting Pascal subprograms must be arranged in the proper order before compilation. Scheme programmers never have to worry about such syntactic issues during program development.

Note that user-defined functions can have a variable number of arguments; they are defined by a syntactic structure which accommodates a varying number of "arguments;" and the function call "(square n)", that is, its usage, is identical to its specification in the call to **define**. Hence, there is a degree of symmetry and consistency in Scheme that is lacking in many other languages.

1.8 ((((((()))))))

Scheme employs parentheses to define the bounds of a list. Although nested parentheses can be cumbersome, most languages have syntax-related language components that can be awkward. Moreover, most Scheme systems provide direct assistance with parentheses balancing.

As mentioned, both data and functions are specified in list form. This has many advantages. One of the most important advantages is that it allows programs to create other programs, and this is an especially powerful feature for AI programming. This power is completely absent from many "syntax-bound" languages, such as C, Pascal, and PL/I, and is not readily appreciated by those new to LISP programming.

1.9 Symbolic Processing

Scheme (LISP) differs from other languages in its facility for working with symbols. In more traditional languages we think of identifiers as symbols. In fact, the term "symbol table" is used for the compiler's temporary array of identifier information. As with other languages, Scheme variables and procedures exist as symbols; but in addition, Scheme provides a facility for processing alternative symbols, namely, symbols that are not assigned a value.

The provision for this type of symbol(ic) processing is tied directly to LISP's origin as an AI support language. In AI applications it is convenient to have a facility for processing symbols like **john**, **mary**, **employee**, **chair**, etc., without having to define a variable before assigning it a value. For example, it is possible to set up something like the following in a Scheme program:

```
'(employee bill engineer 28000)
```

Typically, symbols represent what could be called entities, or objects, and their attributes. However, the term "object" is used in a variety of ways, as we will see in later chapters.

The single quote in the preceding example is essentially a directive to Scheme that the items that follow in the list are to be taken at face value, that is, they are not variable names. Thus, instead of searching an internal Scheme table for the current *value* of some variable **employee**, **employee** is used directly. Symbols are typically indexed internally for rapid look-up. In this way, symbols can be used as a form of nonnumeric constant, in addition to the more traditional string constant.

This kind of "data type" is foreign to, and typically not needed in, languages such as FORTRAN and COBOL. Symbolic processing is explored more fully in later chapters.

1.10 PC Scheme and the Listener

In this introduction to Scheme we use PC Scheme (Texas Instruments, 1987) running on a microcomputer for demonstration purposes. If you are using some other Scheme implementation, or even a mainframe computer, there should be very few incompatibilities. In this text we are primarily interested in standard Scheme, and PC Scheme serves as a vehicle for exploring the standard. Occasionally, it is convenient to provide an example program that uses a PC Scheme primitive, for example, a DOS directory listing. However, most dialects support equivalent primitives, possibly under a different name. Example of Scheme programs that use such PC Scheme primitives are clearly marked.

Scheme, as we mentioned, is an interactive, interpreter-like language. Thus, most Scheme implementations will interact with the user by way of a visual prompt, which signifies that the interpreter is ready to process (interpret) additional commands. This interactive cycle between (user) commands and (system) responses is sometimes called a read-evaluate-print (REP) loop (REPL). Sometimes the component of Scheme that handles this is called the *listener*, or *waiter*.

For example, interaction with your Scheme system might appear as follows:

```
==> (+ 3 2)
5
==> (load "examples.s")
#t
```

```
==> (square 2)
4
```

The arrow simply means "ready." User input is shown to the right of the arrow prompt and Scheme output follows on the next line. Of course, the exact nature of the prompt is of no particular consequence here. Most implementations differ from this in some way. However, since we employ PC Scheme, and its prompt is quite different, a brief example is provided.

The following is a subset of an interaction with PC Scheme:

```
[1] (+ 3 2)
5
[2] (load "examples.s")
OK
[3] (square 2)
4
[4] (%c 1)
(+ 3 2)
[5] (%d 1)
5
[6] (+ (%d 1) (%d 3))
9
[7] (exit)
```

PC Scheme is initiated by typing "pcs" at the operating system prompt. The PC Scheme logo appears first (not shown here) and is followed ultimately by "[1]".

Output from PC Scheme is in uppercase. The first prompt shown is "[1]". The same operations were performed as in the previous, generalized example, plus others. Some Scheme systems may provide a response such as "#t" after loading a file of source code, indicating that all went well. (**#t** is the standard Scheme, Boolean constant for true.) PC Scheme responds: "OK".

Technically, Texas Instruments refers to PC Scheme as an "incremental" compiler, which means that it dynamically compiles Scheme code to a "distilled" form, as necessary. This improves the run-time performance of PC Scheme. We can still think of it as an interpreter, in the sense that it interprets each command that we give it.

In the above dialog, we request the summation of 3 and 2, using Scheme's list notation with the addition operator as the first item, followed by two arguments (prefix form). At prompt [2] Scheme is requested to load a file of Scheme source code, which is processed dynamically: any user-defined functions present in the source code are automatically compiled. One of these user-defined functions, **square**, is used later at prompt [3].

PC Scheme provides a way of referring to previous interactions with Scheme by use of the primitives **%c** and **%d**, hence, the need for prompt numbering. **%c** recalls a previous command to Scheme and **%d** recalls a previous Scheme response, depending on the numeric argument that is provided. For example, at prompt [1], "(+ 3 2)" requests the sum of 3 and 2; the result is 5. At prompt [4], "(%c 1)" recalls the command at prompt [1]. At prompt [6], "(%d 1)" recalls the output, or returned value, from the command at prompt [1], which is 5. Prompt [6] recalls previous Scheme output to compute a sum, returning a value of 9. In general, we do not make programmatic use of the prompt feature; however, the numbering scheme is convenient for discussion purposes.

Exercises

1. In your opinion, what are the advantages and disadvantages of a small language, i.e., a language with a minimum number of language primitives, such as Standard Pascal (ISO, 1980) and standard Scheme (Rees and Clinger, 1986). Consider for example, the following question: With respect to code portability is it better to have a small language that most implementers extend (Scheme), or a large language that many implementers can't fully accommodate (Common LISP)?

2. Do you agree with the comments made in this chapter about interpreters and compilers? Are you aware of interpreters that perform no optimization, compilers that incorporate incremental compilation, compilers that provide little or no program development support, and compilers that do provide extensive development support? Provide a classification of the language software that you've used with respect to such categorizations.

3. Contrast languages that are relatively syntax free, such as Scheme, and languages that are "syntax bound," such as Pascal.

4. Familiarize yourself with the standard Scheme reference document (Rees and Clinger, 1986). Knowledge of its contents is important when attempting to write Scheme programs that are highly portable.

5. At this point you should familiarize yourself with the documentation for your Scheme system. Questions of interest include:

- **a.** Does your system supply an interpreter or a compiler?
- **b.** Does it have a built-in editor?
- **c.** Does it support extensions to standard Scheme?
- **d.** Does it provide operating system interface primitives?

Chapter 2

Scheme Basics

2.1 Introduction

In this chapter we overview basic interaction with Scheme. In particular, we are concerned with the user environment that supports interactive processing, the Scheme listener, and basic Scheme primitives that assist such exploration.

2.2 The Scheme Listener

The command or technique required to initiate Scheme varies from system to system. Once this command is executed, the Scheme prompt should appear, possibly preceded by some logo:

```
Scheme -- An Uncommon LISP -- Version 1.1

==> _
```

At this point, you can communicate directly with the Scheme listener. There are three basic operations that are performed by the listener as part of the interactive cycle:

1. Read – Scheme reads each expression typed by the user.
2. Evaluate – Scheme then evaluates each expression.
3. Print – Scheme prints the result of each evaluation.

The result of such an evaluation is typically the returned value of the highest-level function call. For example, consider the following:

```
[1] (+ 3 2)
5
[2] _
```

Scheme reads the expression, in the form of a list, evaluates the expression, and prints the result, "5". Evaluation involves processing the first item in the list as an operator, or function call, and subsequent items as arguments. In this case, the first item is the Scheme primitive for addition; the arguments are integer constants. Thus, evaluation involves executing the Scheme primitive for addition against two arguments; each constant evaluates to "itself." That is, Scheme reads and converts the character representation of numeric constants to (binary) numeric form. It would be inconceivable to store every possible constant in the universe in a table and then perform a look-up operation to "evaluate" its numeric value – constants are processed "on the spot."

Expressions can involve nested (sub-) expressions. For example:

```
[2] (+ 3 (* 2 4))
11
[3] _
```

In this case, the first item evaluates to the addition operator and the second item to a constant, as before. However, the next argument is an expression, and Scheme must determine its value *before* it can continue with the addition operation. Likewise, the inner expression's evaluation leads to the same kind of activity. The evaluation of the inner expression differs in that the result is not printed; instead, it is returned as the value of the second argument to the outer expression. In this manner the evaluation process may recur. Each time a new (nested) expression is encountered, Scheme must temporarily suspend its previous evaluation activity and take up a new evaluation. i.e., recursive expression evaluation. At the top level, the returned value is simply printed by the listener.

You can view the evaluation process as one in which an evaluation tree is built, each nested expression constituting a subtree. Thus, the following expression

```
[3] (+ (* 2 3) (- 3 (/ 10 2)))
4
[4] _
```

corresponds to the expression tree given in Figure 2.1. A postorder traversal yields the final value, 4. (See the exercises for an explanation.)

In some cases, the evaluation of an expression leads to side effects. Consider the following.

```
[4] (square 2)

[VM ERROR encountered!] Variable not defined in current
environment
SQUARE
```

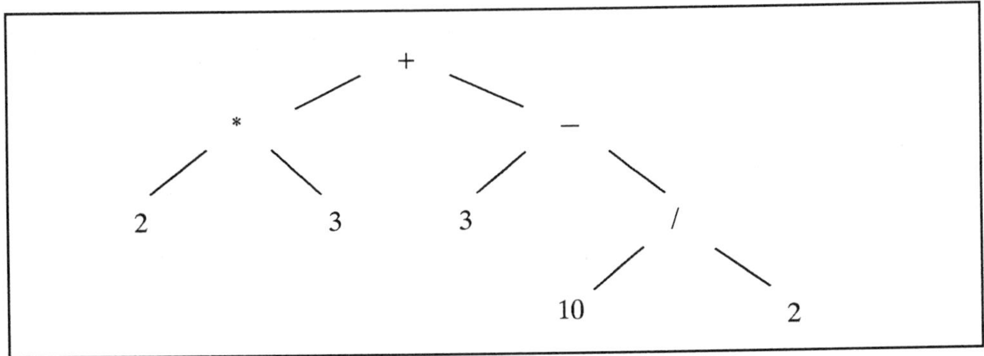

Figure 2.1 An Expression Tree

```
[Inspect] Quit
[5] (load "examples.s")
OK
[6] (square 2)
4
[7] (exit)
```

The action at prompt [4] indicates that **square** is not currently defined. Next, the **load** primitive directs Scheme to read Scheme source code from the file "examples.s". During the process of evaluating the source code, any number of side effects may occur. For example, as is the case here, functions (e.g., **square**) may be defined by the source code. Ultimately, Scheme returns a value at the top level signaling that everything is "OK". The **exit** primitive, which is implementation-specific, causes the ultimate side effect, termination of Scheme. Note that it accepts no arguments.

Another type of side effect is an interruption of the evaluation process, for example, due to a user error:

```
[2] (+ 3 "string")

[VM ERROR encountered!] Non-numeric operand to arithmetic
operation
(+ 3 "string")

[Inspect] Quit
[3] (+ 3 2)
5
[4] (exit)
```

Scheme cannot perform such an addition and must take some prescribed action at this point. In the case of PC Scheme, control is passed to the "inspector" (the bug exterminator). At this point, we don't need to do any debugging, the error is obvious, so we quit and return to the top-level Scheme listener, continuing the normal REP loop.

2.3 Simple Arithmetic

Scheme is one of the best languages for numeric processing, providing several numeric primitives that are nonexistent in most languages. Try the following operations:

```
[2] (+ 3 2)
5
[3] (+ 3.0 2.0)
5.
[4] (+ 3.0 2)
5.
[5] _
```

Scheme, like most modern languages, can automatically handle both integers and real operands to most numeric primitives; in particular, the four basic numeric primitives. Mixed operands are converted to a common numeric data type.

Many Scheme primitives accept more than two operands (this may vary from one implementation of Scheme to another).

```
[5] (+ 1 2 3 4 5)
15
[6] (* 3.2 3 1)
9.6
[7] _
```

Try some of the following expressions. You should get the same response on your system.

```
[7] (/ 10 2)
5
[8] (/ 5 2)
2.5
[9] (* 1000 1000)
1000000
[10] (* 10000 10000 10000)
1000000000000
[11] _
```

Standard Scheme recommends the provision for "bignums" (big numbers), that is, arbitrarily large integers. The largest possible number varies among implementations, but is typically very large. Bignums are represented internally in list form. (Once you get used to bignums, it is surprisingly difficult to accept the integer limits, such as 32767 or 2147483647, that are common with more traditional languages.)

Try a few more Scheme primitives. Most of these are commonly available in other languages.

```
[11] (abs -3)
3
[12] (abs -5.2)
5.2
[13] (quotient 5 2)
2
[14] (remainder 5 2)
1
[15] (remainder -5 2)
-1
[16] (modulo -5 2)
1
[17] (round 10.4)
10
[18] (round 10.5)
11
[19] (truncate 10.5)
10
[20] (floor -4.2)
-5
[21] (floor 4.2)
4
[22] (ceiling 4.2)
5
[23] (exp 1)
2.71828182845905
[24] (log 2)
0.693147180559945
[25] (log (exp 1))
1.
[26] _
```

The precision of the result returned by expressions involving real number operations varies among implementations, but is typically quite supportive of scientific computation. The availability of this kind of numeric support on microcomputers using a relatively inexpensive Scheme product (PC Scheme) is quite extraordinary.

Scheme provides support for relational operations as well.

```
[26] (> 3 4)
()
[27] (< 3 4)
```

```
#T
[28] (= 3 3)
#T
[29] (= 3 3.0)
#T
[30] (<= 10 5)
()
[31] _
```

Scheme implementations differ with respect to their representation of the Boolean constants true and false. Standard Scheme proposes the constants: **#t** and **#f**, respectively; however, some Scheme implementations were developed prior to the most recent report on standard Scheme. PC Scheme 2.0, for example, defined the Boolean constants **#!true** and **#!false**, whereas, PC Scheme 3.0 uses those suggested by standard Scheme. However, due to a LISP tradition, the empty list, "()" is substituted for **#f** in PC Scheme. (This is the case with most LISPs.) Hence, in the above dialog, since three is (numerically) less than four, "(> 3 4)" evaluates to "()", or false.

Implementation note: Older LISP dialects treated the empty list "()" and the symbol **nil** equivalently. The interpretation of "()" differed based on context; that is, during list processing operations "()" represented the empty list, and during Boolean operations it represented false. Any "non-nil" value represented true. Thus, this tradition lives on to some extent with Scheme, mostly in the form of redundant ways of expressing true and false conditions. Some Scheme implementations provide the variables **t** and **nil**, initialized to their respective Boolean constants for true and false. This convention provides a measure of portability among LISP and Scheme implementations.

There are other Scheme primitives that return Boolean values. The following built-in functions are among those supporting numeric processing.

```
[31] (integer? 3)
#T
[32] (integer? 3.0)
()
[33] (number? 3.0)
#T
[34] (real? 3.0)
#T
[35] (rational? 3.0)
()
[36] _
```

Most Scheme primitives that return Boolean values end with a "?", signifying their Boolean function. However, there are exceptions to this rule, e.g, the relational operators. In Scheme, these functions are called *predicates*.

In later chapters we will investigate the power provided by such predicates. Briefly, Scheme supports the development of functions that can "on demand" operate on varying data types. For example, we can write a bubble sort function that sorts integers, reals, character strings, and so on. Such a function must perform run-time checking of data types; the preceding predicates are among those that provide such assistance.

Standard Scheme also provides several ancillary mathematical functions:

```
[36] (gcd 41 2)
1
[37] (gcd 3 9)
3
[38] (lcm 10 3)
30
[39] (lcm 3 9)
9
[40] (lcm 123 234592)
28854816
[41] _
```

The preceding functions evaluate their arguments and return the greatest common divisor and least common multiple, respectively.

2.4 Lexical Components

Thus far our discussion of Scheme has informally introduced various lexical conventions. At this point, a more formal discussion is useful.

2.4.1 Whitespace and Comments

Whitespace characters include the space character, formfeed, tab, and newline character(s). Comments are signaled by a ";". That is, on a given line, anything after a ";" is ignored. Using Scheme, evaluate the following.

```
[2] (+ 23)
23
[3] (+ 2 3)
5
[4] (+ 2
3)
5
[5] ;(+ 2 3)
(+ 2 3)
5
```

```
[6] (+ 2 3) ;two plus three is five
5
[7] _
```

At prompt [2] the two adjacent characters are interpreted as a single integer. At prompt [3] they are distinguished as separate integers, due to an intervening space character. At prompt [4] they are separated by a newline sequence. (Evaluation doesn't begin until the carriage return after the closing parenthesis is typed.) At prompt [5] the first expression is ignored, since it is preceded by a ";". The second expression is picked up by Scheme since it began on a new (uncommented) line. At prompt [6] the text after the ";" has no impact on the preceding expression evaluation.

2.4.2 Constants

The term "constant" is used in computer science and mathematics for items that are taken at face value, that is, cannot be further evaluated. The term "literal" is also used for such indivisible, self-evaluating expressions. It is sometimes said that literals evaluate in such a manner that the printed representation is equivalent to the literal expression itself.

In Scheme, literals include numbers, strings, and characters. (A "quoted symbol," which we've briefly mentioned, is somewhat like a literal, in that it isn't evaluated like a variable.) The following are all literals

Literal	Explanation
`-23`	`;(negative) integer`
`17.2`	`;real`
`"Scheme is great!"`	`;(propagandized) string`
`#t`	`;standard Scheme for Boolean true`
`#!true`	`;PC Scheme 2.0 for Boolean true`
`#f`	`;standard Scheme for Boolean false`
`#!false`	`;PC Scheme 2.0 for Boolean false`
`#!null`	`;PC Scheme 2.0 for empty list--same` `;as #!false.  Its use is discouraged.`
`#\x`	`;a lowercase "x"`
`#\T`	`;an uppercase "t"`
`#\(`	`;a left parenthesis`
`#\space`	`;the single character "space",`
`#\ `	`;alternate (inferior) way to write a` `;space (occupies three columns)`
`#\newline`	`;represents newline sequence`
`#\return`	`;represents carriage return (not` `;the same as newline)`

```
#\backspace            ;represents backspace
#\page                 ;represents a form feed
#\rubout               ;represents the rubout character
#\tab                  ;represents tab
```

The character "#" (sharp, or pound, sign) is used in a variety of ways depending on the character that follows it. Followed by "t" or "f" in standard Scheme it represents the Boolean constants true and false, respectively. Followed by "!" in PC Scheme 2.0 it signals a special constant, e.g., either "true", "false", or "null". Followed by "\" it signals a (single) character constant. Followed by "(" it signals the beginning of a vector (discussed later). And followed by any one of several characters: "o", "d", "x", and so on, it signals the radix of a number. (See your Scheme's documentation.)

The preceding "control" characters may be different on your host computer system. We make use of some of these in later examples.

2.4.3 Identifiers

Scheme has very flexible rules regarding the formation of identifiers. Typically, identifiers begin with a character and may be followed by multiple characters or digits. (This includes certain nonalphabetic characters; see your documentation.)

In Scheme certain identifiers may be reserved as syntactic keywords, such as

and or begin do else if define let set! quote cond ...

Depending on the implementation, these may not be allowed as variable or function names.

There are two nonalphabetic characters that should only be used in Scheme identifiers in restricted ways: "?" and "!", due to LISP and/or Scheme convention. "?" is used as the last character in an identifier that is a predicate, i.e., returns a Boolean value. "!" is used as the last character in an identifier that causes some "destructive" modification (discussed later).

2.4.4 Literal Expressions

We've mentioned Scheme literals and alluded to the possibility of something called a symbol. Consider the following interaction with Scheme.

```
[1] 123
123
[2] "123"
"123"
[3] "abc"
```

```
"abc"
[4] #\space
#\SPACE
[5] #t
#T
[6] #f
()
[7] #!null
()
[8] #\t
#\t
[9] #\T
#\T
[10] _
```

This of course represents the simplest case of expression evaluation—that of self-evaluating literals. In evaluating these literal expressions, Scheme merely has to return their printed representation.

The result of evaluating the string "abc" at prompt [3] is the string itself. Scheme doesn't strip the delimiting quotes, because, in general, when a string is returned its string nature should be preserved. For example, in order to write a string to a file and provide for its subsequent retrieval, the delimiting quotes must be retained. (Scheme provides specific functions for printing strings without surrounding quotes.)

Normally Scheme returns output in uppercase form. By enclosing characters in a string, or by using the special designation for single characters, e.g., "#\t" at prompt [8], it is possible to retain the lowercase form.

Also, note the equivalence between PC Scheme's **#f**, **#!null**, and the empty list; at prompts [6] and [7] it returns the latter.

Now suppose we type "abc", but without the quotes:

```
[10] abc

[VM ERROR encountered!] Variable not defined in current
environment
ABC

[Inspect] Quit
[11] _
```

Since **abc** isn't recognized as a literal, Scheme assumes that it must be a variable and attempts to evaluate it (look up its value). This results in an error, of course—we haven't defined this variable—and the inspector is called, which we then terminate.

We alluded that in some types of programming (symbolic processing) it is convenient to use nonnumeric symbols, just as we use numeric constants. This is one of the features of symbolic processing languages, such as LISP and PROLOG. The only problem is: How does Scheme distinguish between a symbol and a variable?

(Throughout the text we use "symbol" in this restricted sense, even though we recognize that an identifier is of course a symbol.) The single quote is used to signify this usage of a symbol; it prevents its evaluation as a variable. Try the following.

```
[11] 'abc
ABC
[12] '(a b c)
(A B C)
[13] '(employee bill accounting 28000)
(EMPLOYEE BILL ACCOUNTING 28000)
[14] _
```

Scheme returns the printed representation of symbols much as it does for other literals. Note that placing a single quote before a list causes Scheme to "turn off" evaluation for the entire list. (Later, we will investigate a Scheme provision for turning on evaluation within selected positions of a list.)

It is even possible to "quote" true literals, as follows.

```
[14] '123
123
[15] '"123"
"123"
[16] '#t
#T
[17] '#\a
#\a
[18] _
```

In order to provide compatibility with older LISPs, Scheme supports an alternate specification of a quoted expression:

```
[18] (quote abc)
ABC
[19] (quote #\x)
#\x
[20] _
```

Finally, as expected, the quote prevents Scheme's evaluation of expressions with Scheme primitives in the first position of a list.

```
[20] (+ 3 2)
5
[21] '(+ 3 2)
(+ 3 2)
[22] _
```

2.4.5 Others

Other lexical conventions, e.g., delimiters, are best introduced informally. We've already seen the use of parentheses to delimit lists, a single quote to signal literal use of a symbol, and double quotes to delimit character strings.

2.5 Atoms, Lists, Forms, and S-expressions

So far we've mostly investigated Scheme's facility for working with literals—variables are discussed in the next chapter. Sometimes alternate terminology is used, especially in AI applications.

The list is the basic, composite data structure in Scheme; and lists can be nested, as we've mentioned. Consider the following:

```
(* 3 4)
(* (+ 3 2) 7)
'(a (b c) d)
```

In the first case, each item in the list is indivisible, that is, atomic. In this case, each item is called an *atom*. In the second and third cases, all but the second item is an atom (atomic). However, the respective nested lists are each composed of atoms.

Each of these three lists is commonly referred to as an *s-expression*, because they are composed of symbols (symbolic-expressions). In addition, s-expressions that are intended to be evaluated are called *forms*. Above, the first two lists are forms.

Finally, you may find it convenient to make a distinction between forms that initiate calls to built-in functions, e.g., **+**, **-**, **truncate**, and so on, and forms that contain a syntactic keyword in the first position, e.g., Scheme reserved words:

and or begin do else if define let set! quote cond ...

The latter are not procedures, just as **begin** is not a procedure in either Pascal or PL/I. Forms containing such keywords are typically called *special forms*, or *syntactic forms*.

Exercises

1. Explain each step of the REP loop with respect to:

```
(* 3 (+ 2 3))
```

2. We said that a postorder traversal and evaluation of an expression tree yields the expression value. A postorder traversal of a tree is one in which, for a given tree node, each subtree is visited before the current subtree root. Postorder traversals are provided for the following trees.

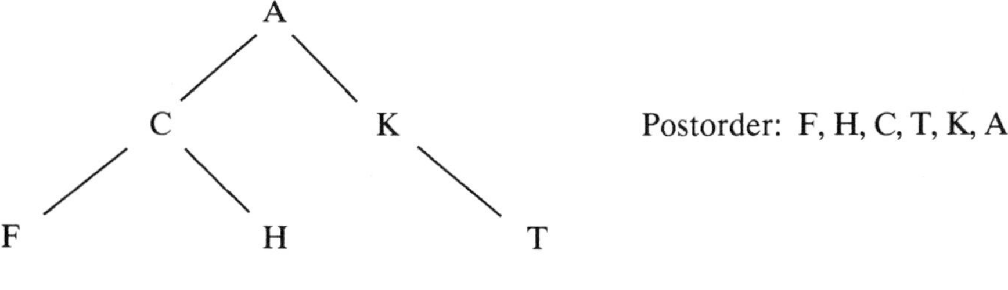

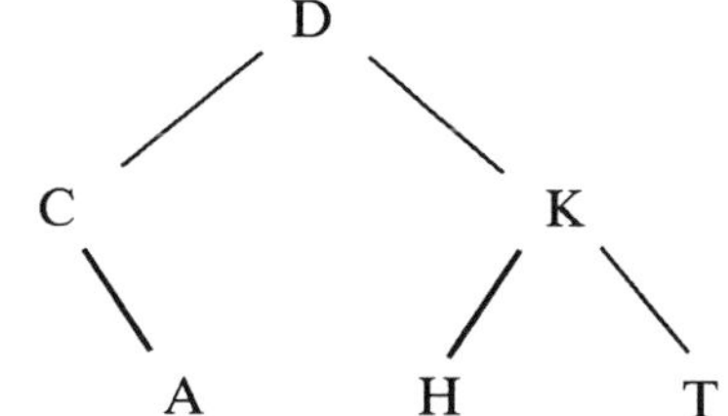

Postorder: A, C, H, T, K, D

Consider the following subtree where we've replaced the letters with expression components.

In this case, a "visit" to C after F and H (postorder) simply means that we evaluate the subtree root (*) after evaluating subordinate subtrees (here, 4 and 3). Thus, 4 and 3 are multiplied to produce 12 which then replaces the entire subtree.

Draw expression trees and evaluate each of the following.

```
a. (* 3 (+ 4 5))
b. (- (* 3 4) 9)
c. (* (* 2 (- 5 (+ 3 4))) (+ (/ 10 2) 9))
```

3. Read your Scheme documentation concerning how to enter and exit Scheme and then test each of the following with your Scheme system:

```
a. (5 / 9) * (F - 32)
```

You should substitute a Fahrenheit temperature for **F**, say, 212, 32, etc. Scheme returns the Celsius temperature.

```
b. [(9 / 5) * C] + 32
```

You should substitute a Celsius temperature for **C**, say, 0, 100, etc. Scheme returns the Fahrenheit temperature.

```
c. 3.14159 * R * R
```

You should substitute a radius for **R**, say, 2, 5, etc. Scheme returns the area of a circle.

4. Read your Scheme documentation concerning how to enter and exit your Scheme system and then use Scheme to evaluate each of the expressions in Exercise 2.

5. Test your Scheme system's support for real numbers and its level of precision by evaluating the following:

```
==> (log (exp 1))
```

6. Test your Scheme system's support for bignums by trying multiplication operations with large integers, e.g., 121332323.

7. What are the restrictions for identifier names for your Scheme implementation?

8. Consider the lists below. How many elements, not counting subelements, does each list have?

```
a. (a b c)
b. ((a b) c)
c. ((a b c))
d. ((a b) c (d e))
```

Check your answer, using Scheme, as demonstrated for the preceding first list:

```
==> (length '(a b c))
```

9. Which of the following forms also qualify as syntactic forms?

```
a. (and 'you 'i)
b. (truncate 14.3)
c. (or 'him 'her)
d. (if 'him 'her)
e. (3 4)
f. (define x 4)
```

Chapter 3

Defining Variables and Functions

3.1 Introduction

Scheme provides the programmer with a very rich set of language primitives. Even so, one of the most important aspects of a language is its provision for extending the language—for building user-defined functions. Scheme provides a single directive, **define**, for establishing both variable and function definitions. Scheme's lexical scoping facility provides for both global and local variable and function definitions. Several aspects of function and variable definitions are investigated in this chapter.

3.2 The Global Environment

One aspect of interpreter-like programming environments differing from that found with compilers is the top-level, or global environment. With most interpreter-like Scheme systems, there is no main procedure within which all other procedures and variables are defined. Instead, Scheme provides a global environment in which the user can define both functions and variables. As new variables and functions are defined, the global environment becomes populated and Scheme must maintain an organization that allows efficient storage and retrieval of both programs and data.

For example, PC Scheme makes a distinction between the top-level user global environment and the top-level system environment, where the latter contains all global system bindings. In PC Scheme these two environments are formally bound to the variables **user-initial-environment** and **user-global-environment**, respectively. We use the environment terminology in a rather generic way here.

Other (sub-) environments, or *frames*, may be defined within the user-initial environment using special Scheme forms, analogous to internal procedure definitions in languages such as Pascal; that is, via lexical scoping. Each frame is analogous to a lexical block in other languages. The lexical scoping aspect of Scheme is discussed in more detail in the chapter on debugging. For now, we simply make the point that within lexically scoped languages, such as Scheme, for each identifier that is established at some point in a program, say, inside a function definition, there is a region where a reference to that identifier has particular meaning.

3.3 Using define

Scheme provides a single language primitive, **define** for defining both variables and functions. (**define** is technically called a *special form.*) Try the following:

```
[1] x

[VM ERROR encountered!] Variable not defined in current
environment
X

[Inspect] Quit
[2] _
```

This generates an error because **x** hasn't been defined; that is, it has no top-level definition. We can use **define** to provide a top-level definition.

```
[2] (define x 3)
X
[3] x
3
[4] _
```

x has been bound to the integer 3 at prompt [2]. Prompt [3] shows a simple type of expression evaluation, namely, evaluation of a single variable. Note that we should not, in this context, put **x** in parentheses, as the parentheses would signal Scheme to process **x** as a function.

We can define any number of global variables in this manner, and use them as arguments in function calls.

```
[4] (define y 6)
Y
[5] (+ x y)
9
[6] '(+ x y)
(+ X Y)
[7] _
```

As we've already seen, the single quote directs Scheme to turn off evaluation temporarily.

Now define a function, **double**, which takes one argument as input and multiplies it by two.

```
[7] (define (double x) (* x 2))
DOUBLE
[8] (double 5)
10
[9] (double x)
6
[10] '(double x)
(DOUBLE X)
[11] _
```

As discussed in Chapter 1, the keyword **define** is the first item in the list, the function-call structure appears next as a (nested) list, and the body of the function appears after that, in this case, as a single expression with a call to the multiplication operator. Scheme responds with "DOUBLE", which indicates that the definition is at least free of major syntactic errors. Note that we don't have to specify explicitly that a value should be returned – Scheme is a functional language and always returns a value. This is the first example we've seen of an environment other than the global user environment, namely, the environment local to the function **double**. Thus, the lexical scoping of Scheme provides **x** with a special meaning inside the function **double**, namely, any reference to **x** inside **double** is a reference to the parameter of **double**, even if there is some other **x** defined elsewhere in the program. This particular **x** is said be *local* to **double.**

Now make a mistake and see what happens:

```
[11] (define (square n (* n n))
)

[Syntax Error] Invalid bound variable name
(* N N)
[Returning to top level]
[12] _
```

First, we attempt to define the function **square**. Note that we failed to add the closing parenthesis after the parameter **n**. Thus, after we've entered a carriage return, Scheme fails to respond – because the parentheses are not balanced. In this case, there aren't enough right parentheses, so Scheme is still building the definition of **square**. Typing another closing parenthesis terminates the definition; however, its specification is incorrect, yielding a Scheme error.

This particular error occurs because a right parenthesis following the parameter **n** is required to direct Scheme to establish a *local* variable for the function **square**. In this particular case, the local variable is a parameter. This is an example of a local environment, an environment local to the function **square**.

Let's define **square** and illustrate a few things about functions.

```
[12] (define (square n) (* n n))
SQUARE
[13] (define square-2 (lambda (n) (* n n)))
SQUARE-2
[14] _
```

The first point is that the syntax we've been using for function definitions isn't "essential," according to standard Scheme. However, it is presented in the Scheme standard, and it's likely to be present is most implementations of Scheme. The definition of **square-2** shows the "essential" syntax, which should be present in all Scheme implementations, even, say, public-domain versions.

The latter form makes use of the **lambda** special form, which we aren't ready to discuss in detail. If you don't have the former capability for defining functions, simply note the differences in syntax and substitute the latter. Namely, the function name is given as the second item in the list, and the third item is a list containing the keyword **lambda**, which signals the occurrence of a function with parameters as given in the second position in the lambda list, and with a function body following the parameters.

You can think of **lambda** as a synonym for "function." For example, compare the following.

f(x) = x * x	(high school math class)
(lambda (x) (* x x))	(LISP)

Thus, **lambda** corresponds to "f" in "f(x)" or "function of x," except that everything is in prefix form. And,

```
(define square-2 (lambda (n) (* n n)))
```

simply means to define an identifier **square-2** to be the function given by the lambda expression. Since **square-2** is defined to be a function, we can use it as the first item in an expression—see below. We will discuss the **lambda** syntactic form in detail in a later chapter. At this point, we can use either of the functions we've defined.

```
[14] (square 3)
9
[15] (square (+ x y))
81
[16] (square-2 3)
9
```

```
[17] _
```

We can use one of these functions in the definition of another function. **square-3** is defined in terms of **square**:

```
[17] (define (square-3 n) (square n))
SQUARE-3
[18] (square-3 5)
25
[19] _
```

Scheme doesn't require that **square** be defined before **square-3** is defined; this is particularly convenient for the programmer. However, **square** must be defined before **square-3** can be executed.

To illustrate environments and lexical scoping, we can define a function with another function local to it.

```
[19] (define (square-4 n)
       (define (sqr n) (* n n))
         (sqr n))
SQUARE-4
[20] _
```

For readability, we've provided some indention using the space bar on the keyboard; Scheme of course doesn't need the indention. The function **sqr** has been defined internal to **square-4**; most Scheme implementations should allow this, provided that such internal function definitions are placed directly after the parameter list. The function body for **square-4**, consisting of a call to **sqr**, is placed directly after the internal definition of **sqr**. (The function body for **square-4** should occur last in the definition.)

Try the following:

```
[20] (square-4 5)
25
[21] (sqr 5)

[VM ERROR encountered!] Variable not defined in current
environment
SQR

[Inspect] Quit
[22] _
```

When we execute **square-4** it works properly, by calling **sqr** to perform the multiplication. However, if we attempt to use **sqr** directly from the top level, we get a Scheme error. This happens because **sqr** is only defined local to **square-4**.

3.4 Latent Typing

You may have noticed that we haven't given any specification regarding the data type of arguments to our functions. This is because Scheme employs *latent typing*. That is, certain decisions are made at run-time regarding which data types can legitimately be passed to a function (run-time type checking). As we will see in later chapters, this aspect of Scheme yields a great deal of power not present in many languages.

A certain amount of flexibility with respect to data typing is automatically incorporated into Scheme. This is true not only for Scheme primitives, but for user-defined functions as well. For example:

```
[1] (+ 3 2)
5
[2] (+ 3.1 2.1)
5.2
[3] (define (square n) (* n n))
SQUARE
[4] (square 3)
9
[5] (square 3.3)
10.89
[6] (square "string")

[VM ERROR encountered!] Non-numeric operand to arithmetic
operation
(* "string" "string")

[Inspect] Quit
[7] _
```

In general, Scheme arithmetic operators can accommodate multiple data types, in this case, integer and real. Likewise, the user-defined **square** function inherits the same capability. Naturally, this flexibility toward data types does not allow a mathematical operation to be performed on a string argument. Note in particular that the error above is trapped inside the function prior to the multiplication, and not at the time the string argument is passed to **square**. Again, this is part of Scheme's scheme for run-time flexibility, which we will take advantage of in later chapters.

3.5 Modifying Definitions

So far we've addressed creating new variable and function definitions. In general, the most straightforward way to modify a function is simply to establish a new definition. In addition, variables can be modified in Scheme by using the **set!** primitive. The "!" in "set!" is a mnemonic for a destructive, i.e., a permanent, modification.

The **set!** primitive is essentially equivalent to the assignment operator in other languages. That is, **set!** assigns (destructively binds) a new value to a variable. Try the following.

```
[1] (define x 3)
X
[2] (define y)
Y
[3] (set! y 4)
4
[4] (+ x y)
7
[5] (set! x 1)
1
[6] (+ x y)
5
[7] (define $ +)
$
[8] ($ x y)
5
[9]
```

At prompt [1] we define **x** and initialize it with a value of 3. At prompt [2] **y** is defined but not initialized (it is unbound). At prompt [3] we use **set!** to "set" **y** equal to 4. Note that **set!** can be used to perform the initial binding of a variable, here **y**, or to bind a variable to a new value; in this case, at prompt [5] **x** is bound to 1.

Scheme, as we will see later, is very flexible with respect to how variables and functions are treated. In particular, Scheme is noted for treating functions as "first-class" data objects. That is, it is very easy in Scheme to manipulate functions. For example, functions can be passed as arguments, just like variables, without any special effort on the programmer's part. One aspect of this flexibility is easily demonstrated at this point. Namely, we can use **define**, or **set!**, to bind a Scheme primitive to a new name. As an example, at prompt [7] we bind the addition primitive to the identifier **$**.

The **set!** primitive can be used to bind values to either global or local variables. In the case above, global variables equate to top-level variables. However, Scheme provides language features that promote/encourage the use of other techniques to establish variable bindings. In later chapters we minimize the use of **set!**, especially with local variables.

3.6 Loading Externally-defined Functions

It's obvious that the definition of functions "on the fly" during REP loop processing is tedious at best, since it is very easy to make typing mistakes. Moreover, it is important to be able to save function definitions (programs) on disk for later processing. Every

Scheme implementation should provide the **load** primitive for loading (and evaluating) function definitions from an external disk file.

At this point, you should experiment with **load** by first developing a function outside of Scheme using your preferred program editor, and second, using **load** to make its definition known to Scheme. As an example, consider the following function named **greeting**, which makes use of Scheme's **read** and **display** primitives to greet the user. (Input/output functions are discussed in a later chapter; here, we take advantage of the simple and intuitive nature of **read** and **display**.)

```
;;;;    greeting.s    ;;;;;;;;;;;;;;;;;;;;;;;;;;;;;;;;;;;;;;;;

;;;;;;;;;;;;;;;;;;;;;;;;;;;;;;;;;;;;;;;;;;;;;;;;;;;;;;;;;;;;;;;
;; GREETING prompts for and reads the user's name (in sym-
;; bol form--first character lowercase), and then greets
;; the user.
;;;;;;;;;;;;;;;;;;;;;;;;;;;;;;;;;;;;;;;;;;;;;;;;;;;;;;;;;;;;;;;

(define (greeting)
  (define name)
  (display "Your (first) name please:  ")
  (set! name (read))
  (display "Hello ")
  (display name)
  (display "!"))
```

In **greeting**, which has no parameters, we first define the local variable, **name**. The local variable definition should be placed first in the function definition. At this point, **name** cannot be given a value because it is necessary to first issue a prompt to the user, thus, **name** is established without a value. After using **display** to prompt the user for a name, **set!** assigns to **name** the result of the function call to **read**, which reads one symbol from the console. At this point, **display** is used to print the greeting.

In this text we attempt to minimize the use of **set!**. However, in the program above, the objective is to write a simple program similiar to what we could write in a language such as Pascal or C. At this point we haven't introduced certain Scheme language constructs that facilitate non-**set!** programming. Later, we will compare programs that use **set!** to programs with alternative Scheme constructs that make **set!** completely unnecessary in many programming situations.

This is the first program that we've written which illustrates the idea of throwing away the returned value, or if you prefer, executing a function for side effect only. Earlier in this chapter we illustrated **set!** in the top-level REP loop; recall that **set!** always returns the value assigned to the identifier. In **greeting** the **set!** function returns this value, but no use is made of it—since the function call is buried inside another function with sequentially-executed expressions, the returned value is discarded. In other words, we always have the option of using a function's returned value, except at the top level where it is always returned. Normally, a function such as **greeting** returns the value of the last expression. However, **display** is somewhat special; in PC Scheme **dis-**

play returns a null value, so as not to clutter up the screen during console output operations. (C is another language with similar characteristics for returning function values. In C, the programmer can define a function as "void", an explicit indication that it's always executed for side effect only.)

Having stored **greeting** in a file named "greeting.s", we can use it as follows.

```
[1] (load "greeting.s")
OK
[2] (greeting)
Your (first) name please:  jerry
Hello JERRY!
[3] (exit)
```

Exercises

1. At the top level in your Scheme system define each of the following variables with the corresponding assigned values:

```
a. w := 3
b. x := 5
c. y := 13
d. z := 15
```

Then evaluate the following expressions:

```
a. (* 3 (/ z w))          ;; integer result
b. (* 3 (/ w z))          ;; real result
c. (* (/ 1 3) y x)        ;; three operands to *
```

2. Define the function **general-greeting** as a function of no parameters that prints the message "Hello world!". Use the **display** function, as given in this chapter, to print the message.

3. Define the functions **f->c** and **c->f** for temperature conversion, as given by the following formulas:

```
a. F = [(9 / 5) * C] + 32
b. C = (5 / 9) * (F - 32)
```

Test each function for correctness by converting Fahrenheit to Celsius and Celsius back to Fahrenheit.

4. Define a function **circumference** that computes the circumference of a circle given the constant **pi** and a single parameter, the diameter.

5. Define the function **fourth-power** to be the product of the parameter squared and the parameter squared; if you haven't done so already, you will have to define **square** also.

6. Rewrite Exercise 4 so that the user is prompted for the diameter. Read the value typed by the user with **read**. Print the output to the screen with **display**.

7. At this point you should become familiar with the editor accompanying your Scheme system. This includes techniques for writing Scheme functions within the editor, saving them to a file, evaluating functions from within the editor, and so on.

- **a.** As an exercise, develop the preceding temperature conversion functions with comments and save them in a file.

- **b.** Use the Scheme **load** directive (or equivalent) to load the functions from disk and test them from the Scheme top level.

Chapter 4

List Processing

4.1 Introduction

Up to this point, we've used the Scheme list structure primarily for expressions and for function definitions. However, one of the primary strengths of Scheme (LISP) is its overall facility for (symbolic) list processing. In this chapter, we explore Scheme's list processing primitives, mostly by looking at list processing in isolation. In subsequent chapters, list manipulation will become a basic part of our programs.

4.2 car and cdr

Probably the two most frequently used list processing functions are **car** (pronounced like the synonym for automobile) and **cdr** (pronounced "could-er"). The names "car" and "cdr" have little mnemonic value and are holdovers from earlier LISP dialects.

Given an arbitrary list, **car** returns the first element of the list and **cdr** returns the rest of the list, that is, all but the first element. For example:

```
[1] (car '(a b c))
A
[2] (cdr '(a b c))
(B C)
[3] (car '(just-one-element))
JUST-ONE-ELEMENT
[4] (cdr '(just-one-element))
()
[5] (car '())
```

```
()
[6] (cdr '())
()
[7] _
```

As an argument to **car** at prompt [1], we pass a list containing three symbols: **a**, **b**, and **c**. Since we're passing a "literal" list, that is, one that should not be evaluated, **quote** is required (the quote syntax in abbreviated form). The first element in the list is **a** (an atom), and thus is returned by the function call to **car**. Next, at prompt [2] **cdr** is used to return the rest of the list, in this case, **(b c)**. (As mentioned, many Scheme implementations print their console output in uppercase form.)

Suppose there is just one element in the list (prompts [3] and [4]). Then **car** returns that element and **cdr** returns the rest, which is the empty list. How would **car** and **cdr** handle the empty list as an argument? The first element of the empty list is, from one point of view, undefined. However, if an empty list is passed to **car**, Scheme handles this by simply returning the empty list. Likewise, the **cdr** of an empty list is the empty list.

At this point we should reemphasize that Scheme always evaluates each element of a symbolic expression, unless we apply **quote**. Sometimes this evaluation is exactly what we want. For example, if we bind a list to a variable, so that we don't have to use the list itself, the argument to **car** or **cdr** must be evaluated. Typically, this is the case – that is, list processing functions are applied to lists passed as arguments to some function.

Try the following:

```
[7] (define example-list '(a b c))
EXAMPLE-LIST
[8] (car example-list)
A
[9] (cdr example-list)
(B C)
[10] example-list
(A B C)
[11] _
```

Note that **car** and **cdr** are nondestructive functions; that is, they return a copy of their arguments' components. At prompt [10], after the application of **car** and **cdr** to **example-list**, an evaluation of **example-list** demonstrates that the original binding is still intact. (This is part of the call-by-value philosophy of Scheme.)

Let's bind a list to a variable (for convenience) and try several more-sophisticated examples, where the list elements are not atoms, but are lists instead.

```
[11] (define current-list '((1 2) (3 4) (5 6)))
CURRENT-LIST                      ;a list of lists
[12] (car current-list)           ;first element is a list
(1 2)
```

```
[13] (cdr current-list)        ;rest is a list of lists
((3 4) (5 6))
[14] (car (car current-list)) ;first element of the first
1                              ;element is an atom
[15] (cdr (car current-list)) ;rest of the first element is
(2)                            ;still a list
[16] (car (cdr (car current-list)))     ;wow!
2
[17] _
```

Lists can be composed of lists or atoms, in any combination. In the preceding case, **current-list** has a fairly uniform structure – each element is a list of two elements. **car** and **cdr** are provided for taking lists apart. They can be applied to any list, in any manner of nested function calls, to extract the desired list component.

Typically, you use **cdr** to work your way down the list, and then apply **car** to extract the desired element. For example, consider the following list of numbers. (We've reused **current-list** simply to illustrate **set!**.)

```
[17] (set! current-list '(1 2 3 4))
(1 2 3 4)
[18] current-list              ;the value of current-list has
(1 2 3 4)                      ;been permanently modified
[19] (car (cdr current-list)) ;extract second element
2
[20] (cadr current-list)       ;extract second element
2
[21] (car (cdr (cdr current-list))) ;extract third element
3
[22] (caddr current-list)           ;extract third element
3
[23] (caddr '())                    ;boundary condition is
()                                  ;the empty list
[24] _
```

At prompt [19] **cdr** is used first to "drop" the first element from the list, and then **car** is applied to the returned value to extract its first element, which is the second element of the original list. At prompt [21] a double application of **cdr** sets us up to extract the third element, and so on.

Prompts [20] and [21] illustrate that Scheme provides short-hand functions for the most common combinations of nested **car** and **cdr** function calls. Note that the intervening characters between "c" and "r", i.e., the **x...x** in **cx...xr**, may be combinations of "a" and "d", where "a" means a call to **car** and "d" means a call to **cdr**, as can be seen by comparing the examples at prompts [21] and [22]. LISP dialects and implementations differ with respect to how many of these actually exist as built-in functions. Standard Scheme provides: **caar**, **cadr**, ... , **cdddar**, **cddddr**. When you need to perform a straightforward retrieval of the *n*th element of a list, it is wise to use other Scheme built-in functions for list processing that have been provided for programmer convenience and for increased readability.

4.3 cons, list, and append

car and **cdr** are used to tear down a list. Scheme provides another built-in function, **cons**, to build up a list. It too is non-destructive; **cons** does its work by building a new (temporary) list, which can then be passed to another function, returned, bound to a variable, etc.

Let's take a look at **cons** in action.

```
[1] (cons 'x '(y z))
(X Y Z)
[2] (cons '(w x) '(y z))
((W X) Y Z)
[3] (cons 'a (cons 'b '(c)))
(A B C)
[4] (cons 'a (cons 'b '()))
(A B)
[5] (cons 'a '())
(A)
[6] (cons '() '())
(())
[7] _
```

The function **cons** **cons**tructs a new (temporary) list by appending its first argument to its second argument. At prompt [1] a symbol is appended to a two-element list. At prompt [2] a list is appended to a list. Thus, the first argument to **cons** becomes the first element of the new list, and this may be a symbol or list. In the latter case, the list structure of the first argument is retained, yielding a nested list structure.

There is no practical limit to the amount of **cons**ing that can be done. Prompts [3], [4], and [5] illustrate that lists of arbitrary length can be built by nested, consing operations. Note that the empty list is a legitimate list, therefore, consing together two empty lists yields a nested list structure, not the empty list. This is somewhat unlike the behavior of **car** and **cdr**, for which an operation on the empty list serves as a boundary condition, i.e., (car (car ... (car '())...) – > ().

We can easily illustrate that **cons** is nondestructive. For example:

```
[7] (define x '(a b c))
X
[8] (cons 'z x)
(Z A B C)
[9] (cons 'x x)
(X A B C)
[10] x
```

```
(A B C)
[11] (define y)
Y
[12] (set! y (cons 'z x))
(Z A B C)
[13] x
(A B C)
[14] y
(Z A B C)
[15] _
```

At prompt [8] **cons** creates a new list by appending the symbol **z** to the list **(a b c)**, which has been bound to **x**. Once this value is returned by the **cons** function, it is, in essence, thrown away (printed by the top-level REP loop). At prompt [10] **x** still has the value bound to it by **define**. Of course we can capture the value returned by **cons** in a number of ways. At prompt [12] the list returned by the consing operation is bound to the variable **y**.

Using **cons** is potentially more inefficient than, say, **car** or **cdr**, in the sense that the latter return a subset of an existing list, whereas **cons** must construct a new list from scratch. However, if the main objective in using **cons** is to create a permanent list, say, for future use, then **cons** in this sense cannot be considered inefficient. On the other hand, the indiscriminant use of **cons**, merely to get from one structure to another, may be unwise.

Using **cons** to build a list of, say, 100 symbols, can be quite awkward. Scheme provides another function, **list**, for this specific purpose. Try the following:

```
[15] (cons 'a (cons 'b (cons 'c (cons 'd '()))))
(A B C D)
[16] (list 'a 'b 'c 'd)
(A B C D)
[17] (list 'a 'b)
(A B)
[18] (cons 'a 'b)
(A . B)
[19] _
```

At this point we briefly mention another Scheme structure, the *pair*, or *dotted pair*. Prompts [17] and [18] provide a contrast between a list and a pair. As we'll see later, there is a special relationship between lists and pairs. For now, when we cons together two symbols, the result is a pair, not a list. A pair is specified by putting a "." between its first and second elements, delimited by spaces. Without looking ahead, use the information provided in prompts [15] through [18] to formulate a list using "pair" notation. You can test your lists simply by submitting them for evaluation.

Scheme provides another function, **append**, for constructing lists. **append** differs from **cons** in that typically its arguments are lists. **append** merges its arguments to form a new list. (Some Scheme implementations may restrict **append** to two arguments; most support multiple arguments.)

```
[19] (append '(a b) '(c d))
(A B C D)
[20] (append '(a) '(b c d) '(e f g))
(A B C D E F G)
[21] _
```

4.4 Other List Processing Functions

Scheme provides several additional functions for working with lists; we briefly overview a few of the most useful ones at this point.

reverse is a nondestructive function that returns a new list constructed by reversing the order of its (list) argument. As shown below, **reverse** can be combined with **set!** to reverse a list "in its own space."

```
[21] (reverse '(1 2 3))
(3 2 1)
[22] (define x '(1 2 3 4))
X
[23] (reverse x)
(4 3 2 1)
[24] x
(1 2 3 4)
[25] (set! x (reverse x))
(4 3 2 1)
[26] x
(4 3 2 1)
[27] _
```

As an exercise, determine what happens if the argument contains nested lists.

Another useful function is **length**, which returns the number of elements in a list.

```
[27] (length x)
4
[28] (length '((a b) c d))
3
[29] _
```

As an alternative to nested **car-cdr** operations, **list-ref** can be used to extract specific elements from a list. For example:

```
[29] (set! x (reverse x))
(1 2 3 4)
```

```
[30] (car (cdr x))
2
[31] (list-ref x 1)
2
[32] (list-ref '((1 2) (3 4) (5 6)) 1)
(3 4)
[33] _
```

list-ref is zero-based, i.e., the first element is the 0th element. Note that it retrieves top-level elements only.

Scheme provides destructive functions for list processing also. Consider the following two:

```
[33] (set-car! x 10)
(10 2 3 4)
[34] x
(10 2 3 4)
[35] (set-cdr! x 20)
(10 . 20)
[36] x
(10 . 20)
[37] _
```

set-car! directly modifies **x**, replacing its first element (its "car", to use common terminology) with the value of the second argument, 10. Likewise, **set-cdr!** directly modifies the "cdr" of **x**, replacing it with the atom (constant) 20. Note that **set-cdr!** has turned our list **x** into a dotted pair. (We haven't specifically investigated dotted pairs yet, but from these two modifications to **x** it appears that a dotted pair is simply a **car-cdr** combination.)

In general, as with most LISP dialects, destructive functions should be used with some caution. It is easy to produce code that is hard to maintain over time but, from a performance view, such functions are sometimes necessary.

4.5 List Processing Predicates

Earlier we looked at Scheme predicates for numeric processing. Scheme also provides several predicates (Boolean functions) to assist the programmer with symbolic list processing. One such predicate is **null?**, which tests whether or not its argument is the empty list.

```
[37] (define y '(a b c))
Y
[38] (null? y)
()
[39] (null? '())
```

```
#T
```

Another function, **member**, isn't a true predicate. **member** checks for the occurrence of its first argument in its second argument.

```
[41] (member 'a y)
(A B C)
[42] (member 'b y)
(B C)
[43] (member 'c y)
(C)
[44] (member 'k y)
()
[45] (member 'c '((a b) (c d) (e f)))
()
[46] _
```

If the search is unsuccessful, **member** returns the Boolean constant for false; if successful, it returns the rest of the list (inclusive), beginning at the point where the match occurs. Thus, it is not a true predicate due to its method of handling the successful condition. (PC Scheme users: For an unsuccessful search, note that the empty list is returned, due to PC Scheme's equating of the empty list with Boolean false. This is common in other dialects as well.)

4.6 (Dotted) Pairs and List Representation

We've alluded to the relationship between a dotted pair and a list. Now that we've concluded our overview of list processing, we can examine this further.

```
[46] (pair? '(a . b))
#T
[47] (pair? y)                          ;defined at prompt [37]
#T
[48] (pair? 123)
()
[49] (pair? '(a . (b . (c . '()))))
#T
[50] _
```

The last structure, built from nested pairs, is evidently a pair. How would Scheme print it out upon evaluation? We can find out simply by binding it to a variable.

```
[50] (define nested-pairs '(a . (b . (c . '()))))
NESTED-PAIRS
[51] nested-pairs
```

```
(A B C QUOTE ())
[52] _
```

When we evaluate **nested-pairs**, Scheme returns a list, but with **quote** in the last position, due to its use inside the nested pair structure. The innermost **quote** isn't necessary because the entire data structure has been **quoted**. What would have happened if **nested-pairs** had been built without the innermost use of **quote**?

```
[52] (set! nested-pairs '(a . (b . (c . ()))))
(A B C)
[53] _
```

In this case, Scheme returns the list **(a b c)**. The data structure bound to **nested-pairs** at prompt[50] is called an *improper list*; that is, it is a chain of pairs that does not end with the empty list. The data structure given at prompt [52] is sometimes called a *proper list*.

There are three points. First, a list is just a special case, or special usage, of (nested) dotted pairs, where the innermost pair's cdr component is the empty list. Second, you should be careful how you use **quote**; use it only when needed to avoid evaluation. Contrast the examples given here with the example given at prompt [15]. Third, as pairs are a generalization of lists, there are quite a few situations in Scheme where a function will accept either one; **car** and **cdr** are perhaps the simplest examples.

```
[53] (define simple-pair '(a . b))
SIMPLE-PAIR
[54] (car simple-pair)
A
[55] (cdr simple-pair)
B
[56] (car nested-pairs)
A
[57] (cdr nested-pairs)
(B C)
[58] (exit)
```

Exercises

1. Show the result (returned value) for each of the following:

```
a. (car '(a b c))
b. (cdr '(a b c))
c. (car '((a b) (c d) (e f)))
d. (cdr '((a b) (c d) (e f)))
e. (car (cdr '(1 2 3)))
f. (cdr (car '(1 2 3)))
```

```
g. (cadr '(1 2 3))
h. (cdar '(1 2 3))
```

2. Define the variable **simple-list** to be **'(a b c)**. Then use the **car** and **cdr** primitives to extract the first element and the list of all but the first element.

3. Define the function **first** as a function of one parameter, a list, that returns the first element from a list passed as an argument.

4. Define the function **rest** as a function of one parameter, a list, that returns a list composed of all elements of the list passed as an argument, except the first element.

5. Define the functions **second, third**, and **fourth** as functions of one parameter each that return the second, third, and fourth elements of their argument, respectively.

6. Write two functions, **pop** and **push**, that operate on a list-based stack. That is, they should operate as outlined:

```
(define lst '(1 2 3))

(pop lst) --> 1          ;"-->" means "returns"

(push 4 lst) --> (4 1 2 3)
```

Both functions should work nondestructively. That is, there should be no permanent modifications to **lst**; in other words, only the returned values reflect the pop and push operations.

7. Show the returned value, or error, if appropriate, for each of the following:

```
a. (cons '3 '(1 2 3))
b. (cons '(3) '(1 2 3))
c. (cons '() '(1 2 3))
d. (cons () '(1 2 3))
```

8. Show the returned value, or error, if appropriate, for each of the following:

```
a. (list 1 2 3)
b. (list (1 2 3))
c. (list '(1 2 3) '(4 5 6))
d. (list (cons '(1 2) '(a b c)))
```

9. Show the returned value, or error, if appropriate, for each of the following:

```
a. (append 3 '(1 2 3))
b. (append '(1 2) '(3 4))
```

```
c. (length '(1 2 3))
d. (length (append '(1 2) '(3 4)))
e. (length (list '(1 2) '(3 4)))
f. (reverse (list '(1 2) '(3 4)))
```

10. Develop a function, **reverse-3**, with one parameter, a list of three elements, that returns the result of reversing the elements of the passed argument. Assume that each element in the passed argument is atomic, that is, nested lists are not allowed.

11. Suppose you have a function with a list as a parameter. What happens when you use **set!** to modify permanently a list passed as an argument to this function, where the passed list is defined at the top level? Why? Does **set-car!** or **set-cdr!** have a different effect? Why?

12. Develop two functions, **pop!** and **push!**, similar to **pop** and **push**, except that they permanently modify the argument. Hint: One method of doing this employs **set-car!** and/or **set-cdr!**.

13. Why does **member**, upon finding a match, return the remaining elements in the list instead of **#t**? What is the impact of this philosophy of returning a value other than **#t**, for Scheme programs that could be relying on a Boolean value being returned?

14. Explain the difference between an improper list and a proper list, especially with respect to the predicate **pair?**.

Chapter 5

Conditional Execution

5.1 Introduction

In previous chapters we've seen several occasions where Scheme primitives return Boolean values: relational operations, numeric predicates, list predicates, and so on. So far, we've primarily written one-line functions/programs, but in particular all of our programs including the "greeting" program have involved sequential execution of program code. In this chapter we explore Scheme's features for supporting conditional program execution, which of course, depends directly on the testing of Boolean values.

To assist in our exploration of conditional execution, we also introduce the logical operators, plus the **equal?** predicate.

5.2 Logical Operators

Scheme supports the three logical operators **and**, **or**, and **not**. Scheme provides the first two as syntactic forms; that is, language constructs that are not procedures, but are built from lower level primitives. **not**, on the other hand, is implemented as a procedure. Although the logical operators are predicates (in the sense that each returns a Boolean result when applied to Boolean expressions), they may also be used with non-Boolean expressions, and therefore do not follow the predicate naming convention with respect to the last character, i.e., **<predicate>?**.

You may want to try several examples with each of the logical operators; for example:

```
[1] (and (< 3 4) (< 4 3))
```

```
()
[2] (and (< 3 4) (> 4 3))
#T
[3] (or (< 3 4) (< 4 3))
#T
[4] (not (< 4 3))
#T
[5] (<= 8 10)
#T
[6] _
```

First, consider the logical operators with expressions that evaluate to Boolean values. At prompt [1] the result is false because the second of the two relational expressions is false. Both **and** and **or** evaluate expressions from left to right—as long as evaluation is necessary. For example, as soon as **and** encounters an expression that evaluates to false, the evaluation process is terminated and the result of the last evaluation is returned. At prompt [3] the first relational expression within the **or** is true. Since the first expression satisfies the **or**, Scheme does not have to evaluate subsequent expressions.

We can use **or** to develop an equivalent of the **< =** (less than *or* equal) predicate.

```
[6] (or (< 8 10) (= 8 10))
#T
[7] (define (le x y) (or (< x y) (= x y)))
LE
[8] (<= 3 4)
#T
[9] (le 3 4)
#T
[10] (<= 4 3)
()
[11] (le 4 3)
()
[12] (define (le x y) (not (> x y)))
LE
[13] (le 4 3)
()
[14] (le 3 3)
#T
[15] _
```

Prompt [6] first illustrates this usage of **or**; at prompt [7] we define our own "less than or equal to," named **le**. As an illustration of **not**, we redefine **le** at prompt [12].

Following LISP tradition, the logical operators may also be used with non-Boolean values. In essence, *Scheme treats non-false values as true*.

```
[15] (and 1 2 3)
3
[16] (or 1 2 3)
1
[17] (not 1 2 3)

[VM ERROR encountered!]
Invalid argument count: Function expected  1 argument(s)
but was called with  3 as follows:
(#<PROCEDURE NOT> 1 2 3)

[18] (not 3)
()
[19] (and 1 2 'x)
X
[20] (and 1 #f 3)
()
[21] (or 1 #f 3)
1
[22] (or #f 2 3)
2
[23] _
```

At prompt [15] Scheme evaluates expressions left to right, but finds no false expressions and thus terminates after the last evaluation, returning its value. At prompt [16] a non-false expression is encountered immediately; this satisfies the **or** and no further evaluation is attempted. The left-to-right evaluation is further illustrated at prompts [19] through [22].

Consider **not** at prompts [17] and [18]. First, **not** only allows one argument, which makes sense. Second, the opposite of a non-false value (the constant 3) is false.

The left-to-right-evaluation rule used by Scheme is convenient, in the sense that a programmer may want to formulate an **and** with several subordinate expressions, where the ith expression has an unbound value(s) initially, but is properly bound prior to evaluation of the ith expression, say, at the jth expression, $j < i$. You can assure yourself that Scheme works left to right and proceeds only as far as necessary by trying something similar to the following.

```
[23] (or #f 2 error-since-not-bound)
2
[24] (exit)
```

Here, the variable **error-since-not-bound** is not evaluated. You may recall that some high level languages evaluate every expression, say, in an **if** statement with a compound logical expression, even when unnecessary.

5.3 equal?

At this point, primarily to be less restricted to numerical examples, we introduce the **equal?** predicate. **equal?** is similar to =, which we used earlier for testing numerical equality, except that it's typically used in nonnumerical situations. It is one of a class of predicates for testing equality called *equivalence predicates*, which we will discuss later. **equal?** is quite common in program code that provides conditional execution.

Consider the following examples.

```
[1] (equal? 'x 'y)
()
[2] (equal? 'x 'x)
#T
[3] (define x 3)
X
[4] (define y 6)
Y
[5] (equal? x y)
()
[6] (equal? (* x 2) y)
#T
[7] (define employee 'bill)
EMPLOYEE
[8] (define instructor 'bill)
INSTRUCTOR
[9] (equal? instructor employee)
#T
[10] (define sister "Janet")
SISTER
[11] (equal? sister "Janet")
#T
[12] _
```

Typically, **equal?** isn't used for numerical comparisons, although you can see that it works for the examples given at prompts [5] and [6]. **equal?** is quite convenient for symbolic processing, say, in AI or database applications. It works with both symbols and strings as demonstrated by prompts [7] through [11].

5.4 if

The **if** construct is the most common tool for altering program flow in most computing languages. Older LISP dialects did not provide **if**, but provided the more general construct **cond** instead. Scheme provides both.

There are typically two legal **if** forms, only the first of which is essential in standard Scheme:

```
(if <logical-test> <true-action> <false-action>)

(if <logical-test> <true-action>)
```

Try the following examples with your Scheme system.

```
[12] (if #t 't 'f)
T
[13] (if #f 't 'f)
F
[14] (if 'any-non-false 't 'f)
T
[15] (if #t 't)
T
[16] (if #f 't)
()
[17] (if employee employee)
BILL
[18] (if (equal? sister "Janet") 'hi-sis 'hi)
HI-SIS
[19] _
```

First, try **if** with the Boolean constants true and false. (You must substitute your system's true and false values.) Since we've used Boolean true directly at prompt [12], **<logical-test>** evaluates to true and **<true-action>** is executed (evaluated). Likewise, **<false-action>** is evaluated at prompt [13]. Again, any non-false value evaluates to true (prompt [14]).

Note that PC Scheme supports the use of **if** without a **<false-action>**; at prompt [16] no action is specified for the false condition, therefore the result of the **if <logical-test>** is simply returned.

Try defining a function which makes use of **if.** To do so, you may want to invoke your editor, so that proper indention is easily supplied.

For the sake of illustration, we can define our own version of the absolute value function. **absolute** illustrates the use of a single **if**; **safe-absolute** illustrates nested **ifs**.

```
;;;;     absolute.s     ;;;;;;;;;;;;;;;;;;;;;;;;;;;;;;;;;;;;;;;;;;;

;;;;;;;;;;;;;;;;;;;;;;;;;;;;;;;;;;;;;;;;;;;;;;;;;;;;;;;;;
;; ABSOLUTE returns the absolute value of a number.
;; There is no error checking.
;;;;;;;;;;;;;;;;;;;;;;;;;;;;;;;;;;;;;;;;;;;;;;;;;;;;;;;;;

(define (absolute n)
```

```
  (if (< n 0)
      (* n -1)
      n))


;;;;;;;;;;;;;;;;;;;;;;;;;;;;;;;;;;;;;;;;;;;;;;;;;;;;;;;;;;;;;;
;; SAFE-ABSOLUTE returns the absolute value of a number.
;; It checks to make sure the argument is numeric.
;;;;;;;;;;;;;;;;;;;;;;;;;;;;;;;;;;;;;;;;;;;;;;;;;;;;;;;;;;;;;;

(define (safe-absolute n)
  (if (number? n)
      (if (< n 0)
          (* n -1)
          n)
      (display "argument must be a number")))


[19] (e)
OK
[20] (absolute -3)
3
[21] (absolute sister)

[VM ERROR encountered!] Non-numeric operand to arithmetic
operation
(>? 0 "Janet")

[Inspect] Quit
[22] (safe-absolute sister)
argument must be a number
[23] (safe-absolute 5)
5
[24] (exit)
```

5.5 cond

The most widely used LISP syntactic form for **cond**itional execution is **cond**; it has the following syntax.

```
(cond <clause>...)
```

where each **<clause>** has the form

```
(<logical-test> <expression>...)
```

and the last **<clause>** may substitute the keyword **else** for **<logical-test>**.

```
(else <expression>...)
```

Less formally, the form is

```
(cond
  (<logical-test> <exp-1> <exp-2> ... <exp-n>)
  (<logical-test> <exp-1> <exp-2> ... <exp-n>)
  ...
  ...
  (else <exp-1> <exp-2> ... <exp-n>))
```

Each **<clause>** is evaluated in turn until a **<clause>** is encountered with a true (non-false) **<logical-test>**, or until the **else** **<clause>** is encountered, which always evaluates to true. When the first non-false **<clause>** is encountered, each associated **<expression>** is evaluated in left-to-right order; the result of the last **<expression>** evaluation is returned as the result of the **cond**.

Note that if no **<expression>**s are specified in a **<clause>**, the result of the **<logical-test>** is returned. If all **<logical-test>**s are false, and there is no **else**, the returned result is unspecified (implementation-dependent).

We can rewrite **safe-absolute** as **safe-abs** using (in this case) one **cond**.

```
;;;;     absolute.s     ;;;;;;;;;;;;;;;;;;;;;;;;;;;;;;;;;;;;;;;;;

;;;;;;;;;;;;;;;;;;;;;;;;;;;;;;;;;;;;;;;;;;;;;;;;;;;
;; SAFE-ABS returns the absolute value of a number.
;; It checks to make sure the argument is numeric.
;;;;;;;;;;;;;;;;;;;;;;;;;;;;;;;;;;;;;;;;;;;;;;;;;;;

(define (safe-abs n)
  (cond
    ((number? n) (if (< n 0)
                     (* n -1)
                     n))
    (else
      (display "argument must be a number"))))
```

In **safe-abs** the first logical test checks to make sure that the argument is numeric. If so, the **if** is evaluated and its result is returned as the result of the **cond**. If the argument is not numeric, the **else** (always true) is evaluated; the evaluation of **display** results in an error message.

```
[1] (load "absolute.s")
OK
[2] (safe-abs 3)
```

```
3
[3] (safe-abs "any string")
argument must be a number
[4] (safe-abs -5)
5
[5] (exit)
```

As another example, consider **change** which simulates the "brain" of a change machine.

```
;;;;    laundry.s    ;;;;;;;;;;;;;;;;;;;;;;;;;;;;;;;;;;;;;;;;

;;;;;;;;;;;;;;;;;;;;;;;;;;;;;;
;; CHANGE makes change at the
;; neighborhood laundromat.
;;;;;;;;;;;;;;;;;;;;;;;;;;;;;;

(define (change money-tendered)
  (cond
    ((equal? money-tendered 'dollar)
     (display "quarter quarter quarter ")
     (display "dime dime nickel"))
    ((equal? money-tendered 'half-dollar)
     (display "quarter dime dime nickel"))
    ((equal? money-tendered 'quarter)
     (display "dime dime nickel"))
    ((equal? money-tendered 'dime)
     (display "nickel nickel"))
    (else
      (display "insert dollars, half-dollars, ")
      (display "quarters, and dimes only"))))
```

Note that **display** does not generate a carriage return after printing its output; we've used multiple **display**s in the program simply to keep the margins clear of code. **change** uses **cond** to test for each type of legitimate monetary input; **else** is the "catch-all" clause for any nonacceptable input.

```
[1] (load "laundry.s")
OK
[2] (change 'dollar)
quarter quarter quarter dime dime nickel
[3] (change 'quarter)
dime dime nickel
[4] (change 'penny)
insert dollars, half-dollars, quarters, and dimes only
[5] (change 'two-dollar-bill)
```

```
insert dollars, half-dollars, quarters, and dimes only
[6] (change 'dime)
nickel nickel
[7] (exit)
```

5.6 case

The **case** syntactic form is the last major language construct for conditional execution. It is similar to Pascal's **case**, PL/I's **select**, and C's **switch**. It has the following syntax:

```
(case <key> <clause>...)
```

where each **<clause>** has the form

```
((<datum>...) <expression>...)
```

and the last **<clause>** may substitute the keyword **else** for **(<datum>...)**.

```
(else <expression>...)
```

Less formally, the syntax is

```
(case <key>
  ((<datum-1> ... <datum-n>) <exp-1> ... <exp-n>)
  ((<datum-1> ... <datum-n>) <exp-1> ... <exp-n>)
  ...
  ...
  (else <exp-1> ... <exp-n>))
```

Recall that each **<clause>** in a **cond** has a corresponding test expression that determines whether or not subsequent expressions in that **<clause>** are executed. A **case** differs in that there is a preliminary test expression, or **<key>**, that is evaluated. The result of this evaluation is "saved" and compared to the first component of a **<clause>**; the first component is in list form and contains one or more **<datum>**s. If the result of evaluating **<key>** matches any **<datum>** for a particular **<clause>**, the expressions in the corresponding **<clause>** are evaluated in turn and the result of the last expression is returned. As with **cond**, the **else** **<clause>** serves in an "otherwise-do-this" capacity. Each **<datum>** must be *coded* in its "external representation," e.g., a symbol should not be quoted when coded.

As an example, let's modify **change** to use a **case** instead of a **cond**.

```
;;;;     change.s     ;;;;;;;;;;;;;;;;;;;;;;;;;;;;;;;;;;;;;;;;;;;;

;;;;;;;;;;;;;;;;;;;;;;;;;;;;;;;;
;; CHANGE makes change at the
```

```
;; neighborhood laundromat.
;;;;;;;;;;;;;;;;;;;;;;;;;;;;;;;;

(define (change money-tendered)
  (case money-tendered
    ((dollar)
     (display "quarter quarter quarter ")
     (display "dime dime nickel"))
    ((half-dollar)
     (display "quarter dime dime nickel"))
    ((quarter)
     (display "dime dime nickel"))
    ((dime)
     (display "nickel nickel"))
    (else
      (display "insert dollars, half-dollars, ")
      (display "quarters, and dimes only"))))
```

Here, there is only one **<datum>** for each **<clause>**. Note that the symbols are not quoted: **dollar**, ..., **dime**. Of course, to execute **change** the argument must be quoted as before to prevent evaluation. When executed, **change** will produce the same output as the example implemented with **cond**.

As an example of multiple **<datum>**s per **<clause>**, let's write a predicate, **vowel?** that determines if its argument is a vowel.

```
;;;;     vowel.s     ;;;;;;;;;;;;;;;;;;;;;;;;;;;;;;;;;;;;;;;;;;;

;;;;;;;;;;;;;;;;;;;;;;;;;;;;;;;;;;;;;;;;;;
;; VOWEL? is a predicate for vowels.
;; It works with lowercase letters only.
;;;;;;;;;;;;;;;;;;;;;;;;;;;;;;;;;;;;;;;;;;

(define (vowel? char)
  (case char
    ((#\a #\e #\i #\o #\u)
     #t)
    ((#\w #\y)
     'maybe)
    (else
      #f)))
```

Recall our earlier discussion of the character data type; a character is specified by the sequence **#\\<char>**, for any **<char>**acter. (Most languages typically require three characters to specify a particular character, e.g., Pascal: **'<char>'**.)

Next, we can use Scheme interactively to test **vowel?**.

```
[1] (load "vowel.s")
OK
[2] (vowel? #\i)
#T
[3] (vowel? #\y)
MAYBE
[4] (vowel? #\t)
()
[5] _
```

We can also "mimic" characters with single-character symbols.

```
;;;;;;;;;;;;;;;;;;;;;;;;;;;;;;;;;;;;;;;;
;; VOWEL-S? is a predicate for vowels.
;; It works with symbols only.
;;;;;;;;;;;;;;;;;;;;;;;;;;;;;;;;;;;;;;;;

(define (vowel-s? sym)
  (case sym
    ((a e i o u)
     #t)
    ((w y)
     'maybe)
    (else
      #f)))


[5] (vowel-s? 'i)
#T
[6] (vowel-s? 'y)
MAYBE
[7] (vowel-s? 't)
()
[8] (exit)
```

To reiterate, **case** is special in that, in the code, **<datum>**s are not quoted. However, note that at prompts [5] through [7] each argument to **vowel-s?** must be quoted.

5.7 begin

Both **cond** and **case** allow multiple expressions per condition/clause. In both cases, multiple expressions are executed left to right. However, **if** provides for only a single expression for either **<true-action>** or **<false-action>**.

begin provides for the substitution of a group of expressions at any point where a single expression is normally expected. The syntax for **begin** is

```
(begin <expression>...)
```

Each **<expression>** is evaluated from left to right—in sequence. More generally, **begin** is useful anytime you want to guarantee sequential execution of a group of expressions.

As an example of the utility of **begin**, consider the following. Suppose you would like to print a fairly complete error message in the event of illegal input to a function. **display**, which we used earlier, prints only one item at a time, i.e., allows only one argument. Also, it does not provide for output on separate lines.

Typically, an error routine prints some generic statement, plus something specific to the data at hand, possibly over multiple lines. To provide conditional execution, plus interwoven messages, using the **display** function, we must sequence the output using **if** and **begin**, as illustrated by the code below.

```
;;;;    recip.s    ;;;;;;;;;;;;;;;;;;;;;;;;;;;;;;;;;;;;;;;;;;;;

;;;;;;;;;;;;;;;;;;;;;;;;;;;;;;;;;;;;;;;;;;;;;;;;;;;;;;;;;;;;;;;;
;; RECIPROCAL returns the reciprocal of a legal number, or
;; "false" in the event of an illegal argument (0).
;;;;;;;;;;;;;;;;;;;;;;;;;;;;;;;;;;;;;;;;;;;;;;;;;;;;;;;;;;;;;;;;

(define (reciprocal n)
  (if (zero? n)
      #f
      (/ 1 n)))


;;;;;;;;;;;;;;;;;;;;;;;;;;;;;;;;;;;;;;;;;;;;;;;;;;;;;;;;;;;;;;;
;; RECIPROCAL-TAKER is a driver program for demonstrating
;; the function RECIPROCAL.
;;;;;;;;;;;;;;;;;;;;;;;;;;;;;;;;;;;;;;;;;;;;;;;;;;;;;;;;;;;;;;;

(define (reciprocal-taker)
  (define number)
  (newline)
  (display "Enter a number:  ")
  (set! number (read))
  (if (zero? number)
      (begin
        (newline)
        (display "Zero is illegal input.  For example, the")
        (newline)
        (display "reciprocal of 5 is 1/5, or 0.2.  Division")
        (newline)
        (display "by zero is not allowed."))
      (begin
```

```
        (newline)
        (display "The reciprocal of ")
        (display number)
        (display " is ")
        (display (reciprocal number)))))
```

First, we define a stand-alone reciprocal function, **reciprocal**, which returns false in the event of an invalid argument, and the numeric result otherwise.

The flexibility and power of Scheme's treatment of Boolean values is evident. In a sense, we've defined a function that can return two types of output: Boolean and numeric; this isn't possible with some languages. Of course this flexibility is a direct result of Scheme's classification of Boolean values: false and non-false; the numeric output is non-false.

The programmer can take advantage of this flexibility in many circumstances. For example, a function call to **reciprocal** could be nested inside other function calls without disastrous results in the case of "bad" data.

```
[1] (load "recip.s")
OK
[2] (display (reciprocal 0))
()
[3] (display (reciprocal 5))
0.2
[4] (define x (reciprocal 0))
X
[5] (if x (display "perform appropriate calculation here")
(display "perform error action here"))
perform error action here
[6] _
```

Getting back to the use of **begin** for delimiting expression groups, consider **reciprocal-taker**, which prompts the user for input. We define a local variable, **number**, for holding the input, since we need it at multiple points in the program.

reciprocal-taker takes one of two possible actions based on the user's input; hence, **if** is an appropriate control structure. In both cases, there are several statements to execute, and **begin** provides a convenient means of grouping them.

We use **read** to read a numeric value from the console, assigning the returned value to **number**. **newline** is a Scheme primitive for generating a newline sequence, and is required to force output from a **display** to a new line. **reciprocal-taker** works as follows.

```
[6] (reciprocal-taker)

Enter a number:  5

The reciprocal of 5 is 0.2
```

```
[7] (reciprocal-taker)

Enter a number:  0

Zero is illegal input.  For example, the
reciprocal of 5 is 1/5, or 0.2.  Division
by zero is not allowed.
[8] (exit)
```

Later, we discuss Scheme I/O in detail; for now, the primitive functions **newline** and **display** are sufficient and quite convenient, since I/O is of secondary interest at this point.

Exercises

1. Why don't **and**, **or**, and **not** follow the same naming conventions as other predicates?

2. Show the returned value for each of the following:

```
a. (and (> 3 2) (< 3 2))
b. (and (> 3 2) (< 2 3))
c. (or (< 3 2) (> 3 2))
d. (not (> 4 3))
e. (not (not (< 3 2)))
```

3. Define the function **ge** (greater than or equal to) using logical operators only.

4. Show the returned value for each of the following:

```
a. (if (> 3 4))
b. (if (> 3 4) 't)
c. (if (> 3 4) 't 'f)
d. (if 1 1)
```

5. Define the function **sort-3** with three parameters that sorts its arguments in ascending order. Assume numeric arguments and use **if** to implement the function.

6. Develop the function **month->integer** that takes a symbol argument and returns the proper integer between 1 and 12, inclusive. Use **cond** to implement this function.

7. Develop the function **month->#days** that takes a symbol argument and returns the number of days for that particular month. Use **case** to implement this function.

8. Define the function **score->grade** that accepts a numeric score between 0 and 100 inclusive and returns a letter grade using the following scheme:

```
90 - 100 --> A
80 -  89 --> B
70 -  79 --> C
60 -  69 --> D
 0 -  59 --> F
```

9. Define the function **buy-a-vowel** which behaves as follows:

```
[1] (buy-a-vowel)
I'd like to buy a vowel...
OK, which vowel?...                <--- user types a single
OK, good choice!                        character

[2] (buy-a-vowel)
I'd like to buy a vowel...
OK, which vowel?...                <--- here also, but incorrect
That's not a vowel.
[3] (exit)
```

Use a **case** to implement this function. The single character that is typed in response to the prompt can be read, without console echo, using **read-char**.

10. Define the function **square** that accepts one argument and tests it with **number?** before squaring the argument. If the argument is not numeric, use **begin** with **display** to sequence a friendly response.

11. Define the function **hypo** that computes the hypotenuse of a right triangle, given the sides **a** and **b** as parameters. Recall that the relationship is

$$h^2 = a^2 + b^2$$

Use conditional execution syntax to ensure that **a** and **b** are legal.

12. Using conditional execution syntax and the number processing functions described in Chapter 2, develop the function **perfect-square** that accepts an integer argument and returns either (1) its integer square root, if it's a perfect square, or (2) false, if it isn't a perfect square.

Chapter 6

Repetitive Execution

6.1 Introduction

In this chapter we introduce some of Scheme's features for repetitive execution. Scheme provides several language constructs for performing repetition that are quite different from other LISP dialects. Perhaps the most distinguishing characteristic of a Scheme program, as compared to programs written with other languages, is the widespread use of recursion.

Scheme's support for recursion is so extensive and elegant that traditional "do loop" programming, which is common with most traditional languages plus many LISP dialects, is uncommon, unnecessary, and generally discouraged. In fact, Scheme provides very few language constructs for iterative execution. For programmers switching to Scheme from other LISP dialects, this aspect of Scheme requires considerable attention.

In this chapter we introduce repetitive execution in Scheme, including iteration and simple recursion. Powerful applications of recursion require the **let** syntactic form, which will be introduced later.

6.2 Iteration Using do

The Scheme syntactic form **do** is roughly analogous to the Pascal syntactic form **for** and/or **while**. Whereas traditional languages typically provide separate constructs for iteration, that is, with or without control (index) variables, Scheme combines these capabilities into a single syntactic form, **do**, with the following syntax (Common LISP has a similar construct):

```
(do ((<variable> <initial-value> <update>)...)
    (<termination-test> <expression>...)
  <statement>...)
```

Unlike languages that require the programmer to declare storage for control variables elsewhere in the program, for example, at the beginning of the surrounding procedure block, Scheme provides for control variables *local* to the **do**. Each **do** has a list of initial variable bindings, plus a list describing loop termination. The former list may specify optional update actions for each cycle; the latter list may specify multiple expressions which are evaluated in sequence. An important point is that each variable-binding list nested within the initialization list is handled independently, e.g., you can't count on the second one being evaluated before the third one. In other words, they are evaluated in unspecified order.

Execution of **do** proceeds as follows. First, in an unspecified order, each **<initial-value>** is evaluated and bound to the corresponding **<variable>**. Second, the body of the **do**, that is, zero or more **<statement>**s, are executed in sequence, contingent on a pretest evaluation of **<termination-test>**. In other words, the body of the **do** is executed only if **<termination-test>** fails.

Subsequent to each execution of the loop body, each **<variable>** is updated, based on evaluation of any corresponding **<update>** expression. Updating occurs in an unspecified order and **<update>** expressions are optional.

If the pretest of **<termination-test>** evaluates to true, execution of the body is not performed; instead zero or more **<expression>**s are evaluated left to right, and the value of the last **<expression>** is returned as the value of the **do**. If no expressions are specified in the loop termination list, the returned value of the **do** is unspecified.

In the following example **one-to-n** is a function that sums the integers between one and some arbitrary integer (provided as an argument).

```
;;;;     one-to-n.s     ;;;;;;;;;;;;;;;;;;;;;;;;;;;;;;;;;;;;;;;

;;;;;;;;;;;;;;;;;;;;;;;;;;;;;;;;;;;;;;;;;;;;;;;;;;;;;;;
;; ONE-TO-N illustrates looping, the use of control
;; variables, and loop termination.
;; It sums the numbers from one to N (which is
;; more easily determined from:  n * (n + 1) / 2).
;;;;;;;;;;;;;;;;;;;;;;;;;;;;;;;;;;;;;;;;;;;;;;;;;;;;;;;

(define (one-to-n n)
  (do ((i 1 (+ i 1))       ;; initial value 1, incr. = 1
       (sum 0))            ;; initial value 0, no increment
      ((> i n) sum)        ;; if i > n then return the sum
      (set! sum (+ sum i))))
```

one-to-n has two local variables, **i** and **sum** (in addition to the parameter **n**); **i** is initialized and updated after each looping operation, whereas **sum** is initialized but not updated. The looping action is terminated as soon as **i** exceeds **n**, and the value of **sum** is returned. Could you write this function with fewer variables?

one-to-n has only one **<statement>** in the loop body. This version of **one-to-n** is a good example of the *misuse* of **set!**. **set!** has been used to update the value of **sum**; however, **do** has a built-in **<update>**ing facility. A more elegant version of **one-to-n** can be written by taking advantage of **do**'s variable updating capability. In this particular case, eliminating the **set!** eliminates the entire body of the **do**. Body-less **do**s are quite common in Scheme.

```
;;;;     one-to-n.s     ;;;;;;;;;;;;;;;;;;;;;;;;;;;;;;;;;;;;;;;;

;;;;;;;;;;;;;;;;;;;;;;;;;;;;;;;;;;;;;;;;;;;;;;;;;;;;;
;; ONE-TO-N illustrates looping, the use of control
;; variables, loop termination, and bodyless do's.
;; It sums the numbers from one to N (which is
;; more easily determined from:  n * (n + 1) / 2).
;;;;;;;;;;;;;;;;;;;;;;;;;;;;;;;;;;;;;;;;;;;;;;;;;;;;;

(define (one-to-n n)
  (do ((i 1 (+ i 1))     ;; initial value 1, incr. = 1
       (sum 0 (+ sum i)))  ;; initial value 0, incr. = i
      ((> i n) sum)))    ;; if i > n then return the sum
```

one-to-n illustrates the idea of unspecified order of processing the **<update>**s. Here, **sum** is updated using **i**—both appearing in the list of variable bindings. The important point is that **<update>**s are evaluated independently of each other, based on the variable bindings from the previous iteration.

The local variable provision within a **do** enhances code readability. In many cases, a repetitive action requires multiple working variables, in addition to those specifically required for loop control. For example, **sum** is used as an accumulator in the above function. Scheme's **do** syntax allows us to set up a variable in close proximity to its usage. In contrast, some languages require all variable definitions at the beginning of a procedure, even when a particular variable is used at a quite remote location in that procedure. In fact, this is a primary motivation for the trend toward smaller and smaller procedures in modern programming—keeping variable definitions close to their point of usage.

Our functions work as follows:

```
[1] (load "one-to-n.s")
OK
[2] (one-to-n 10)
55
[3] (one-to-n 0)
0
[4] (one-to-n 5)
15
```

```
[5] _
```

Next, consider a list processing example. We can use **do** to build user-defined equivalents of the **length** primitive.

```
;;;;    l-length.s    ;;;;;;;;;;;;;;;;;;;;;;;;;;;;;;;;;;;;;;;;;;;

;;;;;;;;;;;;;;;;;;;;;;;;;;;;;;;;;;;;;;;;;;;;;;;;;;;;;;;
;; L-LENGTH determines the length of a list.
;; It makes unnecessary use of SET!.
;;;;;;;;;;;;;;;;;;;;;;;;;;;;;;;;;;;;;;;;;;;;;;;;;;;;;;;

(define (l-length lst)
  (do ((len 0 (+ len 1)))
      ((null? lst) len)
      (set! lst (cdr lst))))
```

If you are accustomed to languages like Pascal and C that require the programmer to make frequent use of assignment statements, you may be inclined to use **set!**s unnecessarily. Again, we've written **l-length** with an unnecessary **set!** to emphasize this point. A better approach is to update the list as follows:

```
;;;;    l-length.s    ;;;;;;;;;;;;;;;;;;;;;;;;;;;;;;;;;;;;;;;;;;;

;;;;;;;;;;;;;;;;;;;;;;;;;;;;;;;;;;;;;;;;;;;;;;;;;;;;;;;;;;;;
;; LIST-LENGTH determines the length of a list.
;;;;;;;;;;;;;;;;;;;;;;;;;;;;;;;;;;;;;;;;;;;;;;;;;;;;;;;;;;;;

(define (list-length lst)
  (do ((len 0 (+ len 1))
       (reduced-list lst (cdr reduced-list)))
      ((null? reduced-list) len)))
```

reduced-list is initially bound to **lst**. Eventually, it is reduced to the empty list and the value of **len** is returned. Both versions produce the same output:

```
[5] (load "l-length.s")
OK
[6] (l-length ())
0
[7] (l-length '(1 2 (3 3) 4))
4
[8] (list-length '(1 2 (3 3) 4))
4
[9]
(list-length '(1 2 3))
```

```
3
[10] (exit)
```

6.3 Simple Recursion

There is an alternative, and more common, technique for controlling repetition in Scheme, namely, *recursion*. Recursion is a technique whereby a procedure calls itself, either directly or indirectly. Some people believe that recursion is harder to understand than nonrecursive repetition, however, many people disagree. In fact, in some cases the recursive approach is simpler, in the sense that there is less syntax associated with loop management. Regardless of your opinion, recursion is a common programming technique, is supported by most modern languages, and is central to Scheme programming. The latter point is emphasized in this and subsequent chapters.

In Scheme simple program repetition can be achieved via recursion by having a function call itself after performing the action that constitutes the loop body – no special syntax is required. In order to control repetition of a process at least two things are required:

1. a means of (ultimately) terminating the repetition
2. a means of initiating each repetitive cycle

The first is easily provided by the conditional execution constructs discussed earlier; the second, as mentioned, is achieved via procedural self-reference.

The easiest way to discuss recursion is by considering several examples. The first example illustrates a means of initiating each repetitive cycle, but without a provision for termination [(1)]; that is, it produces infinite recursion. Don't try it unless you know how to abort a runaway program on your Scheme system.

Implementation note: The following example uses **read-ln**, a user-defined function that is discussed in a later chapter. You really don't need to run this program, since a sample dialog is given. However, if you would like to do so, you must include either the **read-ln** function or a similar function provided by your Scheme implementation.

```
;;;;     why.s     ;;;;;;;;;;;;;;;;;;;;;;;;;;;;;;;;;;;;;;;;;;;

;;;;;;;;;;;;;;;;;;;;;;;;;;;;;;;;;;;;;;;;;;;;;;;;;;;;;;;;;;;;;;
;; Demonstration of the "why syndrome" that mysteriously
;; appears in two-year-olds.
;;;;;;;;;;;;;;;;;;;;;;;;;;;;;;;;;;;;;;;;;;;;;;;;;;;;;;;;;;;;;;

(define (eat-your-green-beans)
  (display "Matthew, please eat your green beans.")
  (why?))
```

```
(define (why?)             ;this predicate illustrates
  (newline)                ;infinite recursion
  (display "Why?")
  (newline)
  (read-ln)
  (why?))
```

Recursive functions can be used in a variety of ways, e.g., as stand-alone functions or as support functions. In this case, the function **why?** mimics an inquisitive two year old child, and can be triggered in a seemingly endless number of ways, perhaps by something like **eat-your-green-beans**. (**why?** really isn't a predicate, but the "?" seem appropriate nevertheless.)

If we execute **eat-your-green-beans**, the following dialog takes place:

```
[1] (load "why.s")
OK
[2] (eat-your-green-beans)
Matthew, please eat your green beans.
Why?
Because they're good for you.
Why?
Because they contain a variety of important nutrients.
Why?
Because nature works that way.
Why?

[VM ERROR encountered!] User keyboard interrupt
()

[Inspect] Quit
[3] (exit)
```

There are several important points here. First, **eat-your-green-beans** is *not* recursive; it employs simple sequence. Its first action is to print a message and its second and last action is to call **why?**. Next, **why** is directly recursive, that is, it calls itself. **why?** employs sequential execution to print a prompt ("Why?") on a separate line and to read a line of input. This sequentially-executed action constitutes the body of the loop, i.e., the action that is to be repeated. Subsequent to the sequential action, the function call to **why?** causes this action to be repeated, i.e., causes the function to recur. Since we have attached no condition to the repetition, it continues indefinitely. (With PC Scheme, for example, a <control-break> keystroke initiates a user interrupt.)

Clearly, this means of producing repetition is quite straightforward and easily programmed. Moreover, in order to control the infinite recursion, all that is required is the addition of conditional execution syntax. The following program illustrates recursion plus "graceful" program termination.

```
;;;;     cookie.s     ;;;;;;;;;;;;;;;;;;;;;;;;;;;;;;;;;;;;;;;;;;;;

;;;;;;;;;;;;;;;;;;;;;;;;;;;;;;;;;;;;;;;;;;;;;;;;;;;;;;;;;;;;;;;;;;;
;; COOKIE-MONSTER illustrates simple tail recursion.
;;;;;;;;;;;;;;;;;;;;;;;;;;;;;;;;;;;;;;;;;;;;;;;;;;;;;;;;;;;;;;;;;;;

(define (cookie-monster n)
  (if (= n 0)
      (begin
        (newline)
        (newline)
        (display "Do you have more cookies?"))
      (begin
        (newline)
        (display "Munch Munch Cookie #:  ")
        (display n)
        (cookie-monster (- n 1)))))
```

cookie-monster uses **if** as a means of terminating the repetition. That is, if there are no more cookies, terminate the loop and display a message; otherwise, display a message and repeat the process by calling **cookie-monster** again. The output from **cookie-monster** is

```
[1] (load "cookie.s")
OK
[2] (cookie-monster 5)

Munch Munch Cookie #: 5
Munch Munch Cookie #: 4
Munch Munch Cookie #: 3
Munch Munch Cookie #: 2
Munch Munch Cookie #: 1

Do you have more cookies?
[3] (exit)
```

Parenthetically, **cookie-monster** is an example of a *tail recursive* function, that is, the recursive function call is the last action that occurs *during a particular invocation*. In other words, there is nothing to be done in a particular invocation of the function subsequent to the recursive call: there is no need to return for further execution to the ith invocation of the function after the recursive call to the $(i + 1)$st invocation. Language implementations that take advantage of this situation are said to be *properly tail recursive*. This issue is discussed in a later section.

There are at least two views of a recursive function. We can view the function **cookie-monster** *externally* as a program that performs a repetitive action based on a single parameter **n**. Typically, repetitive execution is contingent upon some parameter. Here, **cookie-monster** gobbles up **n** cookies, for infinitely large **n** – a function call to **cookie-monster** must specify the number of available cookies, **n**.

However, there is another view of **cookie-monster**: the *internal* view, dealing with its implementation. In an implementation sense, we are concerned with how to carry out the repetition process using recursion. In this case, the proper way to view the repetitive process is "one step at a time." That is, the first step is to consume one cookie. Next comes the realization that the remaining task is a subset of the initial task, namely, consuming n - 1 cookies. Hence we can apply the same process (cookie consumption – the body of the loop) over again, but on a task of reduced dimension. It is this view of our task, the internal or implementation view, that dictates that **cookie-monster** recur.

Confusing these two views of a recursive function initially makes recursion hard to grasp for those who are unfamiliar with recursion and/or are used to iterative programming techniques (**do**). Sometimes it is more convenient to view a repetitive *process* as an iterative one, sometimes as a recursive one. Recursion can be used to *implement* either type of repetition, and in this sense is more flexible and powerful than iteration. A classic example is the factorial function, which we discuss later.

With respect to the preceding examples, there is nothing inherently recursive in the continual repeating of "Why? ... Why?," yet the program can be implemented via recursion. (Try adding a termination condition.) On the other hand, even though the cookie monster program could be implemented with **do**, the process seems somewhat naturally recursive, in that the task can be reduced to a subset of the original task, and thus is a prime candidate for a recursive implementation. (Implement **cookie-monster** with **do**.)

To illustrate that iterative and recursive implementations can be mixed, consider the following example.

```
;;;;     dogscats.s     ;;;;;;;;;;;;;;;;;;;;;;;;;;;;;;;;;;;;;;;;

;;;;;;;;;;;;;;;;;;;;;;;;;;;;;;;;;;;;;;;;
;; DOGS and CATS illustrate recursion,
;; plus recursion termination.
;;;;;;;;;;;;;;;;;;;;;;;;;;;;;;;;;;;;;;;;

(define (cats)           ;CATS is the driver function.
  (newline)
  (display "mmeeoowwwww")
  (newline)
  (dogs)                 ;Provoke the dogs.
  (display
    "Wilma, should we let the cat in (y/n)? ")
  (case (read-char)
    ((#\y #\Y)
     (newline)
     (display "Here kitty, kitty..."))
    (else
```

```
      (newline)
      (display "No Fred, go to sleep.")
      (newline)
      (cats))))            ;CATS is invoked recursively.

(define (dogs)             ;DOGS is an iterative function.
  (do ((i 3 (- i 1)))
      ((zero? i)
       (newline)
       (newline))
      (display "woof woof!! ")))
```

Here, **cats** is recursive, but **dogs** is not. Also, **dogs** is called by the recursive function **cats**. **dogs** is a function implementing a repetitive task via an iterative **do**. However, it is called as part of the sequential execution of the body of **cats**.

Note that the recursive call in **cats**, and hence its ultimate termination, is controlled by the **case** syntax. The **<key>** expression in the **case** is simply a call to the Scheme function that reads a single character from the screen; **read-char** returns the next character typed at the screen. The returned character is compared to two **<datum>**s; if it matches either a lower- or uppercase "y", the recursion is terminated. As you can see from the code, Fred and Wilma aren't going to get any sleep until they let the cat in.

```
[1] (load "dogscats.s")
OK
[2] (cats)

mmeeoowwwwww
woof woof!! woof woof!! woof woof!!

Wilma, should we let the cat in (y/n)?
No Fred, go to sleep.

mmeeoowwwwww
woof woof!! woof woof!! woof woof!!

Wilma, should we let the cat in (y/n)?
No Fred, go to sleep.

mmeeoowwwwww
woof woof!! woof woof!! woof woof!!

Wilma, should we let the cat in (y/n)?
Here kitty, kitty...
[3] (exit)
```

Note that **read-char** doesn't echo the typed character to the screen. (Exercise: Develop a variation of **read-char** that performs echo keyboard input. Hint: There are several ways to do this; however, we've already demonstrated the use of **display**, and it is adequate.)

6.4 Additional Examples Using Recursion

Let's further illustrate recursion with some numerical examples. The traditional example of recursion in introductory computer science textbooks is the factorial function, described by the formula

```
n! = 1,                          for n = 0
   = n * (n - 1)!,               for n > 0
```

Note that the *definition* is inherently recursive; therefore, the factorial function is a good candidate for a recursive implementation. A straightforward recursive implementation is:

```
;;;;    examples.s    ;;;;;;;;;;;;;;;;;;;;;;;;;;;;;;;;;;;;;;;;

;;;;;;;;;;;;;;;;;;;;;;;;;;;;;;;;;;;;;;;;;;;;;;;;
;; FTL implements the standard, recursive
;; factorial function.
;;;;;;;;;;;;;;;;;;;;;;;;;;;;;;;;;;;;;;;;;;;;;;;;

(define (ftl n)
  (cond
    ((zero? n) 1)
    (else (* n (ftl (- n 1))))))
```

ftl uses a **cond** to control the recursion; however, there are only two conditions here and thus an **if** is equally appropriate. Note that adding a third condition, namely, checking for illegal input, is straightforward with a **cond**.

ftl is a direct implementation of the preceding formula. If the argument has a value of zero, the result is one: (ftl 0) – > 1. (N = 0 is called the *boundary condition*.) If the argument has value 3, the result is given by the **else** clause, namely, (ftl 3) – > (* 3 (ftl 2)). However, Scheme's evaluation of "(ftl 2)" results in a recursive invocation of **ftl**. The recursive call and return process for **ftl** is outlined in Figure 6.1.

There's a lot to be said for modern languages that allow a direct coding of the original task as in **ftl**. Sometimes, primarily for program readability and maintenance, a direct coding is preferable. A substantial portion of the code that exists in FORTRAN for scientific computing is devoted to expressing naturally recursive mathematical tasks in an iterative form. (FORTRAN doesn't support recursion.)

However, there are other implementation issues. An important one is program efficiency. In the case of **ftl**, note that each time the function recurs the previous invoca-

```
(ftl 3)-->(* 3 (ftl 2))
          (ftl 2)-->(* 2 (ftl 1))
                    (ftl 1)-->(* 1 (ftl 0))
                              (ftl 0)--> 1
                         (* 1 1)--> 1
                 (* 2 1)--> 2
      (* 3 2)--> 6
```

Figure 6.1 Recursion in the Factorial Function

tion must be saved, or preserved, so that the multiplication can be performed upon return. In other words, **ftl** is *not* tail recursive by our earlier definition. Thus, there is a concern for both space and time efficiency, for large n.

Scheme is a properly-tail-recursive language, which means that tail recursive functions are optimized for efficiency by avoiding the unnecessary preservation and management of data (variables) associated with each recursive invocation—when possible. However, some burden is *on the programmer* to provide tail recursive versions of functions, when such an implementation is possible.

In our opinion, the recursion that we've done so far is simpler than functionally equivalent iterative implementations. However, providing tail recursive versions of recursive implementations requires a little more thought. Nevertheless, their coding is still quite straightforward; we can easily write a tail recursive version of the factorial function, in which case Scheme can perform what is called *tail recursion elimination.*

```
;;;;    fact.s    ;;;;;;;;;;;;;;;;;;;;;;;;;;;;;;;;;;;;;;;;;;;

;;;;;;;;;;;;;;;;;;;;;;;;;;;;;;;;;;;;;;;;;;;;;
;; FACT is a tail recursive version of the
;; factorial function.
;;;;;;;;;;;;;;;;;;;;;;;;;;;;;;;;;;;;;;;;;;;;;

(define (fact n)
  (define (tr-fact result n)              ;; define a helper
    (if (zero? n)                         ;; function
        result
        (tr-fact (* result n) (- n 1))))

  (tr-fact 1 n))                          ;; invoke the helper
```

fact defines a helper function, **tr-fact**, that "builds up the result on the way in." This is achieved by coding **tr-fact** with two parameters: one parameter handles the reduction of **n** and one parameter carries along the result accumulated so far. Thus, if **n** is zero, **tr-fact** returns the current value of **result**; otherwise it is called with updated values of **result** and **n** – via argument/parameter passing. Note that since **tr-fact** is the last (and in this case only) expression evaluation in **fact**, **fact** simply returns the value returned by **tr-fact**. This implementation of the factorial function is tail recursive because as soon as the boundary condition is reached the entire process is complete – all calculations have been made.

Note that this particular usage of tail recursion corresponds to what is traditionally thought of as an iterative definition of factorial, namely,

$$n! = n * (n - 1) * (n - 2) * ... * 1$$

This emphasizes the point made earlier that recursion can be used to implement either recursive or iterative algorithms.

The helper function is necessary only because we prefer to isolate the user from implementation issues. That is, it isn't appropriate to ask a user to use **tr-fact** directly, supplying the constant argument, 1; **fact**'s implementation should reflect its (natural) function. Thus, **fact** is written to accept one argument, **n**, whereas **tr-fact** requires two arguments, **result** and **n**. The (executable) body of **fact** consists of a simple expression, a call to **tr-fact**. Note that this method of using (nested) helper functions provides one means of establishing and initializing local variables. In this case, we use **tr-fact** to establish the local variable **result** and we use a function call to initialize it.

Both **ftl** and **fact** work as follows.

```
[1] (load "examples.s")
OK
[2] (ftl 0)
1
[3] (ftl 3)
6
[4] (ftl 5)
120
[5] (ftl 45)
119622220865480194561963161495657715064383733760000000000
[6] (exit)
```

As you can see from the preceding example, bignums are very convenient.

As another example of this use of helper functions, consider the following tail recursive implementation of **r-l-length**, which determines the length of a list.

```
;;;;     l-length.s     ;;;;;;;;;;;;;;;;;;;;;;;;;;;;;;;;;;;;;;

;;;;;;;;;;;;;;;;;;;;;;;;;;;;;;;;;;;;;;;;;;;;;;;
;; R-L-LENGTH determines the length of a list
;; using a recursive implementation.
;;;;;;;;;;;;;;;;;;;;;;;;;;;;;;;;;;;;;;;;;;;;;;;
```

```
(define (r-l-length lst)
  (define (r-length len reduced-lst)             ;; define a
    (if (null? reduced-lst)                      ;; helper
        len                                      ;; function
        (r-length (+ len 1) (cdr reduced-lst)))) ;;

   (r-length 0 lst))                          ;; invoke the helper
```

The boundary condition is the empty list with length zero; this value is required in the initial call to **r-length**, since the empty list is a legitimate argument. Compare **r-l-length** to **list-length** above. **r-l-length** uses what is called *cdr recursion* to advance through the list element by element. That is, each time **r-length** recurs it does so on a reduced list, the previous list minus its first element, i.e., the **cdr** of the list. This is an important and commonplace approach to list processing in Scheme that should be understood before proceeding. In many cases the contents of the car of the list are used also. In this case, since we are only interested in the number of elements in the list, we merely increment **len** instead of formally processing the car component.

As a final example, consider a function that computes the prime factors of positive integers and returns them in list form.

```
;;;;     examples.s     ;;;;;;;;;;;;;;;;;;;;;;;;;;;;;;;;;;;;;;;;

;;;;;;;;;;;;;;;;;;;;;;;;;;;;;;;;;;;;;;;;;;;;;;
;; PRIME-FACTORS computes the prime factors
;; of positive integers.
;;;;;;;;;;;;;;;;;;;;;;;;;;;;;;;;;;;;;;;;;;;;;;

(define (prime-factors n)
  (define (primes number divisor)
    (cond
      ((< number divisor)
       '())
      ((integer? (/ number divisor))
       (cons divisor (primes (/ number divisor) divisor)))
      (else
        (primes number (+ divisor 1)))))

  (if (< n 1)
      (display "*** number must be a positive integer ***")
      (primes n 2)))
```

The main code for **prime-factors** is the **if** syntactic form. If the argument is legal, i.e., a positive integer, the helper function **primes** is called; **prime-factors** returns the list returned by **prime**. It works as follows:

```
[1] (load "examples.s")
OK
[2] (prime-factors 100)
(2 2 5 5)
[3] (prime-factors 2)
(2)
[4] (prime-factors 0)
*** number must be a positive integer ***
[5] (exit)
```

6.5 car-cdr Recursion

As a final example of recursive processing, we illustrate a type of recursion that we will need in later chapters, namely, *car-cdr recursion*. So far, we've used cdr recursion to advance through a list during recursive processing. Sometimes it is necessary to call a function recursively on both the car and the cdr of its argument, hence, car-cdr recursion.

As an example, consider a function, such as **list-sum** below, that sums the elements of a list, including the situation where lists are nested:

```
;;;;     list-sum.s     ;;;;;;;;;;;;;;;;;;;;;;;;;;;;;;;;;;;;;;;

;;;;;;;;;;;;;;;;;;;;;;;;;;;;;;;;;;;;;;;;;;;;;;;;;;;;;;;;;;;;;;;
;; LIST-SUM sums the elements of a list.  It uses car-cdr
;; recursion to process sublists.
;;;;;;;;;;;;;;;;;;;;;;;;;;;;;;;;;;;;;;;;;;;;;;;;;;;;;;;;;;;;;;;

(define (list-sum lst)
  (cond
    ((null? lst)                                       ;finished
     0)
    ((pair? (car lst))                                 ;nested
     (+ (list-sum (car lst)) (list-sum (cdr lst)))) ;structure
    (else
      (+ (car lst) (list-sum (cdr lst))))))           ;next item
                                                       ;is atomic
```

The boundary condition occurs when a list (or nested list) is empty, i.e., a list is reduced to the empty list through recursion. In this case, zero is returned. Note that the result of each recursive call to **list-sum** constitutes a term in a sum operation using Scheme's addition operator – there is no need for a local variable to hold an intermediate sum.

In **list-sum**, cdr recursion is used to advance through the list element by element. At some point, an element may not be atomic; this is handled by the second **cond** clause, which makes a recursive call on both the car and the cdr of **lst**. In each case, the result of the recursive call becomes a term in an addition operation.

list-sum produces the following output:

```
[1] (load "list-sum.s")
OK
[2] (list-sum '(1 2 3))
6
[3] (list-sum '())
0
[4] (list-sum '(2 3 -5 (4 -4 (2 5) -2 -2 1 1)))
5
[5] (exit)
```

Exercises

1. Develop the function **list-of-element** that accepts two arguments:

```
(list-of-element <element> <count>)
```

and returns a list of **<count>** **<element>**s. Use **do** to implement this function.

2. Develop the function (predicate?) **rose?** that accepts one argument, which can be absolutely anything, and prints the output:

A rose is a rose is a rose is a rose.

Use **display** in conjunction with **do.**

3. Modify the iteration in **one-to-n** so that fewer variables are used.

4. Define the function **i-launch** that prints the following output contingent upon the parameter, **n**, when given the starting count for the countdown. Use **do** to implement **i-launch.**

```
5              ;; here n = 5
4
3
2
1
0
B-L-A-S-T-O-F-F
```

5. Implement **list-of-element** from Exercise 1 using recursion instead of **do.**

6. Implement **r-launch** as a recursive version of **i-launch** from Exercise 4.

7. Define the predicate **list?** that evaluates whether or not its argument is a list, either proper or improper.

8. Modify **list?** in Exercise 7 to return Boolean true for proper lists only.

9. Define your own version of Euclid's GCD algorithm using **if** and simple recursion.

10. Modify **r-l-length** to handle nested lists by using car-cdr recursion.

11. Define your own modified version of **read-char** that echoes the typed character to the console. This can be done quite easily using **display**.

12. Rewrite the factorial function given in this chapter so that it incorporates error detection for negative integers.

13. Using **perfect-square** from the exercises in Chapter 5, write a function **perfect-square-list** that returns a list of all perfect squares between **start** and **stop** inclusive, where **start** and **stop** are two integer parameters.

14. Write a function **reverse-integer** that accepts an integer parameter, **n**, and returns an integer formed by reversing the digits of **n** – both the parameter and returned value are integers, not string representations of integers. Negative arguments should return a negative result. You may find the following useful: **quotient**, **remainder**, and/or **modulo**. Use a **do** to implement an iterative solution.

15. Do Exercise 14 using a tail recursive implementation.

16. Develop a function that estimates the value of pi (3.14159...) by performing the following sum for 100 terms, and then multiplying by 4:

$$(pi / 4) = 1 - (1 / 3) + (1 / 5) - (1 / 7) + (1 / 9) - \ldots$$

17. A good approximation to e^x can be obtained by the sum

$$e^x = 1 + x + (x^2 / 2!) + (x^3 / 3!) + (x^4 / 4!) \ldots$$

provided that a sufficient number of terms are included in the sum. Develop a function, **e-x**, that performs this approximation for the first 100 terms in the sum. Compare your function's result with Scheme's **exp** function. (You must supply a factorial function also.)

18. Develop a function, **prime-factors-list**, that accepts a single argument in list form and returns an alternate list, where every integer in the argument is replaced by a list of its prime factors, and every non-integer in the argument is replaced by '().

Chapter 7

Let Forms

7.1 Introduction

As we've seen, Scheme is a lexically scoped language. A primary advantage of lexical scoping is that it allows the programmer to *localize* variables, i.e., to define variables in close proximity to their point of usage. In earlier chapters we used **define** to create top-level, or global, definitions of variables and functions. In addition, we've used **define** to build user-defined functions in which all (variable) references are to local variables. Up to this point, we've had three mechanisms for providing local variables in functions:

1. function parameters
2. the **do** syntactic form
3. the **define** syntactic form (placed immediately after the parameter list)

We've also defined functions local to other functions.

Scheme provides another major syntactic form for establishing local variable bindings called **let**. In fact, there are several variations of **let**, four of which we consider in this chapter.

7.2 let

The syntax for **let** is

```
(let ((<variable> <initial-value>)...)
  <statement>...)
```

That is, much as with the **do** construct given earlier, multiple local variable bindings are established via a nested list syntax. The body of the **let**, i.e., the statements within the lexical scope of the local variables, is provided immediately after the initializations. Note that the local variable bindings are performed in an unspecified order, and thus should not be interdependent.

As an example of **let**, consider **hello**, a revision of **greeting** from an earlier chapter.

```
;;;;    greeting.s    ;;;;;;;;;;;;;;;;;;;;;;;;;;;;;;;;;;;;;;

;;;;;;;;;;;;;;;;;;;;;;;;;;;;;;;;;;;;;;;;;;;;;;;;;;;;;;;;;;;;;
;; HELLO prompts for and reads the user's name (in symbol
;; form--first character lowercase), and then greets the
;; user.
;;;;;;;;;;;;;;;;;;;;;;;;;;;;;;;;;;;;;;;;;;;;;;;;;;;;;;;;;;;;

(define (hello)
  (let ((name ())
        (prompt "Your (first) name please:  "))
    (display prompt)
    (set! name (read))
    (display "Hello ")
    (display name)
    (display "!")))
```

Two variables are defined local to the **let**: **name** and **prompt**. The first is initialized to a null value (the empty list), and the second is given a string value. The body of the **let** is composed of statements that prompt for the user's name and provide a greeting.

hello uses **set!**, as did **greeting**. However, the **let** provides us with enough flexibility to avoid the use of **set!** in this particular application. The next program, **hi**, illustrates that **let** doesn't necessarily have to occur at the beginning of a function, and it illustrates a more concise coding that avoids **set!**.

```
;;;;    greeting.s    ;;;;;;;;;;;;;;;;;;;;;;;;;;;;;;;;;;;;;;

;;;;;;;;;;;;;;;;;;;;;;;;;;;;;;;;;;;;;;;;;;;;;;;;;;;;;;;;;;;;
;; HI prompts for and reads the user's name (in symbol
;; form--first character lowercase), and then greets the
;; user.
;;;;;;;;;;;;;;;;;;;;;;;;;;;;;;;;;;;;;;;;;;;;;;;;;;;;;;;;;;;;

(define (hi)
  (display "Your (first) name please:  ")
  (let ((name (read)))
    (display "Hi ")
    (display name)
    (display "!")))
```

In this version we display the user prompt first and take advantage of **let**'s flexibility in binding local variables; namely, (almost) any expression is legal for **<initial-value>**. Here, the result of reading a symbol from the console is bound to **name**.

One of the most important uses of **let** forms is for establishing (logical) constants in a program/function. For example, suppose that you are coding a screen I/O function that uses newline sequences in several places, or for that matter, in just one place. Newline sequences differ across computing systems; thus, you could establish **<newline>** (for your computing system) as a constant that could be easily changed by another user, i.e., portable code.

We will code I/O utilities that use **<newline>** s in later chapters, and make use of **let** for code readability and portability. For now, the following serves as an example of using **let** to "set off" constant definitions.

```
;;;;    area.s    ;;;;;;;;;;;;;;;;;;;;;;;;;;;;;;;;;;;;;;;;;;;;

;;;;;;;;;;;;;;;;;;;;;;;;;;;;;;;;;;;;;;;;;;;;;;;;;;;;;;;;;;;;;;
;; AREA calculates the area of a circle, given the radius.
;;;;;;;;;;;;;;;;;;;;;;;;;;;;;;;;;;;;;;;;;;;;;;;;;;;;;;;;;;;;;;

(define (area radius)
  (let ((pi 3.14))
    (* pi radius radius)))
```

Even though **area** is quite simple, it is sufficient to illustrate the use of **let** to promote code readability. Here, we define a program constant, **pi**, at the outset, instead of hard-coding its value into the calculation. Again, we should emphasize that physically, **pi** is a variable. However, we can use the **let** construct to represent *logical* constants.

7.3 let*

let* differs from **let** in one way only: the local variable bindings are performed sequentially from left to right, allowing the ith variable binding to be based on the jth binding, where $j < i$. **let*** is sometimes called *sequential let*. Note that you can view **let*** as a shorthand for multiple nested **let**s. That is, **let*** is functionally equivalent to

```
(let ((<variable> <initial-value>))
  (let ((<variable> <initial-value>))
    (let ((<variable> <initial-value>))
      (let ((<variable> <initial-value>))
        ...
        ...
        <statement>...)...)))
```

The following program provides an example of **let***.

```
;;;;    desktop.s     ;;;;;;;;;;;;;;;;;;;;;;;;;;;;;;;;;;;;;;;;

;;;;;;;;;;;;;;;;;;;;;;;;;;;;;;;;;;;;;;;;;;;;;;;;;;;;;;;;;;;;
;; DESKTOP determines the approximate number of words per
;; page of text, given certain parameters.
;;;;;;;;;;;;;;;;;;;;;;;;;;;;;;;;;;;;;;;;;;;;;;;;;;;;;;;;;;;;

(define (desktop print-type)
  (let* ((total-lines-per-page 60)
         (t-margin 3)
         (b-margin 5)
         (first-print-line (+ t-margin 1))
         (last-print-line (- total-lines-per-page b-margin))
         (printed-lines-per-page (- last-print-line t-margin))
         (elite 12)
         (pica 10)
         (word-size 6)
         (page-width 6.5)
         (chars-per-line (if (equal? print-type 'elite)
                             (* page-width  elite)
                             (* page-width pica)))
         (words-per-line (quotient (truncate chars-per-line)
                                   word-size)))
    (* words-per-line printed-lines-per-page)))
```

desktop illustrates several features of Scheme, in particular, its power and flexibility. **desktop** has one parameter, **print-type**, which should be either **elite** or **pica**, expressed in symbol form. **print-type** is used in the initialization of **chars-per-line**. Specifically, it is part of an **if** which must be evaluated to produce an **<initial-value>** binding for **chars-per-line**. Also, evaluation of the **if** syntax depends on the bindings for **page-width**, **elite**, and **pica**, which are established at earlier points. Note that there are no **set!**s in this function – many languages would require multiple assignment statements in such an application.

desktop illustrates an aspect of Scheme that differs significantly from most other languages. Scheme allows the programmer to isolate much of the mundane code in a program from the principal, and often intricate code, that truly characterizes the program. For example, if **desktop** performed a "real" desktop publishing function, say, printing a page layout, the coding for the page layout could appear in the body of the **let***, separate from the variable initialization code. Scheme's provision for separation, or abstraction, of source code makes it an ideal implementation language for large programming projects.

7.4 Named let

The first two forms of **let** are useful as mechanisms for establishing and initializing local variables. On the other hand, named **let** is useful primarily as a program control mechanism; named **lets** are commonly used by Scheme programmers for implementing repetition. In fact, named **let** is the most general syntactic form available in Scheme for implementing repetition, in that it is a generalization of the **do** syntactic form, yet it also supports recursion. Named **let** is identical to **let**, except that the **let** form is named:

```
(let <name> ((<variable> <initial-value>)...)
  <statement>...)
```

<name> is significant in the sense that any **<statement>** within the **let** body may contain a recursive call to the named **let**. In essence, Scheme can allow the recursive call in a named **let** because it is converted to a procedure. In other words, **<name>** is bound to a function where the function body is defined by **<statement>...**, the function parameters are the **<variable>**s, and the **<initial-value>**s serve as arguments for the first call to **<name>**.

Named **let** is a convenient Scheme construct for coding recursive functions such as the factorial function. To emphasize the elegance of named **let**, the tail recursive version of the factorial function presented earlier, **fact**, is juxtaposed with **ftrl**, a tail recursive implementation of factorial using named **let**.

```
;;;;     fact.s     ;;;;;;;;;;;;;;;;;;;;;;;;;;;;;;;;;;;;;;;;;;;

;;;;;;;;;;;;;;;;;;;;;;;;;;;;;;;;;;;;;;;;;;;;;;;;;;;;;
;; FACT is a tail recursive version of the
;; factorial function.
;;;;;;;;;;;;;;;;;;;;;;;;;;;;;;;;;;;;;;;;;;;;;;;;;;;;;

(define (fact n)
  (define (tr-fact result n)                ;; define a helper
    (if (zero? n)                           ;; function
        result
        (tr-fact (* result n) (- n 1))))

  (tr-fact 1 n))                            ;; invoke the helper


;;;;;;;;;;;;;;;;;;;;;;;;;;;;;;;;;;;;;;;;;;;;;;;;;;;;;;;
;; FTRL is a tail recursive version of the
;; factorial function that uses a named let.
;;;;;;;;;;;;;;;;;;;;;;;;;;;;;;;;;;;;;;;;;;;;;;;;;;;;;;;
```

```
(define (ftrl n)
  (let tr-fact ((result 1) (n n))
    (if (zero? n)
        result
        (tr-fact (* result n) (- n 1)))))
```

In **ftrl** the name **tr-fact** is bound to the **let**, allowing the recursive reference in the otherwise clause of the **if**. **tr-fact** begins execution with the argument "1" passed to the first parameter **result**; or, if you prefer the alternate view, **result** is initialized to one. Also, the argument to **ftrl** is evaluated and passed as an argument to the second parameter in **tr-fact**, namely, **n**. The fact that both of these are named "**n**" is completely immaterial; i.e., in the following code the value of **i** is passed to **n**.

```
(define (ftrl i)
  (let tr-fact ((result 1) (n i)) ...
```

To reiterate, named **let** is a powerful and elegant Scheme construct. We use it repeatedly throughout this text and at this point, for emphasis, we provide additional examples. We can provide another numerical example and also review recursion by demonstrating three versions of an arbitrary function, **power**. We consider the ordinary recursive version, a tail recursive version using a locally-**define**d helper function, and a named-**let** version.

```
;;;;    power.s    ;;;;;;;;;;;;;;;;;;;;;;;;;;;;;;;;;;;;;;;;;;;

;;;;;;;;;;;;;;;;;;;;;;;;;;;;;;;;;;;;;;;;;;;;;;
;; POWER returns the value of M raised
;; to the Nth power.
;;;;;;;;;;;;;;;;;;;;;;;;;;;;;;;;;;;;;;;;;;;;;;

(define (power m n)
  (cond
    ((< n 0) (display "*** exponent must be nonnegative ***"))
    ((zero? n) 1)
    (else (* m (power m (- n 1))))))


;;;;;;;;;;;;;;;;;;;;;;;;;;;;;;;;;;;;;;;;;;;;;;;;
;; POWER-TR returns the value of M raised
;; to the Nth power.
;;;;;;;;;;;;;;;;;;;;;;;;;;;;;;;;;;;;;;;;;;;;;;;;

(define (power-tr m n)
  (define (power m count result)
    (if (zero? count)
        result
```

```
        (power m (- count 1) (* m result))))

  (if (< n 0)
      (display "*** exponent must be nonnegative ***")
      (power m n 1)))


;;;;;;;;;;;;;;;;;;;;;;;;;;;;;;;;;;;;;;;;;;;;;;;;
;; POWER-LET returns the value of M raised
;; to the Nth power -- using LET.
;;;;;;;;;;;;;;;;;;;;;;;;;;;;;;;;;;;;;;;;;;;;;;;;

(define (power-let m n)
  (let power ((number m)
              (exponent n)
              (result 1))
    (cond
      ((< exponent 0)
       (display "*** exponent must be nonnegative ***"))
      ((zero? exponent)
       result)
      (else
        (power m (- exponent 1) (* m result))))))
```

In **power** we employ **cond** to control the recursion, as it allows the specification of multiple conditions: error, boundary, and non-boundary. **power-tr**, on the other hand, checks for an invalid argument before calling the helper function (named **power**), and thus uses the simpler **if** construct in the recursive helper function. Third, **power-let** binds **m** and **n** to **number** and **exponent**, respectively, before checking for illegal values, and thus uses a **cond** construct to provide error checking inside the named **let**.

As a nonnumerical example, consider **chars-til-%**, a function that reads characters from the console, until "%" is typed. It returns a count of the number of characters read, not counting the sentinel.

```
;;;;    percent.s    ;;;;;;;;;;;;;;;;;;;;;;;;;;;;;;;;;;;;;;;;;;;;;;;;;;

;;;;;;;;;;;;;;;;;;;;;;;;;;;;;;;;;;;;;;;;;;;;;;;;;;;;;;;;;;;;;;;;
;; CHARS-TIL-% counts the number of characters typed at
;; the screen until a "%" is typed.
;;;;;;;;;;;;;;;;;;;;;;;;;;;;;;;;;;;;;;;;;;;;;;;;;;;;;;;;;;;;;;;;

(define (chars-til-%)
  (let ((percent #\%))
    (let get-char ((next-char (read-char)) (count 0))
      (if (equal? next-char percent)
          (begin
```

```
          (display "Number of characters: ")
          (display count))
        (begin
          (display next-char)
          (newline)
          (get-char (read-char) (+ count 1)))))))
```

In order to illustrate nested **lets**, **chars-til-%** employs an outer **let** to set up the (logical) constant **percent**. An inner, named **let** implements the iteration. **read-char** is a Scheme function that reads and returns one character from the console; it does not echo (print) the character. **chars-til-%** uses the generic **equal?** predicate to compare each character to the sentinel.

Note that **get-char** (the named **let**) uses a pretest looping technique. A character is read by **read-char** and assigned to **next-char**. If **next-char** equals the percent character, the iteration stops. If the first character read is the percent character, the count is zero. Otherwise, each character is displayed on a separate line and the looping continues.

Make sure you understand both of the following:

```
(let get-char ((next-char (read-char)) (count 0)) ;; 1.
  ...
  ...
      (get-char (read-char) (+ count 1)))))))    ;; 2.
```

In the first case **next-char** and **count** are established and initialized, whereas in the second case they are updated only.

char-til-% produces the following action.

```
[1] (load "percent.s")
OK
[2] (chars-til-%)
a
b
c
d
e
Number of characters: 5
[3] (exit)
```

7.5 letrec

letrec is a variation on **let** that allows for mutually recursive initializations, typically, where the initializations involve procedures. In general, it allows for initializations where there is a circular dependency among the identifiers.

As an example of **letrec**, consider the following version of the factorial function.

```
;;;    letrec.s    ;;;;;;;;;;;;;;;;;;;;;;;;;;;;;;;;;;;;;;;;;;;;;;

;;;;;;;;;;;;;;;;;;;;;;;;;;;;;;;;;;;;;;;;;;;;;;;;
;; FTL implements the factorial function
;; using a letrec syntactic form.
;;;;;;;;;;;;;;;;;;;;;;;;;;;;;;;;;;;;;;;;;;;;;;;;

(define (ftl n)
  (letrec ((fact (lambda (n)
                   (if (zero? n)
                       1
                       (* n (fact (- n 1)))))))
    (fact n)))
```

In this case a (lambda) procedure is bound to the identifier **fact** where the lambda procedure references the identifier **fact**. The body of the **letrec** consists of a single expression evaluation of **fact** with the argument **n**, which is a parameter of **ftl**, the driver function.

The classical example of **letrec** is a mutually recursive definition of the predicates **even?** and **odd?**. In the following example, **even-odd** determines whether a number is even or odd and returns the answer in symbol form.

```
;;;;;;;;;;;;;;;;;;;;;;;;;;;;;;;;;;;;;;;;;;;;;;;;;;;
;; EVEN-ODD determines if a number is even or
;; odd and returns the result in symbol form.
;;;;;;;;;;;;;;;;;;;;;;;;;;;;;;;;;;;;;;;;;;;;;;;;;;;

(define (even-odd n)
  (letrec ((even? (lambda (n)
                    (if (zero? n)
                        #t
                        (odd? (- n 1)))))
           (odd? (lambda (n)
                   (if (zero? n)
                       #f
                       (even? (- n 1))))))
    (if (even? n)
        'even
        'odd)))
```

The output from **even-odd** is

```
[1] (load "letrec.s")
OK
```

```
[2] (even-odd 0)
EVEN
[3] (even-odd 121)
ODD
[4] (even-odd 34374783)      ;Would it ever finish?
 ...
```

Don't try the evaluation at prompt [4] unless you're angry at your computer. You might want to try coding **even-odd** to be more efficient. Later chapters provide additional examples of **letrec.**

Exercises

1. Use a **let** to define the function **circumference** that returns the circumference of a circle given the diameter (parameter). That is, use the **let** to establish the value of **pi** as a "logical" constant, instead of coding 3.14 within the expression for the circumference of a circle.

2. Use a **let** to define the function **tri-area** that returns the area of a triangle when passed the arguments **base** and **height**. The (logical) constant **one-half** should be established by the **let.**

3. Define the function **average** with one parameter, a list. The function should calculate the average of a list of numbers provided as an argument. The primitive **length** can be used in the divisor. The sum of the numbers should be accumulated in a local variable established with **let** (family) syntax.

4. Develop your own version of **max**, a function that returns the largest number in a list, passed as an argument. Is it necessary to use a **set!** in this function? Why or why not?

5. Write a function named **add-two** that reads two numbers from the screen and prints the numbers and their sum. The user should be prompted for the numbers in a reasonable manner. Do not use any **set!**s. Hint: Use a **let*** in conjunction with **begin** to prompt for each number. Recall that **begin** returns the result of the last expression. In this manner, **begin** can be used to interleave prompting and read operations without a **set!**.

6. Use a named **let** to write a recursive function for finding the sum of every number in a list, including nested sublists.

7. Develop a function **square-table** that prints a table of integers and their squares for every integer between **small** and **large**, which are the only function parameters. **display** should be used to print a heading and a closing for the table. Also, every integer and its square should appear on a separate line. Multiple **displays** followed by a call to **newline** can be used to achieve this effect.

8. Develop a more efficient version of **even-odd**, given earlier in this chapter. Hint: The division primitive may be useful!

9. Modify the function in Exercise 6 so that it returns a list where every element represents the element-wise sum of the respective elements in the argument passed to the function:

```
==> (sum-list '(1 4 (1 2 3) ((2 3) 6 (3 4 5)) 9))
(1 4 6 (5 6 12) 9)
```

That is, for each top-level element in the list, an atom is simply passed to the returned list undisturbed, simple lists are replaced by the sum of their elements, and nested lists are reduced by one level of nesting only. For example, in the argument to the preceding **sum-list**, 1, 4, and 9 appear in the returned list, since they were atoms in the argument; the simple list (1 2 3) is replaced by the sum of its elements, 6; however, the nested list ((2 3) 6 (3 4 5)) is reduced to (5 6 12), not to 23.

10. Write a function, **sum**, that employs **sum-list** from Exercise 9 to sum every number in a list, including numbers in nested sublists. That is, a recursive algorithm should be applied until the list returned by **sum-list** contains no nested sublists. Note that the elements of the resulting simple list can be summed by using **list** with **sum-list**.

Chapter 8

Characters and Strings

8.1 Introduction

On several occasions we've informally used both the character and string data types. In this chapter we investigate characters and strings more formally, in particular, we look at the Scheme primitives for manipulating characters and strings. In addition, as programming examples we provide several user-defined functions that are not provided by standard Scheme.

At this point in our discussion of Scheme we've accumulated enough prerequisites to begin the development of non-trivial, user-defined functions. Hopefully, some of these functions will prove useful in developing your personal Scheme function library.

8.2 Characters

A character is represented by one of two forms:

1. #\<char>
2. #\<char-name>

<char> is any uppercase character, lowercase character, or nonalphabetic character, e.g., parenthesis, plus sign, digit, and so on. **<char-name>** represents special characters which are named, e.g., **space**, **newline**, **tab**, **page**, **backspace**, etc. The number of and names for legitimate **<char-name>**s varies among implementations; see your documentation. Case is not significant for **<char-name>**, i.e., **#\space** and **#\SPACE** are equivalent.

In the case of <**char**> being alphabetic, Scheme distinguishes between (1) and (2) based on whether or not a delimiter character occurs immediately after <**char**>, e.g.,

```
(char? #\n)    ;the right parenthesis serves as a delimiter

(char? #\newline)
```

Characters are self-evaluating, distinct from symbols, and case-sensitive.

```
[1] #\a                   ;case-sensitive and self-evaluating
#\a
[2] 'a                    ;the symbol a is something different
A
[3] #\A
#\A
[4] #\newline             ;not case-sensitive
#\NEWLINE
[5] _
```

Next, consider the character-based predicates, many of which are designed to help the programmer distinguish among various character classifications.

Implementation note: Many of the character predicates are non-essential, with respect to standard Scheme, and may not exist in your implementation of Scheme. Several of the predicates presented here (those that don't exist in PC Scheme), are given as library functions later in this chapter.

```
[5] (char-alphabetic? #\v)      ;non-false, system-specific
#T
[6] (char-alphabetic? #\3)
()
[7] (char-numeric? #\v)
()
[8] (char-numeric? #\3)
#T
[9] (char-whitespace? #\3)
()
[10] (char-whitespace? #\space)
#T
[11] (char-whitespace? #\ )          ;avoid this usage
#T
[12] (char-whitespace? #\newline)
#T
[13] (char-whitespace? #\tab)
```

```
#T
[14] (char? #\&)                          ;the most general class.
#T
[15] (char? #\newline)
#T
[16] _
```

Some character-based primitives parallel their numerical counterparts, e.g., relational operators. Since Scheme is case sensitive with respect to characters, there are two categories of relational operators, e.g.,

1. **char=?**
2. **char-*ci*=?**

where *-ci* means case insensitive, i.e., ignore case.

```
[16] (char=? #\space #\ )
#T
[17] (char=? #\b #\B)
()
[18] (char-ci=? #\b #\B)           ;ci = case insensitive
#T
[19] (char<? #\b #\c)
#T
[20] (char>? #\d #\c)
#T
[21] (char<=? #\b #\c)
#T
[22] (char-ci<=? #\b #\C)
#T
[23] (char-upper-case? #\a)
()
[24] (char-lower-case? #\a)
#T
[25] _
```

Scheme character-based primitives can be applied to variables as well.

```
[25] (define a #\a)
A
[26] a
#\a
[27] (char? a)
#T
[28] (char=? a #\a)
#T
```

```
[29] _
```

Scheme, like other LISPs, employs latent typing, which means that type checking is delayed until run-time. Thus, we can define the variable **a** and assign it a character value. Later, we can check its type programmatically by using any of the type checking predicates, e.g., **char?**, **number?**. Because of this run-time flexibility, it is quite easy for the programmer to write, for example, one sort routine that works properly for numbers, characters, strings, and so on.

In addition, Scheme provides functions for converting between data types. Some of the numeric functions support automatic conversion between different numeric types. In the case of character data types, it's possible to convert between character and integer, where the correspondence is based on the underlying character codes for the host computing system. For example, on an ASCII computer a lowercase "a" is represented by (decimal integer) 97.

```
[29] (char->integer #\a)
97
[30] (char->integer #\A)
65
[31] (char->integer #\space)
32
[32] (integer->char 98)
#\b
[33] (char->integer (integer->char 32))
32
[34] (char-upcase #\a)
#\A
[35] (char-upcase #\A)
#\A
[36] (char-downcase #\A)
#\a
[37] (char=? (char-upcase #\a) (integer->char 65))
#T
[38] (exit)
```

Conversion is supported in both directions. Also, conversion between cases is supported. With respect to Scheme's function naming convention, note the mnemonic usage of the character sequence "->" in functions that perform conversion. There is nothing "special" about these characters; we will follow the same convention later in developing such functions.

8.3 Strings

Standard Scheme provides extensive support for the string data type. Most Scheme implementations extend this support with additional primitives.

In Scheme, strings are sequences of characters. Strings are delimited by double quotes; a double quote may be included in a string by escaping it with a backslash. A backslash is handled similarly, e.g.,

```
[1] "A string may include:  \" and \\ following a backslash."
"A string may include:  \" and \\ following a backslash."
[2] (define string-example
"A string may include:  \" and \\ following a backslash.")
STRING-EXAMPLE
[3] (display string-example)
A string may include:  " and \ following a backslash.
[4] (string? string-example)
#T
[5] _
```

Scheme provides the traditional string manipulation functions; unlike some languages, Scheme string functions are zero-based.

```
[5] (make-string 5 #\x)  ;strings are composed of characters
"xxxxx"
[6] (define string-of-xs (make-string 5 #\x))
STRING-OF-XS
[7] (string-length string-of-xs)
5
[8] (string-length string-example)
53
[9] (string-set! string-of-xs 3 #\y) ;permanently modifies it
"xxxyx"
[10] string-of-xs                    ;zero-based indexing
"xxxyx"
[11] (string-ref string-of-xs 3)     ;zero-based indexing
#\y
[12] (string-ref string-of-xs 5)     ;common mistake--made
                                     ;deliberately here!
[VM ERROR encountered!] String index out of range
(STRING-REF "xxxyx" 5)

[Inspect] Quit
[13] _
```

Standard Scheme provides relational operators for strings, including case-insensitive versions.

```
[13] (string=? string-of-xs "xxxyx")
#T
[14] (string-ci=? string-of-xs "XXxyx")
```

```
#T
[15] (string<? "Mary Conner" "Mary Conners")
#T
[16] (string-ci<=? "mary ann" "Mary Ann")

[VM ERROR encountered!] Variable not defined in current
environment
STRING-CI<=?

[Inspect] Quit
[17] (define (string-ci<=? str-1 str-2)
       (or (string-ci<? str-1 str-2)
           (string-ci=? str-1 str-2)))
STRING-CI<=?
[18] (string-ci<=? "mary ann" "Mary Ann")
#T
[19] _
```

Note, however, that PC Scheme doesn't define all combinations of **<**, **>**, **=**, and **-ci**. At prompt [16] we get an error stating that **string-ci< =?** isn't defined; at prompt [17] we provide a user-defined version.

The zero-based indexing is quite convenient; however, if you aren't used to this technique, don't overlook the underlying logic. Consider the **substring** function as an example, specifically, the way in which it combines with **string-length**.

```
[19] (substring "0123456789" 1 3)
"12"
[20] (define substring-note "substring is zero based")
SUBSTRING-NOTE
[21] (substring substring-note 3 6)
"str"
[22] (substring substring-note 18 (string-length substring-note))
"based"
```

The syntax for **substring** is

```
(substring <string> <start> <end>)
```

At prompt [19], 1 is the starting position for the string extraction process. The 3 specifies the ending position for the extraction, not substring length. Also, the substring specification is inclusive for its start and *exclusive* for its end. Thus, the difference between these two values is the actual substring length, not substring length minus one. For example, if you've set a "pointer" to a particular position in a string, this technique allows for convenient retrieval of a substring of arbitrary length. This also facilitates retrieval of the remaining characters in a string using **string-length**, e.g., prompt [22].

Another point is that some functions work with copies of strings, others do not. A function such as **string-append** must of course return a new string, which is a copy of multiple strings.

```
[23] (string-append "Scheme" " is " "great")
"Scheme is great"
[24] _
```

However, it is convenient to be able to modify an existing string—destructively, i.e., "in place." Below, **string-fill!** modifies **substring-note** permanently.

```
[24] (string-fill! substring-note #\X)
"XXXXXXXXXXXXXXXXXXXXXXX"
[25] substring-note
"XXXXXXXXXXXXXXXXXXXXXXX"
[26] _
```

Like **string-append**, **string-copy** makes a new copy of an existing string.

```
[26] (define x (string-copy substring-note))
X
[27] x
"XXXXXXXXXXXXXXXXXXXXXXX"
[28] (define y x)
Y
[29] y
"XXXXXXXXXXXXXXXXXXXXXXX"
[30] (string-fill! y #\Y)
"YYYYYYYYYYYYYYYYYYYYYYY"
[31] y
"YYYYYYYYYYYYYYYYYYYYYYY"
[32] x
"YYYYYYYYYYYYYYYYYYYYYYY"
[33] substring-note
"XXXXXXXXXXXXXXXXXXXXXXX"
[34] _
```

At prompt [26] we store a *copy* under the name **x**. At prompt [28] we make **y** a synonym for **x**. You must be careful in choosing between functions such as **define** and **string-copy**, due to unanticipated side effects. For example, a destructive modification to **y** at prompt [30] changes **x** also. On the other hand, there is no impact on **substring-note**'s value as seen at prompt [25].

In general, making new copies of strings can lead to fewer unanticipated side effects; however, each new string must be taken from remaining primary storage. This is the case with other data types as well, but it is perhaps more of an issue with strings, since programmers frequently manipulate long strings.

Finally, Scheme provides two functions for converting between lists and strings; these are of obvious utility with a list processing language.

```
[34] (string->list "abc")
(#\a #\b #\c)
[35] (list->string '(#\S #\c #\h #\e #\m #\e))
"Scheme"
[36] (exit)
```

8.4 Examples of Library Functions

So far in this chapter we've addressed the character and string primitives provided by standard Scheme. Each implementation typically extends the list of predefined functions. At this point, we can provide our own extensions that further illustrate the preceding primitives. Note that we are primarily interested in illustrating Scheme, and less interested in efficiency at the expense of clarity.

Implementation note: There is no way that we can anticipate the names used by your Scheme implementation for extensions to the Scheme standard. Thus, some of our functions may be redundant in your Scheme implementation, and some may redefine existing functions – functions that have been provided for something quite different. This means that if function **a** exists in your library, and is called by function **b**, a redefinition of **a** may render **b** *totally* useless. Moreover, the side effects may be hard to detect.

For this reason, your Scheme system may warn you immediately after redefinition of a library function – at least during top-level processing. However, if (for example) the editor is itself written in Scheme, you may not get such a warning when an editor function is redefined. Because of this, it is difficult to decide on a strategy for naming functions – if we begin our string functions, for example, with **str-**, we are inconsistent with standard Scheme, but if we choose **string-**, we risk redefinition of primitives.

8.4.1 Character Predicates

The following functions, which were demonstrated previously, may not be present in your version of Scheme. In each case, they are quite short, yet potentially useful. They are provided at this point without discussion.

Implementation note: Some of these functions are present in PC Scheme 2.0, but are absent in PC Scheme 3.0.

```
;;;;     charutil.s     ;;;;;;;;;;;;;;;;;;;;;;;;;;;;;;;;;;;;;;;;;;
```

```
;;;;;;;;;;;;;;;;;;;;;;;;;;;;;;;;;;;;;;;;;;;;;;;;;;;;;;;;;;;
;; CHAR-WHITESPACE? tests for a whitespace character.
;;;;;;;;;;;;;;;;;;;;;;;;;;;;;;;;;;;;;;;;;;;;;;;;;;;;;;;;;;;

(define (char-whitespace? char)
  (case char
    ((#\space #\tab #\newline #\page #\return) #t)
    (else #f)))


;;;;;;;;;;;;;;;;;;;;;;;;;;;;;;;;;;;;;;;;;;;;;;;;;;;;
;; CHAR-NUMERIC? determines if its argument is
;; between #\0 and #\9.
;;;;;;;;;;;;;;;;;;;;;;;;;;;;;;;;;;;;;;;;;;;;;;;;;;;;

(define (char-numeric? char)
  (and (char>=? char #\0) (char<=? char #\9)))


;;;;;;;;;;;;;;;;;;;;;;;;;;;;;;;;;;;;;;;;;;;;;;;;;;;;;;;;;;;
;; CHAR-UPPER-CASE? tests for an uppercase character.
;;;;;;;;;;;;;;;;;;;;;;;;;;;;;;;;;;;;;;;;;;;;;;;;;;;;;;;;;;;

(define (char-upper-case? char)
  (cond
    ((and (char>=? char #\A) (char<=? char #\Z)) #t)
    (else #f)))


;;;;;;;;;;;;;;;;;;;;;;;;;;;;;;;;;;;;;;;;;;;;;;;;;;;;;;;;;;
;; CHAR-LOWER-CASE? tests for a lowercase character.
;;;;;;;;;;;;;;;;;;;;;;;;;;;;;;;;;;;;;;;;;;;;;;;;;;;;;;;;;;

(define (char-lower-case? char)
  (cond
    ((and (char>=? char #\a) (char<=? char #\z)) #t)
    (else #f)))


;;;;;;;;;;;;;;;;;;;;;;;;;;;;;;;;;;;;;;;;;;;;;;;;;;;;;;;;;;;;
;; CHAR-ALPHABETIC? tests for an alphabetic character.
;;;;;;;;;;;;;;;;;;;;;;;;;;;;;;;;;;;;;;;;;;;;;;;;;;;;;;;;;;;;

(define (char-alphabetic? char)
  (cond
    ((char-upper-case? char) #t)
```

```
    ((char-lower-case? char) #t)
    (else #f)))
```

8.4.2 String Manipulation Functions

Many languages provide a function that searches a string for a particular character and returns its position, if found. Such a function is easily provided using the Scheme features that we've studied so far; we name our version: **string-index**.

```
;;;;     strings.s     ;;;;;;;;;;;;;;;;;;;;;;;;;;;;;;;;;;;;;;;;

;;;;;;;;;;;;;;;;;;;;;;;;;;;;;;;;;;;;;;;;;;;;;;;;;;;;;;;;;;;;;;;;
;; STRING-INDEX searches for a character in a string, retur-
;; ning its position -- zero-based.
;; Example usage:  (string-index "string" #\i) ==> 3
;;;;;;;;;;;;;;;;;;;;;;;;;;;;;;;;;;;;;;;;;;;;;;;;;;;;;;;;;;;;;;;;

(define (string-index str search-char)
  (let find-it ((str str) (pos 0))
    (cond
      ((= pos (string-length str))      ;; not found
       ())                              ;; return empty list
      ((char=? (string-ref str pos) search-char)
       pos)
      (else
        (find-it str (+ pos 1))))))
```

In this version, **find-it**, a named **let**, is used to perform the iteration. The search begins at position (**pos**) 0 in the string, advancing one position for each iteration. A **cond** is convenient for handling each of the three possible conditions: (1) search character not found and end-of-string has been reached, (2) search character found at the current position, and (3) search character not found and additional character(s) remain. Condition (3) requires a recursive application of **find-it**—for each iteration the original string is reused, but **pos** must be incremented by one. (The first argument in **find-it** could be omitted by directly referencing the string passed to **string-index**, i.e., the **str** that is global to the **let**.)

Note that **string-index** is tail recursive and thus can be optimized by Scheme. You should study the usage of **string-length** and **string-ref** before proceeding. In particular, when **pos** is equal to the length of **str**, **find-it** has advanced beyond the string, due to the zero-based indexing. Our function works as follows:

```
[1] (load "strings.s")
OK
[2] (string-index "Scheme" #\s)
()
```

```
[3] (string-index "Scheme" #\S)
0
[4] (string-index "Scheme" #\e)    ;finds first occurrence only
3
[5] (string-index "Scheme" #\t)
()
[6] (exit)
```

Sometimes it's convenient to be able to insert or delete characters from a string. We can easily provide these library functions. PC Scheme users should not overlook the warning in the comment area.

```
;;;;     str-i-d.s     ;;;;;;;;;;;;;;;;;;;;;;;;;;;;;;;;;;;;;;;;;;;

;; WARNING -- Renaming STR-DELETE to STRING-DELETE corrupts
;;            the PC Scheme editor (prior to version 3.0).

;;;;;;;;;;;;;;;;;;;;;;;;;;;;;;;;;;;;;;;;;;;;;;;;;;;;;;;;;;;;;;;;;;;
;; STR-INSERT inserts a string into the "middle" of another
;; string, nondestructively returning a new string.  The
;; insertion occurs before position <pos> (zero-based).
;; Usage:  (str-insert <old-string> <new-string> <pos>)
;; Ex. usage:  (str-insert "abcfg" "de" 3) ==> "abcdefg"
;;;;;;;;;;;;;;;;;;;;;;;;;;;;;;;;;;;;;;;;;;;;;;;;;;;;;;;;;;;;;;;;;;;

(define (str-insert old-string new-string pos)
  (if (> pos (string-length old-string))
      ""
      (string-append (substring old-string 0 pos)
                     new-string
                     (substring old-string
                                pos
                                (string-length old-string)))))


;;;;;;;;;;;;;;;;;;;;;;;;;;;;;;;;;;;;;;;;;;;;;;;;;;;;;;;;;;;;;;;;;;;;
;; STR-DELETE strips an arbitrary number of characters from
;; the "middle" of a string, nondestructively returning a new
;; string.  The characters are removed beginning at position
;; <pos> (zero-based).  <len> characters are removed.
;; Usage:  (str-delete <string> <pos> <len>)
;; Ex. usage:  (str-delete "abcde" 2 2) ==> "abe"
;;;;;;;;;;;;;;;;;;;;;;;;;;;;;;;;;;;;;;;;;;;;;;;;;;;;;;;;;;;;;;;;;;;;

(define (str-delete string pos len)
  (if (> (+ pos len) (string-length string))
```

```
      ""
      (string-append (substring string 0 pos)
                     (substring string
                                (+ pos len)
                                (string-length string)))))
```

Both of these functions are quite short and provide examples of common applications of string functions and zero-based indexing.

In our preceding insertion/deletion functions, the **if** syntax provides a convenient mechanism for error testing—**cond** isn't needed. We have to make some decision about error handling. One approach would involve printing error messages, say, if the user specified an illegal **<pos>** in **str-insert**, e.g., beyond the end of **<old-string>**. A second approach, in the case of a reference beyond the end of **<old-string>**, would be to append **<new-string>** to **<old-string>**, however, this strategy promotes hard-to-detect, hair-raising errors. We've adopted the policy of returning a null string in the event of an illegal function application.

Another point to consider is that in order to insert a single character, it must be specified as a string of length one, e.g., "**<char>**". As an exercise, consider using the run-time type-checking predicates to determine programmatically whether the second argument is string or character, and to proceed accordingly using conditional execution constructs.

We can test our functions as follows:

```
[1] (load "str-i-d.s")
OK
[2] (str-insert "abcfg" "de" 3)
"abcdefg"
[3] (str-insert "abcfg" "de" 20)       ;illegal insertion point
""
[4] (str-insert "abcfg" "de" -3) ;Should we have checked this?

[VM ERROR encountered!] Invalid operand to VM instruction
(SUBSTRING "abcfg" 0 -3)

[Inspect] Quit
[5] (str-insert "abcde" "xx" 0)
"xxabcde"
[6] (str-insert "abcde" "xx" 5)
"abcdexx"
[7] (str-delete "abcde" 2 2)
"abe"
[8] (str-delete "abcde" 20 10)
""
[9] (exit)
```

At some point, we have to make a decision about certain types of error checking. For example, prompt [4] demonstrates that we haven't guarded against a negative position—but neither does the Scheme primitive **substring**.

8.4.3 String Conversion Functions

Standard Scheme provides functions for conversion between upper- and lowercase characters, but not for case conversion between strings. We can use the former to define the latter. One of these, **string-upcase**, follows; you may want to code **string-downcase** for your own library.

```
;;;;     strings.s     ;;;;;;;;;;;;;;;;;;;;;;;;;;;;;;;;;;;;;;;;;;;;

;;;;;;;;;;;;;;;;;;;;;;;;;;;;;;;;;;;;;;;;;;;;;;;;;;;;;;;;;;;;;;;;;;
;; STRING-UPCASE returns a string converted to uppercase.
;;;;;;;;;;;;;;;;;;;;;;;;;;;;;;;;;;;;;;;;;;;;;;;;;;;;;;;;;;;;;;;;;;

(define (string-upcase lower-str)
  (do ((str-len (string-length lower-str))
       (position 0 (+ position 1))
       (upper-str "" (string-append
                        upper-str
                        (make-string
                          1
                          (char-upcase (string-ref
                                          lower-str
                                          position))))))
      ((= position str-len) upper-str)))
```

Quite arbitrarily, and for the sake of illustration, we've used **do** to implement the iteration. **str-len** is initialized to the length of **lower-str**, but never updated, as its only function is in testing for loop termination. **position** is incremented by one each time through the loop. **upper-str** is initialized to the null list; during iteration, each character found in **lower-str** is first converted to a string of length one character, and then appended to **upper-str**.

It's common in Scheme to do most, if not all, of the iterative work outside the loop body. In this case the loop body isn't needed, since only simple iteration and updating are required. **string-upcase** can be used as follows:

```
[1] (load "strings.s")
OK
[2] (string-upcase "")
""
[3] (string-upcase "a")
"A"
```

```
[4] (string-upcase "Abc")
"ABC"
[5] (exit)
```

At this point, we consider the process of converting between string and integer data types. Functions for performing this type of conversion provide good examples of character and string processing in Scheme. Standard Scheme recommends two procedures, **number->string** and **string->number**, which are more general, i.e., accommodate numbers other than integers; however, these may not be provided in all Scheme implementations. We provide **str->int**, a function that converts strings to integers; you are encouraged to develop a function for converting integers to strings.

Consider the task of writing system software. Systems programmers write code that can read a number, either from a file or from the console. Typically, the input is in character form and must be converted to a numeric representation. For example, if we write a compiler for a high level language like Pascal, it must process source code that has been stored in a text file (character form). A typical source code statement is:

```
A := -1234;
```

In order to build the numeric value -1234, a string of five characters must be processed, one by one: first, the sign must be recognized, then the "1" must be recognized as a "thousands" digit, and so on.

No matter what language is chosen to implement system software, it won't provide all the tools needed for a particular project. Scheme is no exception. Perhaps the best measure of a high-level language is its potential for extension – to address the problem at hand. As we've seen, Scheme is a very extensible language.

As another example of character and string processing, let's consider the development of a function, **str->int**, which performs the string to integer conversion described previously. One task that must be addressed is the handling of "signed" integers, i.e., integers in string form with a leading sign character, plus or minus. It will be convenient in our implementation of **str->int** to develop a predicate, **sign-prefix?**, for determining whether or not a sign character is present:

```
;;;;;;;;;;;;;;;;;;;;;;;;;;;;;;;;;;;;;;;;;;;;;;;;;;;;
;; SIGN-PREFIX? determines whether or not the
;; integer has a leading sign.
;;;;;;;;;;;;;;;;;;;;;;;;;;;;;;;;;;;;;;;;;;;;;;;;;;;;
(define (sign-prefix? char)
  (or (char=? char #\+) (char=? char #\-)))
```

That is, we want a procedure which will allow us to treat this task abstractly.

In order to convert a character string into an integer, we must have a way of extracting each character, so that its numeric magnitude and position in the ultimate integer can be determined, i.e., 312 = 3 * 100 + 1 * 10 + 2 * 1. In doing so, we need one helper function to convert individual characters to integer equivalents. Note that we do not want the ASCII equivalent of, say, "3", which is 30 (hex). Instead, we need to convert character "3" to integer 3. The following function will perform this task.

```
;;;;;;;;;;;;;;;;;;;;;;;;;;;;;;;;;;;;;;;;;;;;;;;;
;; NUM-CHAR->INT converts a numeric character
;; to a decimal integer.
;;;;;;;;;;;;;;;;;;;;;;;;;;;;;;;;;;;;;;;;;;;;;;;;

(define (num-char->int char)
  (if (char-numeric? char)
      (- (char->integer char) (char->integer #\0))
      #\?))
```

num-char->int simply determines the character code offset from **#\0** to the character of interest, say, **#\3**, which is 3.

The task of multiplying and summing each digit's contribution to the ultimate integer is performed by **build-integer**:

```
;;;;;;;;;;;;;;;;;;;;;;;;;;;;;;;;;;;;;;;;;;;;;;;;;;;;;
;; BUILD-INTEGER builds up the integer by converting
;; each digit in the string to an integer value and
;; multiplying it into the result.
;;;;;;;;;;;;;;;;;;;;;;;;;;;;;;;;;;;;;;;;;;;;;;;;;;;;;

(define (build-integer result multiplier rev-digits)
  (cond
    ((null? rev-digits)
     result)
    ((char? (car rev-digits))
     -999999999)          ;; error--return a numeric value,
                          ;;         due to the recursion
    (else
      (build-integer (+ result (* (car rev-digits)
                                  (expt 10 multiplier)))
                     (+ multiplier 1)
                     (cdr rev-digits)))))
```

build-integer is designed as a helper function and will be local to **str->int**. For this reason, it is coded as a tail recursive function with the extra parameter **result**; the first time it must be called with an argument of 0 corresponding to **result**. Quite arbitrarily, we have chosen to process the integer, in string form, from right to left. Hence, each time the function recurs, the parameter **multiplier** is increased by a factor of ten. Note that in order to allow cdr recursion, the third parameter takes a list argument with the digits in reverse order. We've written **build-integer** so that, in the event of bad data, it returns a "funny" number, because of the tail recursive implementation and the implied final multiplication.

Now we're ready to put the main function **str->int** together:

```
;;;;     str-int.s     ;;;;;;;;;;;;;;;;;;;;;;;;;;;;;;;;;;;;;;;;;

;;;;;;;;;;;;;;;;;;;;;;;;;;;;;;;;;;;;;;;;;;;;;;;;;
;; STR->INT converts a string to an integer.
;;;;;;;;;;;;;;;;;;;;;;;;;;;;;;;;;;;;;;;;;;;;;;;;;

(define (str->int str)

;;;;;;;;;;;;;;;;;;;;;;;;;;;;;;;;;;;;;;;;;;;;;;;;;;
;; SIGN-PREFIX? determines whether or not the
;; integer has a leading sign.
;;;;;;;;;;;;;;;;;;;;;;;;;;;;;;;;;;;;;;;;;;;;;;;;;;
(define (sign-prefix? char)
  (or (char=? char #\+) (char=? char #\-)))

;;;;;;;;;;;;;;;;;;;;;;;;;;;;;;;;;;;;;;;;;;;;;;;;;;;;;;;;;;;;
;; BUILD-INTEGER builds up the integer by converting
;; each digit in the string to an integer value and
;; multiplying it into the result.
;;;;;;;;;;;;;;;;;;;;;;;;;;;;;;;;;;;;;;;;;;;;;;;;;;;;;;;;;;;;

(define (build-integer result multiplier rev-digits)
  (cond
    ((null? rev-digits)
     result)
    ((char? (car rev-digits))
     -999999999)        ;; error--return a numeric value,
                        ;;        due to the recursion
    (else
      (build-integer (+ result (* (car rev-digits)
                                  (expt 10 multiplier)))
                     (+ multiplier 1)
                     (cdr rev-digits)))))

;;;;;;;;;;;;;;;;;;;;;;;;;;;;;;;;;;;;;;;;;;;;;;; main program ;;;;

  (let* ((sign-num-list (if (= (string-length str) 0)
                            (list #\0)    ;; trap a null string
(string->list str)))
         (sign (if (sign-prefix? (car sign-num-list))
                   (if (char=? (car sign-num-list) #\-)
                       -1                   ;; signed negative
                       1)                   ;; signed positive
                   1))                      ;; unsigned
```

```
        (num-list (if (sign-prefix? (car sign-num-list))
                      (cdr sign-num-list)   ;; strip the sign
                      sign-num-list)))

    (* sign
       (build-integer
        0 0 (reverse (map num-char->int num-list))))))


;;;;;;;;;;;;;;;;;;;;;;;;;;;;;;;;;;;;;;;;;;;;;
;; NUM-CHAR->INT converts a numeric character
;; to a decimal integer.
;;;;;;;;;;;;;;;;;;;;;;;;;;;;;;;;;;;;;;;;;;;;;

(define (num-char->int char)
  (if (char-numeric? char)
      (- (char->integer char) (char->integer #\0))
      #\?))
```

We've adopted a policy here that is convenient, due to Scheme's support for lexical scoping, namely, coding some functions internally and some functions externally. Consider the predicate **sign-prefix?**, which has been coded as an internal function. It's not very likely that **sign-prefix?** would be useful as a library function—its function is fairly specialized—hence, its internal coding. Moreover, coding such functions externally implies that the programmer must be aware of name conflicts with other applications which might use a different **sign-prefix?**. Following the same rationale, **build-integer** has been placed internal to **str->int**.

On the other hand, **num-char->int** has utility as a library function, and thus is coded externally. Note that **num-char->int** differs from standard Scheme's **char->integer** in two ways: (1) its approach to error handling and (2) the type of integer returned. First, we intend to convert a string to an integer, and if a particular character can't be converted properly, we prefer to return a flag character instead of just "bombing out." Second, recall from the earlier demonstration of **char->integer**, that it returns the host computer system's internal representation of a character, e.g., its ASCII code. As mentioned previously, we need a function that accepts, say, the character "3" and returns integer 3. Note also that we've defined a function that can return either of two data types, depending on the characteristics of its argument.

Consider the driver function **str->int**. The primary code for **str->int** begins with the **let*** construct, following the internal function definitions. It begins by converting the string to list form (in the **let***'s initialization code). Overall, there are two possible approaches: (1) work with the string in string form, using string manipulation functions, e.g., **string-ref**, or (2) convert the string to a list of characters and work with list manipulation functions. Which approach is best depends on the application at hand; for the sake of illustration, we've chosen the latter.

After converting the string to a list of characters, nested **if** syntax is used to determine if a leading sign is present, and if so, to determine its sign and remove it from the list. This activity occurs in the **let*** initialization phase. Subsequently, in the body of the **let***, **build-integer** is called to build the integer result, which is multiplied by the value recorded in **sign**.

Having stripped the sign character in an earlier phase, it is straightforward to reverse the list so that we can use cdr recursion to work our way down the list, building up the integer result in the order: units, tens, hundreds, etc. In order to do so, we use **map**, which we haven't yet discussed. (Mapping functions are described in greater detail in a later chapter.) **map**'s syntax is

```
(map <function> <list>)
```

map applies **<function>** to **<list>**, item by item, and returns a list of the individual function applications, i.e., **<function>** is mapped to each item in **<list>**. For example, if we apply **square**, which we defined earlier, to an arbitrary list we get the following result.

```
[1] (map square '(1 2 3 4 5))
(1 4 9 16 25)
```

Thus, **build-integer** is called with a list as the third argument, where each item in the list is either a single-digit integer or the flag character "?".

We will use **str->int** in a miniature systems programming application later on; for now, consider the following dialog.

```
[1] (load "str-int.s")
OK
[2] (char->integer #\3) ;ASCII code for a "3"--not what we need
51
[3] (char->int #\3)        ;our specialized (con)version
3
[4] (char->int #\x)
#\?
[5] (char->integer #\x)
120
[6] (str->int "12")
12
[7] (str->int "1a2")
-999999999
[8] (str->int "-4321")
-4321
[9] (str->int "+1234")
1234
[10] (map num-char->int '(#\a #\1 #\space #\6))
(#\? 1 #\? 6)
[11] (exit)
```

There are several ways to handle invalid strings. In this case, we've chosen to return an integer value, but with an unusual value; see prompt [7]. In general, it would be preferable to return, say, Boolean false. However, in this case we are calling **build-integer** recursively, and returning **#f** would lead to a data type mismatch in certain pending calculations.

Exercises

1. Define the one parameter function **char->str** that accepts a single character and returns a one-character string representation for printable characters and Boolean false for nonprintable characters.

[WARNING: PC Scheme users (prior to version 3.0) should *not* use the function name **char->string**; this function is used by the editor.]

2. Define the function **substr**, a variation of **substring**, that accepts three arguments: a string, a starting position, and a substring length. Note that **substring** differs with respect to the third argument.

3. Define the predicate **null-string?** that returns a Boolean value indicating whether or not a string has length 0.

4. Define the function **int->str** that returns a string representation of any positive or negative integer. One way to accomplish this is to use division and modulo operations iteratively to shift the number to the right digit by digit. Each digit that is "pushed" out of the number can be pushed onto the front of the string representation. The sign must be accommodated also.

5. Rewrite **string-index** so that it uses a **do** instead of a named **let**.

6. Rewrite **string-upcase** to use a named **let** instead of a **do**.

7. Define **string-downcase** as a complement to **string-upcase**. It should be implemented with a named **let**.

8. Rewrite **char-numeric?**, as given in this chapter, so that it uses a nested **if** structure instead of **and**.

9. Write the predicate **punctuation?** that checks a string for presence of any of the punctuation characters **#\\.**, **#\\,**, **#\\:**, **#\\;**, **#\\'**, **#\\"**, **#\\!**, and **#\\?**. It should return either **#t** or **#f**.

10. Provide a function, **string-reverse**, that reverses the characters in a string.

11. Provide a function, **name-reverse**, that reverses a person's name, in string form, by moving the last name to the beginning of the string and adding a comma after the last name:

```
==> (name-reverse "John Q. Doe")
"Doe, John Q."
```

Note the positioning of blanks (**#\space**).

12. Develop a one parameter function, **number->$**, that returns a string of the form "$ nn.nn". That is, a numeric argument is converted to character form and "$ " is appended to the front of it. There should always be two "cents" digits, even for an integer argument.

13. Many word processors display their text unjustified, i.e., with a ragged right margin. Write a function named **ragged-edge** with three parameters: (1) a string of any length, (2) a left margin size, and (3) a right margin size. Your function should scan the string and insert newline sequences (**#\newline**) between appropriate words so that when the string is **display**ed, each word after a **#\newline** begins on a new line. Punctuation characters should be kept with the word that they follow.

Assume that the maximum line length is 80 characters. Thus, the maximum number of characters per line will be 80 - **left-margin** - **right-margin**. The value for the number of characters represented by **#\newline** should NOT be considered in the line length count. Each line should be appended with **left-margin** - 1 blanks. Each time you embed **#\newline** in a string, it must be surrounded by blanks serving as delimiters. Thus, the blank following each **#\newline** will be printed on the subsequent line, making the left margin size equal to **left-margin**.

Words should not be hyphenated. Thus, when the line length, including allowances for left and right margins, exceeds the maximum, you should "drop back" and break the current line before the current word, unless you are between words. Note that while the left margin is handled by appending blanks to the beginning of each line, **right-margin** is only used to calculate where to "break" each line.

Test your function by setting up a global variable such as

```
(define test-string "Words should not be hyphenated...")
```

so that you can invoke your function many times without having to retype the string paragraph. If your editor doesn't allow you to type strings that are longer than one line, then test your function with a 70-character string and very large margins. Your function call should be:

```
==> (display (ragged-edge test-string))
```

Chapter 9

Input and Output

9.1 Introduction

Consider the following classifications for input and output (I/O) processing:

1. interactive, or console, I/O
2. file I/O
   a. sequential
   b. direct

By current standards, early LISP dialects provided only primitive I/O processing. The basic assumption was that most processing, e.g., AI programming, could be done in primary storage. Modern LISPs have enhanced their support for sequential file processing (1) and (2.a). For example, Common LISP (Steele, 1984) provides formatted I/O, something not provided in early LISP dialects. Although Scheme's I/O capabilities are quite primitive, in keeping with the small-language philosophy, e.g., C and standard Pascal, it is easy to extend Scheme's I/O capabilities. For example, standard Scheme does not provide a primitive for reading a line of input from the console; however, we can easily add this capability with a user-defined function.

Although it is straightforward for the programmer to provide extensions for interactive and sequential file processing, extensions supporting direct (random) file processing must be provided by the Scheme implementation. Hopefully, the trend toward larger AI programs will lead to direct file support by LISP dialects in the near future.

Implementation note: PC Scheme 3.0 provides both binary and direct file processing, as an extension to standard Scheme.

So far in this text, we've primarily confined our discussion to standard Scheme. In this chapter, however, we occasionally address implementation-specific issues. Although we attempt to minimize the discussion of these issues, they are important from the standpoint of writing robust code. For example, many Scheme implementations provide a function for testing for the existence of a particular file, since attempting to open a nonexistent file is an error. In order to write robust programs, you must find and use the equivalent function in your Scheme implementation.

9.2 Stream I/O and Scheme Ports

In Scheme, all I/O processing is performed on sequential streams of characters, called *ports* in Scheme, and *streams* in, for example, Common LISP. A general term for such processing is *stream I/O.*

There are two types of I/O primitives supported by Scheme implementations:

1. primitives that work directly with operating system (OS) I/O facilities
2. port-related primitives

One example of the former that we've used already is **load**, which reads and evaluates a file of Scheme source code, without formally setting up a port. As another example, PC Scheme has a function named **dos-delete** that invokes OS primitives to delete a disk file. (DOS stands for disk operating system.) Most Scheme implementations provide extensions for communicating with the OS which fall into this category.

The second category, primitives for accessing ports, is more easily addressed by the Scheme standard, as ports provide a means of abstracting away from the low-level aspects of I/O processing. In fact, the level of abstraction provided by ports makes it easy to have Scheme primitives that can be applied to physically different ports, i.e., the console and a disk file.

For example, so far we've only used **display** to display output at the console. However, there are actually two forms:

```
(display <arg>)

(display <arg> <port>)
```

In other words, **display** accommodates an optional second argument. If **<port>** is omitted, output defaults to the current, or standard, output port – normally, this is the console. Thus, **display** is suitable for writing output to either the console or a disk file. Many Scheme functions, where appropriate, support the optional specification of a port.

Some languages support both binary and character ports/streams. Communication with binary streams involves data transfer only; there is no conversion of data during I/O. For example, in order to write an integer to a binary stream representing a disk file, the integer's primary storage representation is simply copied to disk. (There may be intermediate buffering operations.)

Communicating with character streams is more complicated, in that there must be conversion from one type to another. For example, in order to write an integer to a Scheme port, the system must convert the integer to its character (string) representation, e.g., "-123". In particular, interactive console I/O involves character ports, since (1) data must be converted to human-readable form before printing, and (2) users enter data in human-readable form. In this chapter we investigate standard Scheme's support for I/O processing via ports.

9.3 Standard I/O Port Operations

We can best illustrate and discuss Scheme port activity by examining a sample Scheme dialog.

```
[1] (read)
'anything                           ;waiting for input here
(QUOTE ANYTHING)                    ;the returned value
[2] (read)
"anything"
"anything"
[3] (read)
(+ 2 3)
(+ 2 3)
[4] (eval (read))
(+ 2 3)
5
[5] _
```

read is the most general Scheme function for reading input. We can use it to read symbols, strings, expressions – almost anything that can be evaluated by Scheme. **read** is used by the top-level REP loop. Note that it does not automatically evaluate expressions; however, **eval**, a Scheme function that forces evaluation of an expression, can be applied to the expression returned by **read**.

Earlier we demonstrated **read-char**, which doesn't echo the character typed at the console. At the Scheme top-level REP loop **read-char** simply returns the character.

```
[5] (read-char)
#\x                                ;an "x" is typed at this point
[6] _
```

However, we can define our own version, **read-ch**, which does echo the character. It would be useful, for example, in a program that prompted the user with a one character menu selection, allowing the user to see the character that is typed.

```
;;;;     read-ch.s     ;;;;;;;;;;;;;;;;;;;;;;;;;;;;;;;;;;;;;;;;

;;;;;;;;;;;;;;;;;;;;;;;;;;;;;;;;;;;;;;;;;;;;;;;;;;;;;;;;;;;;;;;;
;; READ-CH reads and displays a single character from the
;; console.  There is no error checking.
;;;;;;;;;;;;;;;;;;;;;;;;;;;;;;;;;;;;;;;;;;;;;;;;;;;;;;;;;;;;;;;;

(define (read-ch)
  (define ch (read-char))
  (display ch)
  ch)                       ;return the character
```

```
[6] (load "read-ch.s")
OK
[7] (read-ch)
x#\x                  ;displays the "x" before returning it
[8] _
```

There are many ways to write this function. For example, write **read-ch** without defining a local variable.

According to standard Scheme, **display** prints its argument in human-readable form and returns an unspecified value.

```
[8] (display #\x)
x
[9] (display (+ 2 3))
5
[10] (display "anything")
anything
[11] (display 'anything)
ANYTHING
[12] _
```

Here, "nothing" is returned, allowing us to print messages without screen clutter. Note that **display** doesn't generate a carriage return/line feed (CR/LF) after printing its output, allowing multiple output activity to a given line. That is, at the top level, the output is on a new line because we had to type a **<return>** in order to process the **display**.

An alternative output function, **write**, is available for writing output in a form that can be reread at a later time.

```
[12] (write #\x)
```

```
#\x
[13] (write (+ 2 3))
5
[14] (write "anything")
"anything"
[15] (write-char #\x)
x
[16] _
```

write does not generate a CR/LF after printing its output. Standard Scheme provides **write-char** for writing characters to, for example, a disk file—without the "#\".

As we've seen, **newline** can be used to break output across lines.

```
[16] (newline)
;generates CR/LF
()                              ;returns empty list
[17] (display #\newline)
;generates CR/LF,
[18] _                          ;but nothing returned
```

Note that **newline** returns an empty list. During top-level processing, this clutters the screen. Typically, this isn't a problem, since it would be used inside a function for its side effect—the returned value is only an issue when **newline** occurs as the last expression.

9.4 User-defined Port Operations

We can create and map an output port to a disk file with **define**.

```
[18] (define export (open-output-file "scheme.dat"))
EXPORT
[19] (input-port? export)
()
[20] (output-port? export)
#T
[21] _
```

At prompt [18] we've created a Scheme port (**export**), opened a disk file for processing (**scheme.dat**), and established a file mapping between the two. This is analogous to establishing a file pointer in a language such as C or Pascal. In Scheme, **open-output-file** is used to establish a pointer to the beginning of an output port; subsequently, the pointer is advanced as output is written to the port. In this particular case, the port (file mapping) is global, having been established by a **define** at the top level. Following, we illustrate using **let** to establish a (local) port.

The primary motivation behind the provision of ports is high level file processing. That is, a disk file can be processed abstractly as a continuous stream of characters. All the low-level details are taken care of by Scheme and the OS access methods. We can view an input port as capable of delivering a stream of characters on demand and an output port as capable of accepting a stream of characters – a sink.

Another point is that ports are a kind of data type. We can assign them to identifiers, e.g., **export**; test whether a port has been opened for input or output processing, or hasn't been opened at all, e.g., prompts [19] and [20]; etc. Other actions against ports are illustrated in subsequent examples.

Let's write some data to the output port created at prompt [18].

```
[21] (write "this is line 1." export)
[22] (newline export)
#<PORT>
[23] (write "this is line 2." export)
[24] (close-output-port export)
#<PORT>
[25] (output-port? export)
()
[26] _
```

We've written a string, followed by a newline sequence, followed by a string. Since **write** preserves the data for later reading, the strings are written with double quotes. Lastly, the port is closed. Note at prompt [25] that **export** is no longer a port. Also, **write** returns nothing and **newline** returns **#<PORT>**, as a mnemonic. It's a good idea to close ports formally (prompt [24]) so that the OS can recover whatever space it allocates for file management, i.e., release temporary file structures.

Next, let's open the same file for input processing.

```
[26] (define import (open-input-file "scheme.dat"))
IMPORT
[27] (input-port? import)
#T
[28] (read import)
"this is line 1."
[29] (read import)
"this is line 2."
[30] (read import)
#!EOF
[31] (close-input-port import)
#<PORT>
[32] _
```

open-input-file returns an input port, named **import**, capable of delivering characters from the associated file. If we use **read** to read from **import**, characters are packaged based on **read**'s knowledge of Scheme data types. Thus symbols, numbers, expressions, and in this case, strings, can be read from the port. Note that **read** automatically skipped the newline sequence, which is considered whitespace, as it does during top-level processing. Note the strings returned by **read**.

Scheme defines two standard (default) ports, one input, one output, both of which are assigned to the console. The functions **current-input-port** and **current-output-port** return the current input and output ports, respectively, and *initially* are assigned to the console. Later, we demonstrate Scheme functions for reassigning the current, or default, ports.

```
[32] (current-input-port)
CONSOLE
[33] (current-output-port)
CONSOLE
[34] (write "anything")
"anything"
[35] (write "anything" (current-output-port))
"anything"
[36] (exit)
```

We've informally illustrated several of the basic console I/O functions in earlier chapters; however, consider an additional example, a program that reads two numbers from the screen and then computes and prints their sum.

```
;;;;     addtwo.s      ;;;;;;;;;;;;;;;;;;;;;;;;;;;;;;;;;;;;;;;;;;

;;;;;;;;;;;;;;;;;;;;;;;;;;;;;;;;;;;;;;;;;;;;;;;;;;;;
;; ADDTWO adds two numbers and prints their sum.
;;;;;;;;;;;;;;;;;;;;;;;;;;;;;;;;;;;;;;;;;;;;;;;;;;;;

(define (addtwo)
  (do ((sum 0 (+ sum (read)))
       (i 0 (+ i 1)))
       ((= i 2)
       (newline)
       (display "The sum is:  ")
       (display sum))
      (display "Enter a number:  ")))
```

Here, the sum is accumulated by using **do**'s update mechanism, avoiding unnecessary **set!**s. **addtwo** works as follows:

```
[1] (load "addtwo.s")
OK
[2] (addtwo)
Enter a number:  34
Enter a number:  43
```

```
The sum is:  77
[3] (exit)
```

9.5 Examples/Utilities Using Ports

We can illustrate several aspects of Scheme I/O by coding a utility for counting characters in a file.

```
;;;;    ccount.s    ;;;;;;;;;;;;;;;;;;;;;;;;;;;;;;;;;;;;;;;;

;;;;;;;;;;;;;;;;;;;;;;;;;;;;;;;;;;;;;;;;;;;;;;;;;;;;;;;;;;;
;; CCOUNT counts the number of bytes/characters in a file.
;;;;;;;;;;;;;;;;;;;;;;;;;;;;;;;;;;;;;;;;;;;;;;;;;;;;;;;;;;;

(define (ccount file)
(let ((in-port (open-input-file file)))
    (do ((char (read-char in-port) (read-char in-port))
         (count 0 (+ count 1)))
        ((eof-object? char)
         (close-input-port in-port)
         (display
           (string-append "file size in bytes for " file ":  "))
         (display count)))))
```

The primary intent here is to illustrate (traditional) file opening, processing, and closing. Below, we address an alternative technique.

First, **ccount** establishes an input port named **in-port**, an abstraction for a physical disk file. The **let** provides a convenient mechanism for establishing **in-port** before it's needed in the initialization clause of the **do**. The **do** iterates over each character (**char**) in the port until end-of-file, incrementing **count** by one on each iteration.

The predicate **eof-object?** is provided by Scheme as a means of detecting end-of-file – in a way that retains code portability across Scheme implementations. In this case, the iteration is terminated upon end-of-file and a message is printed indicating the file size.

```
[1] (load "ccount.s")
OK
[2] (ccount "scheme.dat")
file size in bytes for scheme.dat:  36
[3] (exit)
```

The message, in a way, gives file size in bytes. There are two common interpretations of file size for text (character) files: (1) the file size printed by an operating system utility, such as a directory listing, and (2) the file size reported by some word processing programs. The preceding count does *not* correspond to either of these. Typically, **ccount**'s count will differ from a OS utility's count by one, since it does not count the end-of-file character. **count** will also be different than that reported by a word processor, since the latter typically ignores CR/LFs.

ccount provides a prototype for an application that would perform substantive processing on the contents of a file. However, since we are just counting characters in this application, there are two modifications that can be made to **ccount**. First, **char** is superfluous, since we aren't really doing anything with it; Scheme syntax is sufficiently flexible to avoid **char**'s definition completely. Second, Scheme provides two special port-reassignment functions (one input, one output) for those cases where a port is established for the duration of one function only. **ccount-2** illustrates **with-input-from-file.**

```
;;;;     ccount.s     ;;;;;;;;;;;;;;;;;;;;;;;;;;;;;;;;;;;;;;;;

;;;;;;;;;;;;;;;;;;;;;;;;;;;;;;;;;;;;;;;;;;;;;;;;;;;;;;;;;;;;;;
;; CCOUNT-2 counts the number of bytes/characters in a file.
;;;;;;;;;;;;;;;;;;;;;;;;;;;;;;;;;;;;;;;;;;;;;;;;;;;;;;;;;;;;;;

(define (ccount-2 file)
  (with-input-from-file file
    (lambda ()
      (do ((count 0 (+ count 1)))
          ((eof-object? (read-char))
           (display
             (string-append "file size in bytes for "
                            file ":  "))
           (display count))))))
```

The function **with-input-from-file** has the following syntax:

```
(with-input-from-file <filename> <thunk>)
```

where **<filename>** is a string naming a file and **<thunk>** is a function with *no* parameters.

with-input-from-file establishes a port representing the named file and *temporarily* reassigns the default input port to the newly established port—until **<thunk>** terminates. (**with-output-to-file** works analogously.) **ccount-2** uses this feature to avoid formal specification of an input port, i.e., to avoid **open-input-file, close-input-port,** and **(read-char <port>)**.

As discussed in an earlier chapter, **lambda** creates a "temporary" function. In **ccount-2** a **lambda** function is established that performs all activity with respect to the file processing operation, namely, absorbing characters and incrementing **count**; this function then becomes the second argument to **with-input-from-file.** Note that, due to the port reassignment, a port specification is not needed in the call to **read-char**. Also, as mentioned above, we can invoke **read-char** in the loop termination test to avoid defining a character variable.

Another typical I/O utility is one for making backup copies of files; our version is named **fcopy**.

```
;;;;     fcopy.s     ;;;;;;;;;;;;;;;;;;;;;;;;;;;;;;;;;;;;;;;;;;;

;;;;;;;;;;;;;;;;;;;;;;;;;;;;;;;;;;;;;;;;;;;;;;;;;
;; FCOPY copies files--character by character.
;;;;;;;;;;;;;;;;;;;;;;;;;;;;;;;;;;;;;;;;;;;;;;;;;

(define (fcopy old-file new-file)
  (let ((in-port (open-input-file old-file))        ;file
        (out-port (open-output-file new-file)))    ;definitions
    (let copy-file ((char (read-char in-port)))
      (if (eof-object? char)                        ;finished
          (begin
            (close-input-port in-port)
            (close-output-port out-port)
            (display
              (string-append old-file " copied to " new-file)))
          (begin
            (write-char char out-port)
            (copy-file (read-char in-port)))))))
```

For the sake of illustration we've used a named **let** to implement this version of **fcopy**. The outer **let** provides the port assignments needed to operate on two files, one input and one output. The named **let** provides the iteration over each character in the input file until terminated by the **if** at end-of-file. For each iteration, a character is written to the output port using **write-char**. We get the following output from **fcopy**.

```
[1] (load "fcopy.s")
OK
[2] (fcopy "twolines.dat" "twolines.bkp")
twolines.dat copied to twolines.bkp
[3] (exit)
```

(**twolines.dat** is a simple text file created by a text editor and containing two lines of data.)

Implementation note: There is no way to guarantee the performance of **fcopy** across Scheme implementations, due to each implementation's technique for handling things such as newline sequences. For example, some systems replace a newline sequence of two characters (CR/LF) by a single character (#\newline). This code will work properly with some Scheme systems; however, it does *not* for the Scheme implementation used in this textbook. The output file will have two newline sequences for every newline sequence in the input file.

Apparently, there is an "error" in how PC Scheme (both versions 2.0 and 3.0) processes newline sequences in input files. Note that the file in the introductory dialog of this chapter is created correctly. Also, the following program, which echoes characters typed at the console to disk until a sentinel is typed, works properly as well.

```
;;;;     log-disk.s     ;;;;;;;;;;;;;;;;;;;;;;;;;;;;;;;;;;;;;;;;

;;;;;;;;;;;;;;;;;;;;;;;;;;;;;;;;;;;;;;;;;;;;;;;;;;;;;
;; LOG-DISK writes, or logs, every character that
;; you type to a disk file until the sentinel "%"
;; is typed.
;;;;;;;;;;;;;;;;;;;;;;;;;;;;;;;;;;;;;;;;;;;;;;;;;;;;;

(define (log-disk file)
  (with-output-to-file file
     (lambda ()
       (let get-char ((next-char (read-char)))
         (write-char next-char)
         (if (not (char=? next-char #\%))
             (get-char (read-char))))))
  (newline)
  (display "end of logging"))
```

See the exercises (and answers to the exercises) for more discussion of this issue under PC Scheme. The accompanying programs demonstrate how to overcome this problem.

Next, consider an alternate version of **fcopy**, which illustrates another Scheme feature for port assignment.

```
;;;;     fcopy.s     ;;;;;;;;;;;;;;;;;;;;;;;;;;;;;;;;;;;;;;;;;;;

;;;;;;;;;;;;;;;;;;;;;;;;;;;;;;;;;;;;;;;;;;;;;;;;;
;; FCOPY copies files--character by character.
;;;;;;;;;;;;;;;;;;;;;;;;;;;;;;;;;;;;;;;;;;;;;;;;;

(define (fcopy old-file new-file)
  (call-with-input-file old-file
    (lambda (in-port)
      (call-with-output-file new-file
        (lambda (out-port)
          (do ((char (read-char in-port) (read-char in-port)))
```

```
            ((eof-object? char)
             (display (string-append
                        old-file " copied to " new-file)))
            (write-char char out-port)))))))
```

The function **call-with-input-file** has the following syntax:

```
(call-with-input-file <filename> <proc>)
```

where **<filename>** is a string naming a file and **<proc>** is a function with *one* parameter.

call-with-input-file calls **<proc>** with one argument—the port established after opening **<filename>** for input. The port is closed after **<proc>** returns. The file passed as **old-file** is opened and the lambda function is called; the lambda function incorporates a call to **call-with-output-file**, which is the output analog of **call-with-input-file. call-with-output-file** then establishes an output port and calls a lambda function, which performs the iteration over both ports.

9.6 Strings as Ports

Although not described by standard Scheme, Scheme implementations often support the manipulation of strings as ports. That is, it may be possible to "open" a string as an input (output) port and use I/O functions to process the string. Other traditional languages providing such support include C (**sscanf** and **sprintf**) and PL/I (**get string** and **put string**).

At this point we demonstrate half of Scheme's facility for processing a string as a port, namely, **open-input-string.** You are encouraged to investigate whether or not your Scheme supports **open-input-string** and **open-output-string**. In a later chapter we will further illustrate **open-input-string**.

The syntax for **open-input-string** is:

```
(open-input-string <string>)
```

where **<string>** is any defined Scheme string. As a result of this function call, Scheme returns an input port assigned to the named string.

We've mentioned that Scheme processes input from files as a continuous stream of characters; hence, the provision for treating a string of characters in primary storage in a similar manner. In this case, it is possible to use input functions such as **read-char** to manipulate the string. Of particular note is the treatment of end-of-file; **eof-object?** is true once the last character of the string has been read. String ports need not be closed.

Note that this usage of I/O functions for string processing is sequential in nature, as Scheme provides sequential I/O only. In contrast to files, direct processing of strings is supported by the string manipulation functions that were discussed earlier, e.g., **string-ref**.

As an example of **open-input-string**, consider the following example.

```
;;;;     strings.s     ;;;;;;;;;;;;;;;;;;;;;;;;;;;;;;;;;;;;;;;;;;

;;;;;;;;;;;;;;;;;;;;;;;;;;;;;;;;;;;;;;;;;;;;;;;;;;;;;;;;;;;;;;;
;; STRING-INDEX searches for a character in a string, retur-
;; ning its position -- zero-based.
;; Example usage:  (string-index "string" #\i) ==> 3
;;;;;;;;;;;;;;;;;;;;;;;;;;;;;;;;;;;;;;;;;;;;;;;;;;;;;;;;;;;;;;

(define (string-index str search-char)
  (let ((search-str (open-input-string str)))
    (let next-char ((char (read-char search-str)) (position 0))
      (cond
        ((eof-object? char)
         ())
        ((char=? char search-char)
         position)
        (else
          (next-char (read-char search-str) (+ position 1)))))))
```

string-index is a variation on a function defined earlier. It searches forward in a string looking for the first occurrence of a particular character, returning its zero-based position.

The outer **let** establishes **search-str** as a string port. Next, an inner, named **let** is used to iterate over the string, until end-of-string (= “end-of-file”). **char**, the first parameter in the named **let**, is initially bound to the first character in **search-str** (or **str**); **position** is bound to zero. For each iteration, one of three conditions is true: (1) end-of-string, (2) the search character is matched, or (3) there is no match – continue searching. Compare the use of **(read-char search-str)** here to **string-ref** in the earlier version of **string-index**.

The second and last example (for now) of string ports is not discussed. It is similar to the previous example, and is a variation on an earlier-defined function, **string-upcase**.

```
;;;;     strings.s     ;;;;;;;;;;;;;;;;;;;;;;;;;;;;;;;;;;;;;;;;;;

;;;;;;;;;;;;;;;;;;;;;;;;;;;;;;;;;;;;;;;;;;;;;;;;;;;;;;;;;;;;;
;; STRING-UPCASE returns a string converted to uppercase.
;;;;;;;;;;;;;;;;;;;;;;;;;;;;;;;;;;;;;;;;;;;;;;;;;;;;;;;;;;;;

(define (string-upcase string)
  (let ((lower-str (open-input-string string)))
    (let next-char ((char (read-char lower-str))
                    (upper-str "")
                    (position 0))
```

```
        (if (eof-object? char)
            upper-str
            (next-char (read-char lower-str)
                       (string-append upper-str
                                      (make-string
                                        1
                                        (char-upcase char)))
                       (+ position 1))))))
```

9.7 A Utility for Reading Lines: read-ln

Sometimes it's convenient to read an entire line of text from the console (or from some other port). Standard Scheme provides this in a primitive way; that is, you can use **read** to read any legitimate expression, e.g., a string. Thus, by enclosing everything on a line in double quotes, it's possible to read a line of data into a string.

Providing the double quotes is cumbersome; hence, most Scheme implementations provide a language extension for reading a line of text. For example, PC Scheme provides **read-line**. The following function, **read-ln**, is a utility function that echoes characters, allows backspacing, etc. It has been written for console input only, however, extending it to work with any port is quite easy.

```
;;;;    read-ln.s    ;;;;;;;;;;;;;;;;;;;;;;;;;;;;;;;;;;;;;;;;;;

;;;;;;;;;;;;;;;;;;;;;;;;;;;;;;;;;;;;;;;;;;;;;;;;;;;;;
;; READ-LN reads a line of input from the keyboard.
;; Usage:  (read-ln)
;; Returns:  a string containing the typed input
;; PC Scheme:  cntl-<bs> erases the entire line.
;;;;;;;;;;;;;;;;;;;;;;;;;;;;;;;;;;;;;;;;;;;;;;;;;;;;;

(define (read-ln)
  (let ((backspace #\backspace)          ;system dependent
        (line-reset-char #\rubout)       ;system dependent
        (end-of-line-char #\return))     ;system dependent
    (let next-char ((in-char (read-char)) (input-string ""))
     (cond
       ((char=? in-char end-of-line-char)
        input-string)
       ((char=? in-char line-reset-char)
        (do ((i (string-length input-string) (- i 1)))
            ((zero? i))
            (display backspace))
        (next-char (read-char) ""))
       ((char=? in-char backspace)
        (display backspace)
```

```
        (cond
          ((zero? (string-length input-string))
           (next-char (read-char) input-string))
          (else
            (next-char
              (read-char)
              (substring input-string
                         0
                         (- (string-length input-string)
                            1))))))
      (else
        (display in-char)
        (next-char
          (read-char)
          (string-append input-string
                         (make-string 1 in-char))))))))
```

Implementation note: This version of **read-ln** contains implementation-specific code. Implementing it on your system should be fairly trivial. At worst, you'll have to remove the code supporting backspacing and line rubout, leaving a small amount of code to modify.

---

read-ln supports regular backspacing via the standard backspace key. (On some systems this may be <control-h>.) It also allows you to erase an entire line of text and begin over. (On an IBM PC under PC Scheme, for example, this is initiated by <control-backspace>.)

The outer **let** defines the logical constants, e.g., backspace, line rubout, and carriage return. The inner, named **let** implements the iteration. Nested **cond**s are used to detect special directives, e.g., line rubout, backspace, and carriage return. Characters that aren't later wiped out ultimately comprise a string, **input-string**, which is the value returned by **read-ln**.

Following, **read-ln** is invoked to illustrate its returned value.

```
[1] (load "read-ln.s")
OK
[2] (read-ln)
Can anybody hear me?"Can anybody hear me?"
[3] (display (read-ln))
read-ln allows you to enter strings without the quotes
read-ln allows you to enter strings without the quotes
[4] _
```

At prompt [2] the first sentence is the user's input, which is read by **read-ln**. The quoted string is the returned value. At prompt [3] the returned value is printed without quotes, since the **read-ln** is nested inside a **display**.

At this point, we can rewrite **greeting** so that it supports string input, avoiding the restriction to symbol input. (This one's in French.)

```
;;;;    greeting.s    ;;;;;;;;;;;;;;;;;;;;;;;;;;;;;;;;;;;;;;;

;;;;;;;;;;;;;;;;;;;;;;;;;;;;;;;;;;;;;;;;;;;;;;;;;;;;;;;;;;;;;;
;; BONJOUR greets the user in French.  If the user's
;; response contains multiple words, assume name is
;; the last word.
;;;;;;;;;;;;;;;;;;;;;;;;;;;;;;;;;;;;;;;;;;;;;;;;;;;;;;;;;;;;;;

(define (bonjour)
  (display "Bonjour.  Comment vous appelez-vous?")
  (newline)
  (let ((response (read-ln)))
    (if (> (string-length response) 0)
        (do ((i (- (string-length response) 1) (- i 1)))
            ((or (char=? (string-ref response i) #\space)
                 (zero? i))
             (newline)
             (display "Enchante ")
             (if (char=? (string-ref response i) #\space)
                 (display (substring
                            response
                            (+ i 1)
                            (string-length response)))
                 (display response))))
        (display ""))))
```

In this version, an entire line of text is accepted as a response to the greeting. If it is more than one word, the last word is assumed to be the person's name; it is then extracted and displayed following "Enchante". It the user's response is just a null line, "Enchante" alone is returned.

```
[4] (load "greeting.s")
OK
[5] (bonjour)
Bonjour.  Comment vous appelez-vous?
Je m'appelle Jerry.                    ;line of text typed
Enchante Jerry.
[6] (bonjour)
Bonjour.  Comment vous appelez-vous?   ;null line is typed by
[7] (bonjour)                          ;unfriendly person
Bonjour.  Comment vous appelez-vous?
Jerry                                  ;one word response
Enchante Jerry
```

```
[8] (exit)
```

9.8 Extended Example: calc, A Four-function Calculator

At this point, we've developed enough prerequisites for a fairly simple example of a four-function calculator, **calc**. It's also an example of an interpreter, in the following sense. Each line of source code, an arithmetic expression in infix form, is *compiled* to an intermediate code, i.e., Scheme prefix form, for *interpretation* (execution) by Scheme.

This version of **calc** processes simple infix expressions, e.g.,

```
==> <constant-1> <operator> <constant-2>
```

calc remembers the previous result, and if **<constant-1>** is missing, the previous result is substituted, thus allowing:

```
==> 3 * 5
==> 15
==> + 3
==> 18
```

For convenience, we'll refer to each of these expression components as a *token*.

One of the essential tasks in **calc** is the process of *parsing*, or breaking down, an infix expression for processing. Since Scheme is naturally prefix oriented, a reasonable goal is to disassemble the infix expression and reassemble the tokens in prefix form. The most straightforward way to handling the parsing operation is to assume that each token is separated from the next token by one or more blanks; this is completely reasonable and is similar to how Scheme expressions are processed.

We can approach the development of our program incrementally by viewing each task abstractly (procedural abstraction). First, consider the process of extracting tokens. A simple approach is to scan forward in a line, extracting consecutive characters and concatenating them in a token string. For example, if a line begins with

```
==> -1234  ...
```

five characters occur before the first delimiter character, a blank; in this case, our function should build the string "-1234". However, our **calc** program should be flexible enough to allow a variable number of blanks as a delimiter. For example, expressions such as the following should be acceptable to our parser:

```
==> -1234 + 2
==> -1234   + 2
==> -1234 +     2
==>      -1234 + 2
```

Perhaps the best way to proceed is to assume that every token is preceded by such "annoying" blanks. In this case, all we need is a function to strip blanks from the front of a token:

```
;;;;;;;;;;;;;;;;;;;;;;;;;;;;;;;;;;;;;;;;;;;;;;;;;;;;;;;;;;;;;;;;
;; ABSORB-BLANKS deletes leading blanks from a string.
;;;;;;;;;;;;;;;;;;;;;;;;;;;;;;;;;;;;;;;;;;;;;;;;;;;;;;;;;;;;;;;;

(define (absorb-blanks line)
  (let find-start ((line line) (pos 0))
    (cond
      ((= pos (string-length line))
       "")
      ((char=? #\space (string-ref line pos))
       (find-start line (+ pos 1)))
      (else
        (substring line pos (string-length line))))))
```

To be more specific, we can process each line (expression) in the following manner.

1. Absorb the leading blanks, if present.
2. Extract a token from the line.
3. Perform this same process on the remaining part of the line.

Of course, this cycle is continued until the line is null.

In other words, if **absorb-blanks** is called immediately before the process of extracting each token from a line, token extraction per se is quite straightforward, as illustrated by **get-token**.

```
;;;;;;;;;;;;;;;;;;;;;;;;;;;;;;;;;;;;;;;;;;;;;;;;;;;;;;;;;;;;;;;;;;;;;
;; GET-TOKEN processes a string one character at a time and
;; builds a token.  It returns a list containing the token
;; and the reduced line.
;;;;;;;;;;;;;;;;;;;;;;;;;;;;;;;;;;;;;;;;;;;;;;;;;;;;;;;;;;;;;;;;;;;;;

(define (get-token line)
  (let find-end ((line line) (pos 0))
    (cond
      ((= pos (string-length line))
       (list (substring line 0 pos)
             (substring line pos (string-length line))))
      ((char-whitespace? (string-ref line pos))
       (list (substring line 0 pos)
             (substring line pos (string-length line))))
      (else
```

```
        (find-end line (+ pos 1))))))
```

Assuming that **absorb-blanks** has been applied to a particular line/expression, **get-token** performs step 2 of the parsing process. Note that both of these functions perform their work by returning values that can be used as input to the next part of the parsing process. For example, **absorb-blanks** returns a string, absent any leading blanks. **get-token** returns a list where the first element is the token and the second element is the reduced list. The reduced list can then be used as input to **absorb-blanks**, as stated in step 3 of the parsing process.

At this point, we need a function that can serve as a coordinator of these activities. **parse-input** manages the expression processing, including the task of reading each line/expression. More importantly, **parse-input** allows us to view the overall parsing operation abstractly, and in a top-down fashion:

```
;;;;;;;;;;;;;;;;;;;;;;;;;;;;;;;;;;;;;;;;;;;;;;;;;;;;;;;;;;;;;;;;;;;;;;;;;;
;; PARSE-INPUT reads a line of input in infix form and returns
;; a list of the form:  ("operator" "operand-1" "operand-2").
;;;;;;;;;;;;;;;;;;;;;;;;;;;;;;;;;;;;;;;;;;;;;;;;;;;;;;;;;;;;;;;;;;;;;;;;;;

(define (parse-input)
  (let parse ((token-list (get-token (absorb-blanks (read-ln))))
              (parse-list '()))
    (cond
      ((string=? (absorb-blanks (cadr token-list)) "")
       (re-order (cons (car token-list) parse-list)))
      (else
        (parse (get-token (absorb-blanks (cadr token-list)))
               (cons (car token-list) parse-list))))))
```

Another important point is that we don't need any **set!**s (assignment statements). We've used a functional style that promotes procedure abstraction; in this case, the parsing operation can be viewed as a pipe-and-filter process, of sorts. That is, **absorb-blanks** filters out the blanks and pipes its output to the next stage of the parsing process. This aspect of our program design can be seen in the following function application structure:

```
... (token-list (get-token (absorb-blanks (read-ln)))) ...
```

In this case, the value returned by **read-ln** is piped into **absorb-blanks**; the value returned by **absorb-blanks** is piped into **get-token**; and the value returned by **get-token** is stored in the variable **token-list** for subsequent processing by the named **let parse**.

get-token returns a list where the second element is a reduced list; i.e., the leading token has been removed. Hence, in subsequent iterations of the parsing process, the second element of **token-list** is the appropriate argument to **absorb-blanks** – instead of **read-ln** which was needed in the initial cycle only.

Eventually, the entire expression is consumed. In order to return the list of tokens in prefix form, **parse-input** calls on the function **re-order** to reorder the tokens:

```
;;;;;;;;;;;;;;;;;;;;;;;;;;;;;;;;;;;;;;;;;;;;;;;;;;;;
;; RE-ORDER exchanges the tokens in the expression,
;; which were put out of order by the consing in
;; PARSE in PARSE-INPUT.
;;;;;;;;;;;;;;;;;;;;;;;;;;;;;;;;;;;;;;;;;;;;;;;;;;;;

(define (re-order parse-list)
  (if (= (length parse-list) 2)
      (list (cadr parse-list) (car parse-list))
      (list (cadr parse-list)
            (caddr parse-list)
            (car parse-list))))
```

It is convenient to perform the reordering at this time because the **parse** loop in **parse-input** uses **cons** to build a list of tokens (**parse-list**); these tokens are in a "backward," nonsense order. Additionally, **re-order** must be prepared to deal with an expression of either two or three tokens, as shown by the input/output for **calc**.

Note that there are several details that aren't handled by **parse-input**. For example, each token in the list produced by **parse-input** remains in string form—the details of converting each token, in particular, converting the character form of a numeric constant to an integer, are handled elsewhere.

Several remaining aspects of **calc** are considered after presenting the entire calculator program:

```
;;;;     calc.s     ;;;;;;;;;;;;;;;;;;;;;;;;;;;;;;;;;;;;;;;;;;;;;;;;;;;;;;;;;

;;;;;;;;;;;;;;;;;;;;;;;;;;;;;;;;;;;;;;;;;;;;;;;;;;;;
;; CALC performs simple, four-function calculations.
;; If the first operand is missing, the previous
;; result is used.  E.g.,
;; ===> 3 * 5
;; ===> 15
;; ===> + 3
;; ===> 18              [A null line terminates CALC.]
;; CALC uses the library modules:  str-int.s
;;                                 read-ln.s
;;;;;;;;;;;;;;;;;;;;;;;;;;;;;;;;;;;;;;;;;;;;;;;;;;;;

(define (calc)
  (define (display-prompt)
    (newline)
    (display "CALC -- FOUR-FUNCTION CALCULATOR")
    (newline)
```

```
      (display "===> "))
    (display-prompt)
  (let calc-loop ((op-list (parse-input)) (result 1))
    (cond
      ((null? (car op-list))
       (newline) (display "END CALC"))
      (else
        (newline)
        (display "===> ")
        (display (eval-string-list op-list result))
        (newline)
        (display-prompt)
        (calc-loop (parse-input)
                   (eval-string-list op-list result))))))


;;;;;;;;;;;;;;;;;;;;;;;;;;;;;;;;;;;;;;;;;;;;;;;;;;;;;;;;;;;;;;;;;;
;; PARSE-INPUT reads a line of input in infix form and returns
;; a list of the form:  ("operator" "operand-1" "operand-2").
;;;;;;;;;;;;;;;;;;;;;;;;;;;;;;;;;;;;;;;;;;;;;;;;;;;;;;;;;;;;;;;;;;

(define (parse-input)
  (let parse ((token-list (get-token (absorb-blanks (read-ln))))
              (parse-list '()))
    (cond
      ((string=? (absorb-blanks (cadr token-list)) "")
       (re-order (cons (car token-list) parse-list)))
      (else
        (parse (get-token (absorb-blanks (cadr token-list)))
               (cons (car token-list) parse-list))))))


;;;;;;;;;;;;;;;;;;;;;;;;;;;;;;;;;;;;;;;;;;;;;;;;;;;;;;;;
;; RE-ORDER exchanges the tokens in the expression,
;; which were put out of order by the consing in
;; PARSE in PARSE-INPUT.
;;;;;;;;;;;;;;;;;;;;;;;;;;;;;;;;;;;;;;;;;;;;;;;;;;;;;;;;

(define (re-order parse-list)
  (if (= (length parse-list) 2)
      (list (cadr parse-list) (car parse-list))
      (list (cadr parse-list)
            (caddr parse-list)
            (car parse-list))))
```

```
;;;;;;;;;;;;;;;;;;;;;;;;;;;;;;;;;;;;;;;;;;;;;;;;;;;;;;;;;;;;;;
;; GET-TOKEN processes a string one character at a time and
;; builds a token.  It returns a list containing the token
;; and the reduced line.
;;;;;;;;;;;;;;;;;;;;;;;;;;;;;;;;;;;;;;;;;;;;;;;;;;;;;;;;;;;;;;

(define (get-token line)
  (let find-end ((line line) (pos 0))
    (cond
      ((= pos (string-length line))
       (list (substring line 0 pos)
             (substring line pos (string-length line))))
      ((char-whitespace? (string-ref line pos))
       (list (substring line 0 pos)
             (substring line pos (string-length line))))
      (else
        (find-end line (+ pos 1))))))


;;;;;;;;;;;;;;;;;;;;;;;;;;;;;;;;;;;;;;;;;;;;;;;;;;;;;;;;;;;
;; ABSORB-BLANKS deletes leading blanks from a string.
;;;;;;;;;;;;;;;;;;;;;;;;;;;;;;;;;;;;;;;;;;;;;;;;;;;;;;;;;;;

(define (absorb-blanks line)
  (let find-start ((line line) (pos 0))
    (cond
      ((= pos (string-length line))
       "")
      ((char=? #\space (string-ref line pos))
       (find-start line (+ pos 1)))
      (else
        (substring line pos (string-length line))))))


;;;;;;;;;;;;;;;;;;;;;;;;;;;;;;;;;;;;;;;;;;;;;;;;;;;;;;;
;; EVAL-STRING-LIST evaluates a list of strings.
;;;;;;;;;;;;;;;;;;;;;;;;;;;;;;;;;;;;;;;;;;;;;;;;;;;;;;;

(define (eval-string-list str-list prev-result)
  (if (= (length str-list) 2)
      (set! str-list (list (car str-list)
                           (number->string prev-result
                                           '(int))
                           (cadr str-list))))
  (let ((op (car str-list))
        (opnd-1 (str->int (cadr str-list)))
```

```
          (opnd-2 (str->int (caddr str-list))))
    (case op
      ("+" (+ opnd-1 opnd-2))
      ("-" (- opnd-1 opnd-2))
      ("*" (* opnd-1 opnd-2))
      ("/" (/ opnd-1 opnd-2)))))
```

First, an internal function named **display-prompt** is defined for use in the driver routine **calc**. **calc** uses a named **let**, **calc-loop** to iterate over expressions typed by the user, until a null line is entered. The second argument to **calc-loop**, **result**, is initialized to 1 in the beginning; subsequently **result** is bound to the result of the evaluation of the previous cycle – this implements the feature of **calc** whereby the previous result of an expression evaluation is the default first argument for the next expression evaluation. The first argument to **calc-loop**, **op-list**, is always the value returned by **parse-input**.

get-token returns a data structure in the form:

```
(<token> <rest-of-string>)
```

As an example, if **parse-input** reads the string

```
"              12 +     24"
```

absorb-blanks returns

```
"12 +      24"
```

then **get-token** returns

```
("12" " +     24")
```

This is **token-list**; its **car** is pushed onto **parse-list** and its **cadr** (second element – the reduced line) is used in the next cycle.

Once **parse-list** is built by the recursion process, **re-order** is called to put the elements in prefix order. Since the parsing operation is so simple, only three tokens, we have used car-cdr operations directly to manipulate the elements. For a more complicated situation, it would be a good idea to build special functions with highly mnemonic names for these parsing operations.

The last function that needs mentioning is **eval-string-list**. It is passed a list of tokens, **op-list**, plus **result**, which may or may not be needed depending on the number of elements in **op-list**. Where only two tokens are present and the previous result is to be used, **prev-result** is necessarily in numeric form, and for coding convenience is converted to string form; i.e., so that the **let** initialization is presented with only one form of token list.

The conversion is performed by **number- > string**, a standard Scheme primitive for performing such conversions; a numeric data type must be specified in list form, here, just **(int)** because there are no special conversion/format requirements. (See the documentation for your Scheme.) Try this exercise: Write **int->str** to accompany **str->int**, presented in Chapter 8.

Once the numeric versions of the operands are built, a **case** structure is used to select the appropriate operation. Note that Scheme cannot evaluate

```
("+" <int> <int>)
```

i.e., the string " + " is not the same as the addition operator.

As an aside, we should address the issue of function encapsulation at this point. On several occasions we have demonstrated that helper functions can be defined local to a driver function. For a utility given earlier, **str->int**, we mentioned that helper functions that are specific to the task at hand should be placed internal to the driver function, and that, in some cases, for functions having promise for widespread use, i.e., potential library functions, it may be preferable to keep their definitions external.

Another important aspect of whether or not functions should be local or external is the development cycle. In particular, it may be considerably more awkward to invoke debug facilities on an internal function. Moreover, the interactive development environment that accompanies Scheme systems makes it easy to test external functions via top-level REP loop processing. That is, we can easily test a function such as **get-token** by "feeding" it a series of strings at the Scheme prompt. Once we internalize a function we lose this automatic debugging support.

In this text, we reserve the right to present some programs with helper functions already internalized, while presenting other programs with helper functions that still exist external to the driver function. Obviously, it is a trivial exercise to internalize such external functions. **calc** is an example of a program with associated external functions. You may want to consider extending the capabilities of **calc**, in which case the external status of the central functions is an advantage.

calc produces the following dialog.

```
[1] (load "calc.s")
OK
[2] (load "read-ln.s")                 ;don't forget these two--
OK
[3] (load "str-int.s")                 ;from your library
OK
[4] (calc)

CALC -- FOUR-FUNCTION CALCULATOR
===> 3 * 5
===> 15

CALC -- FOUR-FUNCTION CALCULATOR
===> + 3
===> 18
```

```
CALC -- FOUR-FUNCTION CALCULATOR
===>                                    ;<--- null line to exit
END CALC
[5] (exit)
```

Exercises

1. Rewrite **read-ch** from the beginning of this chapter to use a **let** instead of an internal **define.**

2. Rewrite **read-ch** from the beginning of this chapter so that no local variables are required.

3. Develop a program that prompts the user for lawn and house dimensions and then queries the user whether he/she is a slow, average, or fast worker, and based on this information calculates the time required to mow the lawn:

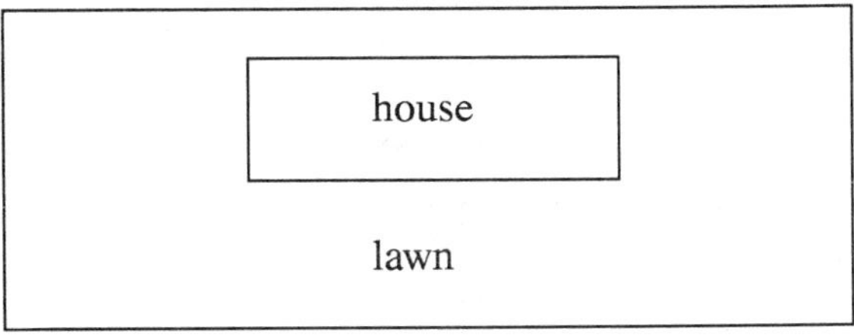

Your program should prompt the user for information using "nice" prompts; this can be done with **display** and **newline.**

4. Develop a program similar to **ccount** for counting lines in a file. Your program should prompt for filename and then report the number of lines in the file. You will have to develop your own technique for detecting end-of-line, or use a Scheme extension. In the case of the former, **#\newline** may be useful. (Also, see the solutions to the two versions of Exercise 10.)

5. Develop a Scheme utility for listing the contents of a disk file at the screen, complete with user prompts.

6. Enhance the utility in Exercise 5 so that the listing pauses after each screen of output.

7. Develop a Scheme printer listing utility that prints a file.

8. Develop a utility that sends a formfeed character to the printer.

9. Write the function **string-downcase** as a companion to **string-upcase**, given earlier in this chapter. Use **open-input-string**.

10. Rewrite **fcopy** from earlier in this chapter to use **with-input-from-file** and **with-output-to-file.**

11. Develop a Scheme utility, **find**, that searches a file (second parameter) line by line for any occurrence of a given string (first parameter). Each line from the file that contains the string should be reported at the console. Assume that strings do not span lines in the file.

12. Write a utility that copies and concatenates files together. Your program should first prompt the user for the name of the new file and then repeatedly prompt the user for the names of files to be added/concatenated to the new file.

13. Develop a utility to compare lines in two text files until two unequal lines are encountered. The first occurrence of unequal lines should terminate the file comparison, with a display of both lines and their respective line numbers. If no unequal lines are found, a message to that effect should be displayed that includes the line count. The occurrence of end-of-file for one file before end-of-file for the other file should be handled "gracefully."

14. Develop a program that returns a list of every unique word in a file and the number of times each word occurred. The format of the returned list should be

```
((a 5) (the 7) (cat 5) (hat 6) (fish 5) ... )
```

All words and their counts should be reported without distinguishing between upper- and lowercase characters.

15. Develop a Scheme function that searches a file of Scheme source code and reports every line that contains **set!**, along with a final tally of the number of occurrences of **set!**. Do not use **set!** in developing this function. Note: You do not need to write this function, if you've never used **set!**.

Chapter 10

Debugging and Lexical Scope

10.1 Introduction

In this chapter we primarily discuss generic techniques for error detection and correction. However, to some extent this chapter is still implementation-dependent, primarily due to the examples provided in PC Scheme. You are encouraged to investigate the debugging facilities available in your Scheme implementation.

Sophisticated, modern software development systems typically provide extensive debugging facilities. However, the provision of extensive debugging support is a difficult and expensive task, and frequently the level of support for debugging is directly related to the cost of an interpreter or compiler. Consequently, the level of support for debugging in your Scheme implementation may vary considerably from that discussed in this chapter.

10.2 Simple Techniques for Debugging

Many inexpensive implementations of a particular language, say, public-domain implementations, provide limited debugging support. Typically, this includes the ability to pretty-print, trace, and break functions.

The term "pretty-print" is used to describe the process of printing out a function (procedure) in a standard format, based on specific syntactic characteristics of the language. For example, in Scheme pretty-printing involves printing a function with controlled indention, based on the order of occurrence and nesting of specific language constructs, i.e., syntactic forms.

The examples given so far reflect the indention provided by the "smart" editor that accompanies the PC Scheme compiler. Scheme programming editors are smart in the sense that they can typically (1) indent syntactic forms based on generic rules of indention and (2) detect certain syntax errors during code entry/evaluation.

However, sometimes a programming editor is unavailable (as in the public-domain versions of software). In this case, the probability is higher that a (logical) syntax error can lead to a subtle error at execution time. In many cases, pretty-printing the function may help illuminate the error.

As an example, consider the following code which was typed with a simple editor, and which includes a logic error.

```
;;;;    debug.s    ;;;;;;;;;;;;;;;;;;;;;;;;;;;;;;;;;;;;;;;;;;;;;;;;

(define (square n)
  (* n n))


(define (one-to-x-sqrd x)
  (if (< x 0)
      (display "number must be nonnegative"))
      (do ((i 1 (+ i 1))
           (sum 0 (+ sum (square i))))
           ((> i x) sum)))
```

The intent here is to print an error message if the argument is negative; otherwise, perform the iteration and return the sum of the numbers squared from one to **x**. Note that the **display** expression has an extra closing parenthesis, which results in a null else condition and an unconditional execution of the **do**.

If we execute the program, the following occurs:

```
[PCS-DEBUG-MODE is OFF]                ;the PC Scheme default
[1] (set! pcs-debug-mode #t)
#T
[2] (load "debug.s")
OK
[3] (one-to-x-sqrd 3)
14
[4] (one-to-x-sqrd -3)
number must be nonnegative0
[5] (pp one-to-x-sqrd)
#<PROCEDURE ONE-TO-X-SQRD> =
(LAMBDA (X)
  (IF (< X 0) (DISPLAY "number must be nonnegative"))
  (DO ((I 1 (+ I 1))
       (SUM 0 (+ SUM (SQUARE I))))
      ((> I X) SUM)))
[6] _
```

First, note that PC Scheme automatically disables debugging when the compiler is first loaded, in order to optimize overall system performance. The overhead associated with maintaining debugging information is considerable; plus, turning on debugging requires that code optimization be turned off, thus adversely affecting run-time performance. Debugging is enabled in PC Scheme by setting the global variable **pcs-debug-mode** to true.

Although we demonstrate other aspects of debugging later, it's necessary to enable debugging at this point, as pretty-printing is associated with debugging in PC Scheme. (Please check your implementation.) After loading a file containing the preceding program, **one-to-x-sqrd** is executed at prompts [3] and [4]. At prompt [4], although the message is correctly printed, a value of zero is returned—which isn't supposed to happen.

Next, we pretty-print the function using **pp**. **pp** prints and indents **one-to-x-sqrd** using prescribed rules. Specifically, expressions that have the same (conditional) execution priority are vertically aligned. In this case, due to the extra parenthesis, the null else condition is immediately apparent. Thus, pretty-printing can be useful during program debugging, especially if a Scheme editor is unavailable.

In order to illustrate breakpoint facilities, let's consider a variation of the previous program, named **one-to-y-sqrd**.

```
(define (one-to-y-sqrd y)
  (do ((i 1 (- i 1))                              ;bug in this line
       (sum 0 (+ sum (square i))))
      ((> i y) sum)
      (bkpt "break in loop body showing i" i)))
```

In **one-to-y-sqrd** the loop variable **i** is improperly updated; **i** should be incremented by one, not decremented. This is of course a logic error that typically can't be anticipated by a Scheme editor. Obviously, when the program is executed, **i** is decremented "forever."

Assume that you've written such a program (without the **bkpt** expression) and can't figure out what's wrong. A good first guess is that something is wrong with the loop control variable **i**, since iteration is involved.

Most Schemes support breakpoint debugging. This means that we can arbitrarily establish breakpoints during execution by placing a breakpoint command inside the function. In this case, we illustrate the process of breaking execution for each iteration.

In some systems a break may place the programmer in a REP loop in which variable values can be examined. PC Scheme's **bkpt** allows the programmer to issue a message and evaluate an expression. Here, we break during each iteration and examine the value of **i**—**i** is the expression to be evaluated, the second argument to **bkpt**:

```
[6] (one-to-y-sqrd 3)

[BKPT encountered!] break in loop body showing i
1
```

```
[Inspect] Go

[BKPT encountered!] break in loop body showing i
0

[Inspect] Go

[BKPT encountered!] break in loop body showing i
-1

[Inspect] Go

[BKPT encountered!] break in loop body showing i
-2

[Inspect] Go

[BKPT encountered!] break in loop body showing i
-3

[Inspect] Quit
[7] _
```

Each break invokes the PC Scheme code inspector. Additionally, the breakpoint message is printed, along with **i**'s current value. Execution can be continued from the breakpoint by typing <control-g> (go). After one or two iterations, it's apparent that **i** is being updated incorrectly, and the proper correction can be made.

The next variation on the preceding program, **one-to-z-sqrd**, demonstrates primitive program tracing using additional debug facilities.

```
(define (sqr n)
  (* n 2))                          ;bug in this line

(define (one-to-z-sqrd z)
  (do ((i 1 (+ i 1))
       (sum 0 (+ sum (sqr i))))
      ((> i z) sum)))
```

Again, a logic error is present that can't be detected by the Scheme system; namely, the argument to **sqr** is doubled instead of being squared.

```
[7] (one-to-z-sqrd 3)
12                                    ;should be:  1 + 4 + 9 = 14
[8] (trace one-to-z-sqrd)
OK
```

```
[9] (one-to-z-sqrd 3)
 >>> Entering #<PROCEDURE ONE-TO-Z-SQRD>
  Argument 1: 3
12
[10] _
```

First, we demonstrate **trace**, which can be used to provide a limited trace of a function's execution activity. Here, we trace **one-to-z-sqrd**; in PC Scheme **trace** prints the values of the arguments each time the traced function is called. This can be useful for a program that contains several interdependent functions; in this case, tracing **one-to-z-sqrd** doesn't help much, since it is only called once. (**untrace** turns off tracing for a function.)

Another possibility involves using one of the "automatic" breakpoint commands: in PC Scheme, **break**, **break-both**, **break-entry**, and **break-exit**. For illustration we show **break-exit**.

```
[10] (break-exit sqr)
OK
[11] (one-to-z-sqrd 3)
 >>> Entering #<PROCEDURE ONE-TO-Z-SQRD>
  Argument 1: 3

[BKPT encountered!] BREAK-EXIT
((#<PROCEDURE SQR> 1) --> 2)

[Inspect] Go

[BKPT encountered!] BREAK-EXIT
((#<PROCEDURE SQR> 2) --> 4)

[Inspect] Go

[BKPT encountered!] BREAK-EXIT
((#<PROCEDURE SQR> 3) --> 6)

[Inspect] Quit
[12] (unbreak-exit sqr)
OK
[13] _
```

Guessing that there may be an error in **sqr**, the procedure that performs the squaring, we break execution upon each *exit* of **sqr**. The inspector shows the returned value in each case. Although we can take any of a number of actions each time the inspector is invoked, we continue execution, observing the returned values from **sqr**. It's obvious after the third break that the value returned from the call to **sqr**, 6, is incorrect for the argument value 3.

An alternate technique for this particular error would be to **trace sqr**. Suppose for illustration we trace both **one-to-z-sqrd** and **sqr**. (We trace **one-to-z-sqrd** using the default technique, **trace**, since there really isn't much to be gained – it's only executed once.)

```
[13] (trace one-to-z-sqrd)
OK
[14] (trace-both sqr)
OK
[15] (one-to-z-sqrd 3)
 >>> Entering #<PROCEDURE ONE-TO-Z-SQRD>
  Argument 1: 3
 >>> Entering #<PROCEDURE SQR>
  Argument 1: 1
 <<< Leaving #<PROCEDURE SQR> with value 2
  Argument 1: 1
 >>> Entering #<PROCEDURE SQR>
  Argument 1: 2
 <<< Leaving #<PROCEDURE SQR> with value 4
  Argument 1: 2
 >>> Entering #<PROCEDURE SQR>
  Argument 1: 3
 <<< Leaving #<PROCEDURE SQR> with value 6
  Argument 1: 3
12
[16] (exit)
```

As you can see, **trace-both** shows the argument value and the returned value for each invocation of **sqr**. If we only intend to examine data flow among function invocations, **trace** commands are more appropriate than break commands, as information is more condensed on the screen and we don't have to respond to the inspector.

Typically, recursive functions can be traced. Try tracing a function such as our first definition of factorial, **ftl**:

```
;;;;;;;;;;;;;;;;;;;;;;;;;;;;;;;;;;;;;;;;;;;;
;; FTL implements the standard, recursive
;; factorial function.
;;;;;;;;;;;;;;;;;;;;;;;;;;;;;;;;;;;;;;;;;;;;

(define (ftl n)
  (cond
    ((zero? n) 1)
    (else
      (* n (ftl (- n 1))))))
```

PC Scheme produces the following trace activity. (Don't forget to disable compiler optimization, if required by your Scheme.)

```
[1] (load "examples.s")
OK
[2] (trace-both ftl)          ;trace both entry and exit
OK
[3] (ftl 3)
 >>> Entering #<PROCEDURE FTL>
  Argument 1: 3
 >>> Entering #<PROCEDURE FTL>
  Argument 1: 2
 >>> Entering #<PROCEDURE FTL>
  Argument 1: 1
 >>> Entering #<PROCEDURE FTL>
  Argument 1: 0
 <<< Leaving #<PROCEDURE FTL> with value 1
  Argument 1: 0
 <<< Leaving #<PROCEDURE FTL> with value 1
  Argument 1: 1
 <<< Leaving #<PROCEDURE FTL> with value 2 ;(* 2 (ftl 1))
  Argument 1: 2
 <<< Leaving #<PROCEDURE FTL> with value 6 ;(* 3 (ftl 2))
  Argument 1: 3
6
[4] (exit)
```

10.3 Debugging in a Lexically Scoped Environment

To emphasize the lexically scoped nature of Scheme we provide a brief overview of PC Scheme's debugging facilities for examining the lexical environments surrounding a particular breakpoint. For simplicity, the program that we examine is *very* contrived, and it executes without error. Again, the primary focus of this section is Scheme's lexical scoping; even though the output is from a particular Scheme implementation, it illustrates lexical environments and frames.

The program that we examine is named **mean-table**; it produces the following output when executed without debugging code:

```
[1] (mean-table 5)
========================================
N   MEAN OF 1 TO N

1          1
2          1.5
3          2
```

```
4           2.5
5           3
========================================
[2] (exit)
```

Line *n* shows the value of **n** and the mean of all integers between one and **n** inclusive.

The code associated with **mean-table** is as follows:

```
;;;;    debug2.s     ;;;;;;;;;;;;;;;;;;;;;;;;;;;;;;;;;;;;;;;;;;;

;;;;;;;;;;;;;;;;;;;;;;;;;;;;;;;;;;;;;;;;;;;;;;;;;;;;;;;;;;;;;
;; The following functions illustrate nested prodecure
;; calls; for simplicity, there is no error checking.
;;;;;;;;;;;;;;;;;;;;;;;;;;;;;;;;;;;;;;;;;;;;;;;;;;;;;;;;;;;;

(define (mean-table high-bound)
  (define header-line
    "========================================")
  (define (print-header)
    (display header-line)
    (newline)
    (display "N    ")
    (display "MEAN OF 1 TO N")
    (newline))

;;;;;;;;;;;;;;;;;;;;;;;;;;;;;;;;;;;;;;;;;;;;;;; mean-table ;;;;
  (print-header)                                          ;;;;
  (do ((n 1 (+ n 1)))                                     ;;;;
      ((> n high-bound)                                   ;;;;
       (newline)                                          ;;;;
       (display header-line))                             ;;;;
      (newline)                                           ;;;;
      (assert (< n 5) "inside math-table")                ;;;;
      (display n)                                         ;;;;
      (display "            ")                            ;;;;
      (display (one-to-n-mean n))))                       ;;;;


;;;;;;;;;;;;;;;;;;;;;;;;;;;;;;; external support functions ;;;;

(define (one-to-n n)
  (assert (< n 3) "inside one-to-n")
  (/ (* n (+ n 1))
     2))
```

```
(define (one-to-n-mean n)
  (let ((location "inside one-to-n-mean"))
    (/ (one-to-n n) n)))
```

There are three "external" functions: **mean-table**, **one-to-n**, and **one-to-n-mean**. **mean-table** contains two local (internal) identifiers: **header-line**, a variable, and **print-header**, a function. Note the **assert** syntactic form, which is used to provide a conditional breakpoint. It has two arguments: (1) a condition (predicate), and (2) a message. A break occurs in execution when the condition *fails*. In this case, we've established an arbitrary breakpoint so that we can inspect the program's lexical environments as soon as **n** becomes equal to three in **one-to-n** (and also when **n** is 5 in **mean-table**).

PC Scheme's debugging inspector can be used to "move around" in the lexical environment. This is especially useful when you have several nested procedure calls and need to examine variable values at a particular point in the execution of the program by moving back and forth between calling procedures and called procedures. In many cases, the more convoluted the programming logic, the more useful the inspector.

Our intent here is only to illustrate the lexical environments through simple examination. Consider the following PC Scheme dialog. Several comments have been appended, along with numbered reference points near the right margin in the form: **@n**, where **n** is the reference number.

```
[PCS-DEBUG-MODE is OFF]
[1] (set! pcs-debug-mode #t)
#T
[2] (load "debug2.s")
OK
[3] (mean-table 5)
========================================
N   MEAN OF 1 TO N

1          1
2          1.5
3                                    ;n = 3, so program breaks
[ASSERT failure!]
(ASSERT () "inside one-to-n")

[Inspect] ?                                ;we type "?" for info @1
   ?    -- display this command summary
   !    -- reinitialize INSPECT
 ctrl-A -- display All environment frame bindings
 ctrl-B -- display procedure call Backtrace
 ctrl-C -- display Current environment frame bindings
 ctrl-D -- move Down to callee's stack frame
 ctrl-E -- Edit variable binding
 ctrl-G -- Go  (resume execution)
```

```
 ctrl-I -- evaluate one expression and Inspect the result
 ctrl-L -- List current procedure
 ctrl-M -- repeat the breakpoint Message
 ctrl-P -- move to Parent environment's frame
 ctrl-Q -- Quit  (RESET to top level)
 ctrl-R -- Return from BREAK with a value
 ctrl-S -- move to Son environment's frame
 ctrl-U -- move Up to caller's stack frame
 ctrl-V -- eValuate one expression in current environment
 ctrl-W -- (Where) Display current stack frame
To enter 'ctrl-A', press both 'CTRL' and 'A'.

[Inspect] All                                ;we type <control-a>  @2
Environment frame bindings at level 0
    N                     3
Environment frame bindings at level 1
    ONE-TO-N              #<PROCEDURE ONE-TO-N>
Environment frame bindings at level 2  (USER-INITIAL-ENVIRONMENT)
    ONE-TO-N-MEAN         #<PROCEDURE ONE-TO-N-MEAN>
    MEAN-TABLE            #<PROCEDURE MEAN-TABLE>
    ONE-TO-N              #<PROCEDURE ONE-TO-N>

[Inspect] Backtrace calls                    ;we type <control-b>  @3
Stack frame for #<PROCEDURE ONE-TO-N>
    N                     3
  called from   #<PROCEDURE ONE-TO-N-MEAN>
  called from   #<PROCEDURE %00000>
  called from   ()
  called from   #<PROCEDURE EVAL>
  called from   #<PROCEDURE ==SCHEME-RESET==>

[Inspect] Up to caller                       ;we type <control-u>  @4
Stack frame for #<PROCEDURE ONE-TO-N-MEAN>
    LOCATION              "inside one-to-n-mean"

[Inspect] Down to callee                     ;we type <control-d>  @5
Stack frame for #<PROCEDURE ONE-TO-N>
    N                     3

[Inspect] Value of: location                 ;we type <control-v>, @6
                                             ;then variable name
[VM ERROR encountered!] Variable not defined in current
environment
LOCATION

[Inspect] Value of: header-line              ;we type <control-v>, @7
```

```
                                        ;then variable name
[VM ERROR encountered!] Variable not defined in current
environment
HEADER-LINE

[Inspect] Go                            ;we type <control-g>  @8
2                                       ;more output
4
[ASSERT failure!]
(ASSERT () "inside one-to-n")

[Inspect] Go                            ;we type <control-g>  @9
2.5                                     ;more output

[ASSERT failure!]                       ;since n = 5
(ASSERT () "inside math-table")

[Inspect] All                           ;we type <control-a> @10
Environment frame bindings at level 0
    N                      5
Environment frame bindings at level 1
    %00000                 #<PROCEDURE %00000>
Environment frame bindings at level 2
    HEADER-LINE        "========================================"
    PRINT-HEADER           #<PROCEDURE PRINT-HEADER>
Environment frame bindings at level 3
    HIGH-BOUND             5
Environment frame bindings at level 4
    MEAN-TABLE             #<PROCEDURE MEAN-TABLE>
Environment frame bindings at level 5  (USER-INITIAL-ENVIRONMENT)
    ONE-TO-N-MEAN          #<PROCEDURE ONE-TO-N-MEAN>
    MEAN-TABLE             #<PROCEDURE MEAN-TABLE>
    ONE-TO-N               #<PROCEDURE ONE-TO-N>

[Inspect] Backtrace calls               ;we type <control-b>
Stack frame for #<PROCEDURE %00000>
    N                      5
  called from   ()
  called from   #<PROCEDURE EVAL>
  called from   #<PROCEDURE ==SCHEME-RESET==>

[Inspect] Value of: header-line              ;we type <control-v>
"========================================"   ;then variable name

[Inspect] Value of: high-bound               ;we type <control-v>
5                                            ;then variable name
```

```
[Inspect] Go                                ;we type <control-g>
5
[ASSERT failure!]
(ASSERT () "inside one-to-n")

[Inspect] Where am I?                       ;we type <control-w>
Stack frame for #<PROCEDURE ONE-TO-N>
    N                      5

[Inspect] Up to caller                      ;we type <control-u>
Stack frame for #<PROCEDURE ONE-TO-N-MEAN>
    LOCATION               "inside one-to-n-mean"

[Inspect] Value of: location                ;we type <control-v>
"inside one-to-n-mean"                      ;then variable name

[Inspect] Down to callee                    ;we type <control-d>
Stack frame for #<PROCEDURE ONE-TO-N>
    N                      5

[Inspect] Value of: n                       ;we type <control-v>
5                                           ;then variable name

[Inspect] Go                                ;we type <control-g>
3
======================================== ;prints last output
[4] (exit)
```

As in our earlier example, the inspector is entered as soon as the program breaks. At reference **@1** we enter a "?" to receive help on inspector commands. Next, at reference **@2** the <control-a> command is chosen to display all environment frames.

In an earlier chapter we mentioned Scheme lexical environments. In brief, a (lexical) *environment* is a set of identifier bindings, with respect to some point of reference. Normally, there are two environments to consider. First, there is the global environment, which is established by the top-level REP loop. As we've seen, global variables can be established and bound to values in the global environment using **define** and/or **set!**. Internal to the global environment, a user-initial environment is established upon activation of Scheme code containing a lexical construct such as a **lambda** form. One of Scheme's most notable features is that procedure and variable identifiers are established in the same environment. In contrast, many languages maintain procedure and variable declarations in different "name" spaces.

Within an environment such as the user-initial environment, variables may be bound to identifiers in contours, i.e., nested lexical blocks; these contours are typically called environment *frames*. For the previous debug dialog, the <control-a> command lists all environment frames. From the listing we can see three frames, 0, 1, and

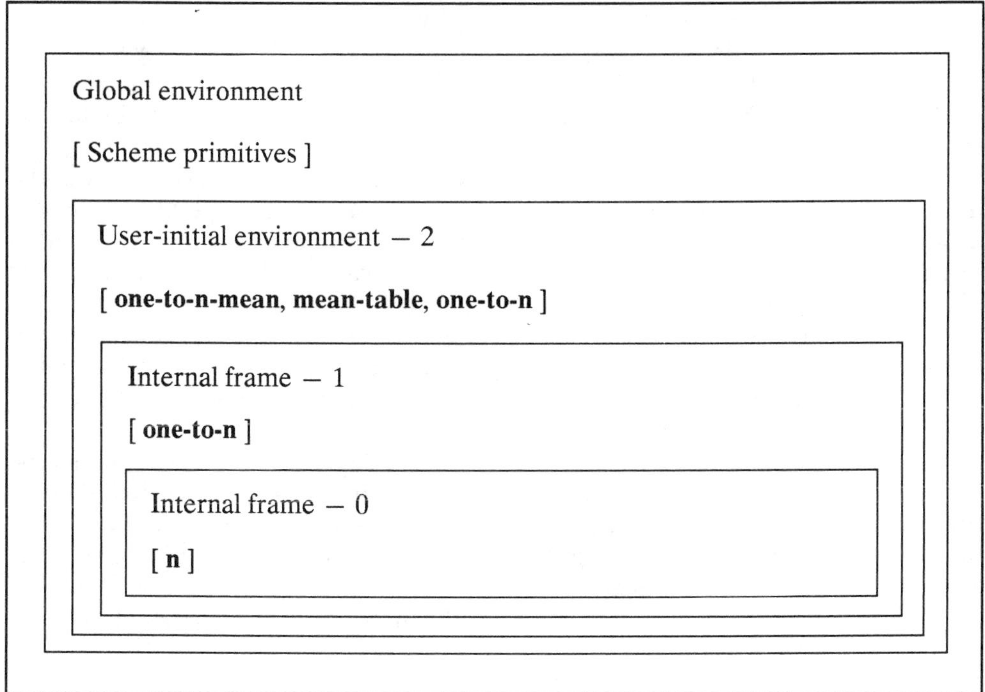

Figure 10.1 Scheme Frames for **mean-table**

2, reflecting the lexical scope of our program. Specifically, the innermost frame describes the bindings local to the function **one- to-n**, in this case, the parameter **n**. There are, for example, no **let** or **lambda** forms within **one-to-n** – this is the innermost frame.

Immediately surrounding frame 0 is frame 1, which describes a binding between the identifier **one-to-n** and the function body, described by a lambda form. Likewise, frame 1 is surrounded by frame 2, the outermost frame with respect to active, programmer-written code containing lexical constructs. This can be seen by reviewing the previous Scheme code or by examining the diagram in Figure 10.1.

It's important to distinguish between all possible legitimate procedural call sequences and actual procedural call sequences reflected by the existing code. This is best exemplified by the relationship between **one-to-n** and **one-to-n-mean**. Both of these functions are established at the same "level," i.e., in the user-initial environment. Legitimately, either procedure could call the other. However, this does not occur in the program above – **one-to-n-mean** calls **one-to-n**, but not the other way around. Thus, the environment frames described by the <control-a> command reflect the calling sequence with respect to the current break in execution.

References @**3**, @**4**, and @**5** illustrate that we can move up and down in the call sequence of code that is currently under execution; i.e., advance from one stack frame to another. This allows us to examine current variable values within a given lexical scope. Note that as we move up and then back down in the call sequence the local variable bindings are automatically displayed for **n**, **location**, and **n**, respectively.

The <control-v> command requests explicit evaluation of an expression typed by the user. At references @**6** and @**7** we illegally request evaluation of identifiers outside the current lexical environment.

At reference points @**8** and @**9** we step forward in the execution cycle until the next (conditional) breakpoint is reached. This occurs at reference point @**10**, where we again display all environment frames. This time the break has occurred within **mean-table**, prior to entry into **one-to-n-mean**. In this case, the lexical contours reflect the fact that **n** is within the lexical scope of the **do** (%00000), and so on.

Note in particular the way in which the "internal" **defines** are handled. Their bindings (one variable, one procedure) are established in an environment frame (frame 2) which is higher than that of the **do** (frame 1). This makes sense with respect to our usage of lexical scoping in previous programs.

The environment frame at level 3 reflects the binding of arguments to parameters; in this case, **high-bound** is bound to 5. Note that this allows for variables in the subordinate levels to reference the passed argument value. Finally, all of this occurs within the environment frame that binds and establishes **mean-table**, which of course exists within the user-initial environment.

As an exercise, you may want to examine other aspects of the debugger output that we have not mentioned here.

10.4 Nested Use of define

In an earlier chapter, we mentioned that **define**-ing a helper function inside another function is sometimes useful as a means of controlling the potential for name conflicts, and also confining specialized procedures to locations near their point of usage.

In light of the previous discussion, it is apparent that the programmer must strike a balance between such "internal" function definitions, which have the aforementioned advantages, and "external" function definitions, which are more easily traced and "broke" from the top-level REP loop. Note that the PC Scheme debugger displays considerable information for both types of definitions.

It is this type of debugging support that motivates programmers to write very small procedures, using Scheme, LISP, C, or whatever language. Although we may have a particular reason for doing so, when we construct a large function, say, with 30 lines of source code, the debugging facilities described in this chapter are of limited utility.

Exercises

1. Define a simple recursive version of the factorial function and trace its execution. You will have to read your documentation to discover the names for tracing functions. There may be a single trace function/directive, or multiple trace functions as with PC

Scheme. In any case, you should be able to duplicate the tracing activity given in this chapter for **ftl**.

2. Define a function that uses cdr recursion to sum all the elements in a list of numbers—nested lists are not allowed. Use your Scheme's trace facilities to illustrate the cdr processing of the list of numbers. Obtain printed output, if possible.

3. Define a function that uses car-cdr recursion to sum all the elements in a list of numbers, including nested lists. Then use your Scheme's trace facilities to illustrate the car-cdr recursion. Obtain printed output, if possible.

Chapter 11

Lambda Forms and Optional Arguments

11.1 Introduction

In this chapter we explore the three basic varieties of **lambda** forms. In particular, we investigate the use of **lambda** for handling optional arguments in a function call. We provide two utilities as examples that contrast two alternative techniques for accommodating optional arguments.

11.2 lambda

Chapter 3 illustrated the use of **lambda** forms as a mechanism for defining procedures. Recall that we described **lambda** as a "synonym" for function, in the sense of some function *f*(*x*). Since Chapter 3 we've primarily worked with a shorthand method for defining procedures in which the **lambda** form is invisible. However, **lambda** forms are more general and powerful than indicated in our earlier description. In this section we work directly with **lambda** and illustrate how to define procedures that can accommodate either a varying number of arguments or optional arguments.

In Scheme, **lambda** is a syntactic form that evaluates to a procedure. The syntax for **lambda** is:

```
(lambda <parameters> <expression>...)
```

where **<expression>...** is the function body and **<parameters>** has one of the following formats:

```
(<variable>...)
```

```
<variable>
```

```
(<variable1> ... <variablen-1)> . <variablen>)
```

The first format is the one we've worked with so far—a fixed number of parameters, e.g.,

```
(define (add x y) (+ x y))              ;shorthand form
```

or

```
(define add (lambda (x y) (+ x y)))    ;lambda form
```

In this chapter we work with latter form.

In the second format the parameters are represented by a single variable name, **<variable>**, e.g.,

```
(define add
  (lambda parms
    (let add-loop ((sum 0) (parm-list parms))
      (if (null? parm-list)
          sum
          (add-loop
            (+ sum (car parm-list)) (cdr parm-list))))))
```

Here, **add** is a procedure that mimics Scheme's addition function; it accepts zero or more arguments. Each argument is collected in a list and bound to **parms**. **add-loop** performs cdr recursion on the list of arguments; for each iteration the first argument is added to **sum** and the list is reduced by the first argument. The processing terminates when the last argument has been extracted, leaving an empty list.

The third format allows for optional arguments. The first n - 1 parameters are fixed; i.e., if any parameters are specified, the corresponding arguments must be provided when the function is called, or an error results. If n - 1 parameters are specified before the period ("."), at execution time any excess arguments, i.e., the nth, n + 1st, etc., are collected in a list and bound to **<variable$_n$>**. As an example, suppose you would like to write a function that mimics **write-char**; recall that **write-char** allows for an optional port specification. We can specify one fixed argument before the period and one optional argument after the period:

```
(define write-ch
  (lambda (char . port)
    (if (null? port)
        (write-char char)
        (write-char char (car port)))))
```

write-ch calls **write-char**, with either one or two arguments. If a second argument is supplied to **write-ch**, it is placed in a list and bound to **port**. Thus, **(car port)** returns the I/O port, which is supplied to **write-char** as the second argument.

11.3 dir: A Utility for Listing Filenames (Implementation-specific)

Many software development systems provide supplemental primitives for working with the OS. A common example is a primitive that returns a name list of files in a disk directory. In this section we describe **dir**, a Scheme function that prints a directory listing at the console:

```
;;;;     dir.s     ;;;;;;;;;;;;;;;;;;;;;;;;;;;;;;;;;;;;;;;;;;;;

;;;;;;;;;;;;;;;;;;;;;;;;;;;;;;;;;;;;;;;;;;;;
;; DIR prints a DOS directory listing.
;; Library:    uses STRING-INDEX
;; PC Scheme: uses DOS-DIR function
;;             uses SORT! function
;; Usage:   (dir [<file-spec>])
;; Example usage:   a. (dir "*.s")
;;                  b. (dir)  [same as a.]
;;;;;;;;;;;;;;;;;;;;;;;;;;;;;;;;;;;;;;;;;;;;

(define dir
  (lambda filespec                    ;put argument in a list,
                                      ;i.e., make it optional
;;;;;;;;;;;;;;;;;;;;;;;;;;;;;;;;;;;;;;;;;;;;;;;;;;;
;; PRINT-FILES prints a list of files vertically,
;; aligned by filename and filetype.
;;;;;;;;;;;;;;;;;;;;;;;;;;;;;;;;;;;;;;;;;;;;;;;;;;;

(define (print-files file-list)
  (if (null? file-list)
      (display "*** no matching files ***")
      (let ((filename-length 8)
            (screen-size 22))
        (display "==============")
        (newline)
        (let print-each ((fname (car file-list))
                         (flist (cdr file-list))
                         (count 1))
          (display (string-append
                     (make-string (- filename-length
                                     (string-index fname #\.))
                                  #\space)
```

```
                    fname))
          (newline)
          (if (null? flist)
              '()
              (if (= count screen-size)
                  (begin
                    (display
                "==============  Press <enter> to continue...")
                    (read-char)
                    (newline)
                    (print-each (car flist) (cdr flist) 1))
                  (print-each
                    (car flist)
                    (cdr flist)
                    (+ count 1)))))
        (display "==============")))))

;;;;     end internal definitions     ;;;;;;;;;;;;;;;;;;;;;;;;;;;;;

    (let ((file-spec (if (null? filespec)
                         "*.s"              ;default filetype
                         (car filespec))))
      (if (string? file-spec)
          (print-files (sort! (dos-dir file-spec) string<?))
          (display
        "*** file specification must be a quoted string ***"))
      (display " "))))
```

The body of **dir** occurs after the comment line that marks the end of internal definitions; in this case, the internal function is **print-files**, which takes care of the details of printing consecutive screens of output. Here, we've assumed that development of **dir** is complete and have moved **print-files** internal to **dir** to prevent potential name conflicts with yet-to-be-developed functions.

Our version of **dir** uses **dos-dir**, a PC Scheme primitive that returns a list of filenames, plus **sort!**, a PC Scheme primitive used to sort the list of filenames. Otherwise, **dir** is written in standard Scheme; you can substitute your Scheme's equivalent primitives, if available. The sorting aspect of **dir** is of course optional and could be eliminated, or you could define your own routine for sorting a list. (See some of the later chapters.) Also, **dir** requires the **string-index** function that we discussed earlier.

dir illustrates the use of **lambda** with provision for a single optional argument. That is, **dir** is written so that the user can type "(dir)" with no arguments, or "(dir <pathname>)". Thus, the second form of **lambda** is required, since it allows zero or more arguments. If an argument is provided at execution time, it is put into a list of length one and bound to **file-spec**.

Although Scheme provides the essential support for optional arguments, it is up to the program to determine their presence or absence and take the steps necessary to continue processing in either case. The technique that we use in the driver function **dir** is to use an **if** structure to determine whether or not the optional argument is present, and if not, to supply the default file specification. The result is bound to **file-spec** using **let** syntax.

If a file specification is provided, it's used directly as an argument to **dos-dir**; otherwise, **file-spec** is set to "*.s", a wildcard specification that matches any filename ending in ".s". Note that a second **if** is used for error detection – to make sure that the file specification is a string, as required by PC Scheme's **dos-dir**. Your system may require something slightly different.

The **print-files** function is used for the actual printing. A variation of **print-files** that simply printed filenames would be much shorter. In this case, most of the code is devoted to aligning filenames vertically based on the period that separates filenames and file types in MS-DOS. This is done by searching each filename for the period, using **string-index**, and then appending the proper number of leading blanks for alignment. In addition, **print-files** pauses when the screen is full for ease of viewing.

Although some Scheme systems may not provide the OS primitives required here, you could use these two functions as a model for tasks that require printing voluminous string output at the screen.

11.4 format: A Utility for Formatted Output

By now you may have grown tired of the **display** statement, especially interleaving multiple **display**s to get the desired output. The third **lambda** form provides the tools necessary for developing our own utility for formatted output. Common LISP provides **format** for formatted output; it is somewhat like C's **printf**. In this section we provide a standard Scheme function that mimics **format**, at least its most basic and common usage. You may want to supplement **format** based on your own preferences. In any case, **format** could be useful in porting Common LISP code to Scheme.

The Common LISP **format** function is very powerful, having an extensive number of formatting directives. Our intent here is to provide a similar function written in standard Scheme that can perform *basic* formatting for the standard output port. Before considering the actual code, we should describe our version of **format**. We start with examples of its usage and then formally discuss its syntax. Consider the following dialog with Scheme:

```
[1] (load "format.s")
OK
[2] (format "Keep off the grass!")
Keep off the grass!
[3] (format "Don't Even Think of Parking Here~%")
Don't Even Think of Parking Here
[4] (format "~%  No Parking~%~%This Means YOU~%~%")

  No Parking
```

```
This Means YOU

[5] (format "Hello ~a~%" "John")
Hello John
[6] (define name "Mary")
NAME
[7] (format "Hello ~a~%" name)
Hello Mary
[8] (format "~a copied to ~a" "xyz.dat" "xyz.bak")
xyz.dat copied to xyz.bak
[9] (format "file size in bytes for ~a:  ~a~%" "scheme.dat" 100)
file size in bytes for scheme.dat:  100
[10] (exit)
```

The simplest usage of **format** is shown at prompt [2] where it is used to print a string in the same way that **display** prints a string—without the double quotes. Prompt [3] illustrates the directive for issuing a newline sequence, ~%; note that it is put inside the double quotes. This capability makes it quite easy to print messages to standard output with interleaved textual output and blank lines. Since the REP loop automatically begins each interaction on a new line, the directives at prompts [2] and [3] have the same effect. Prompt [4] illustrates multiple newline sequences; a new line is generated for each "~%".

The syntax for **format** is:

```
(format <control-string> <arg>...)
```

where **<control-string>** may contain printable characters plus print control directives and **<arg>...** represents zero or more arguments separated by blanks (see prompt [9]).

format uses the character "~" (tilde) to signal a formatting directive. (In order to print a "~", you must enter two "~"s.) A tilde may be followed by any one of several characters which (following a tilde) have special meaning:

Directive	Function
a	output an expression in printed ASCII representation
s	output an s-expression
c	output a character
%	go to a new line
~	output a tilde

Each directive that specifies output of a data item must have a corresponding **<arg>**; they are processed in order; i.e., the first directive requiring a data item uses the first **<arg>**, and so on.

The directive ~**a** requests that output be in ASCII or "display" form; i.e., in the same form as **display** would print it. In contrast, the ~**s** directive prints s-expressions in the same form as **write**, i.e.; in a form that can be read with **read**. The ~**c** directive prints a single character in the same way that **write-char** would, without the "#\".

The standard Scheme code for our simplified **format** is given next.

```
;;;;     format.s     ;;;;;;;;;;;;;;;;;;;;;;;;;;;;;;;;;;;;;;;;;;;;

;;;;;;;;;;;;;;;;;;;;;;;;;;;;;;;;;;;;;;;;;;;;;;;;;;;;;;;;;;;;;;;;;
;; FORMAT is similar to Common LISP's FORMAT and C's PRINTF.
;; There is no error checking.
;; Usage:  (format <control-str> [<arg1> <arg2> ... <argn>])
;; Returns:  nothing
;;;;;;;;;;;;;;;;;;;;;;;;;;;;;;;;;;;;;;;;;;;;;;;;;;;;;;;;;;;;;;;;;

(define (format control-string . objects)
  (let ((input-string (open-input-string control-string)))
    (let get-args ((c (read-char input-string)) (lst objects))
      (cond
        ((eof-object? c)
         (display ""))                              ;return nothing
        ((char=? c #\~)
         (case (read-char input-string)
           (#\a
             (display (car lst))
             (get-args (read-char input-string) (cdr lst)))
           (#\s
             (write (car lst))
             (get-args (read-char input-string) (cdr lst)))
           (#\c
             (write-char (car lst))
             (get-args (read-char input-string) (cdr lst)))
           (#\%
             (newline)
             (get-args (read-char input-string) lst))
           (#\~
             (write-char #\~)
             (get-args (read-char input-string) lst))))
        (else
          (write-char c)
          (get-args (read-char input-string) lst))))))
```

Processing the various options is straightforward and is handled by a **case** structure. **cond** is useful for controlling three situations that arise in processing the control string: (1) end-of-string, (2) special control directive, and (3) ordinary character to be printed.

The third **lambda** form is particularly useful in coding **format** because it allows for the provision of a fixed number of required arguments and additional optional arguments—in this case, one fixed and one optional argument:

```
(lambda (format-string . objects)
```

Executing **format** with no arguments results in an error, that is, the format control string must be supplied. However, if there are no **~a**, **~s**, or **~c** directives, no variables/constants will be supplied and the list **objects** will be null. In **format <arg>...** are automatically collected in list form making it easy for the user in that print objects are simply separated by spaces, and easy for the programmer in that list processing directives are available to process the print objects. This is a good example of how *list processing* can be brought to bear on *traditional applications*.

The programming for the **format** function mostly involves string and character processing. There are two basic choices: (1) use the **open-input-string** facilities for simulated port processing, or (2) use the basic string and character manipulation facilities. Either approach is acceptable; however, since the format control string must be examined from beginning to end, the first approach seems slightly more appropriate. If your Scheme implementation doesn't have **open-input-string**, you can still implement the above function by using the second approach.

Exercises

1. Develop an alternative version of standard Scheme's **make-string**, **make-str**, such that if no fill character is provided, a blank is used.

2. Develop an alternative version of standard Scheme's **substring**, **substrg**, such that if the third argument is missing, the rest of the string is extracted; i.e., the third argument is optional with the default value: "end-of-string."

3. Modify **string-insert** from a previous chapter so that if only two arguments are passed to **string-insert**, the second argument is interpreted as the insert position and the insert string is composed of a one-character string containing a blank (" "). This modification is mostly an exercise in using the second **lambda** form to accommodate optional arguments. Note that the third **lambda** form is useful primarily when the optional parameters occur last in the parameter list. Also, see **dir** in this chapter.

4. Implement the directory utility from this chapter, **dir**, as best you can, given your Scheme's OS interface.

5. Modify **format** so that an optional, alternative output port is accommodated. Use the following call structure, which is similar to Common LISP's (Steele, 1984). (It differs in that Common LISP uses Boolean true to indicate the standard output port, whereas we omit the argument for standard output.)

```
(format [<destination>] <control-string> [<arg>...])
```

<destination> is the optional output port.

6. Modify the version of **format** given in Exercise 5 so that Boolean false as a **<destination>** directs the function to return the output as a string.

7. A common exercise is to develop a program that outputs a monthly calendar. Develop such a function, using **format** to assist with the formatted output. The function should be passed two arguments: the number of days in the month (integer), and the day of the week when the month begins. The latter should be in either symbol or string form. This is primarily a formatting exercise; i.e., because of the information passed as arguments, no special algorithm is needed to determine on which day of the week the month begins. Minimally, your program should output the monthly calendar with day of the week headings and nicely-aligned columns. If available, you may want to call on support routines for additional information. A sophisticated program would output something like the following, possibly requiring additional parameters:

```
# June 1988 ==== 3:47 PM         #
#================================#
# Sun Mon Tue Wed Thu Fri Sat #
#================================#
#                 1   2   3   4 #
#   5   6   7   8   9  10  11 #
#  12  13  14  15  16  17  18 #
#  19  20  21  22  23  24  25 #
#  26  27  28  29  30          #
#================================#
```

8. Add optional, alternative port capabilities to **read-ln**. You must make a decision about whether the output is to be echoed to the console (standard output port). That is, in reading a line from disk file, should that line be written to the console, or just returned? Consider the utility of such a function, say, reading lines of a file in a line count utility where it is undesirable to echo the file contents to the console. You may want to incorporate "character echoing" as an option; consider the next exercise.

9. Modify one of the file listing utilities from the exercises in Chapter 9 to use **read-ln** from Exercise 8 above.

10. Modify the line counting utility from the exercises in Chapter 9 to use **read-ln** from Exercise 8 above.

11. If your version of Scheme has windowing facilities, e.g., PC Scheme, rewrite **calc** as **calc-win**, a program that prompts for input in one window and displays output in another window. You will need to provide a version of **read-ln** that "does windows."

Depending on your Scheme implementation, you may be able to develop one version of **read-ln** that addresses Exercises 8 through 11.

Chapter 12

Lambda Forms and Procedure Application

12.1 Introduction

In this chapter we explore **lambda** forms and function usage in more detail by investigating the programming flexibility provided by Scheme's treatment of functions as first-class data objects. We begin by investigating the ease with which Scheme functions can be passed as arguments to, and returned from, other functions; this includes built-in and user-defined functions.

In the second half of the chapter we consider the use of lambda forms for creating anonymous functions. We discuss several uses of anonymous functions, most of which involve passing functions as arguments, including certain Scheme mapping functions.

12.2 Functions as First-class Data Objects

With respect to programming languages, a first-class data object is one that has no restrictions on its usage. For example, integers can be used in many ways, including:

1. as components in expressions
2. as elements in an array
3. as values bound to identifiers
4. as arguments to functions
5. as values returned by functions.

Most languages do not extend such capabilities to procedures. For example, Pascal does not allow a function to return another function; nor does Pascal allow the programmer to create an array of functions, etc. Many LISP dialects allow functions to be passed as arguments to other functions, including Common LISP. However, passing Common LISP functions as arguments typically requires some special effort, e.g., quoting the function name, **apply**ing extra function evaluations, and so on.

Scheme, on the other hand, treats functions as first-class data objects, meaning that functions can be used in all of the ways mentioned previously. Moreover, by elevating functions to the same status as other data objects, Scheme achieves a measure of consistency and elegance that is absent from other languages. For example, a function is defined (and handled) in the same way as a variable:

```
(define x 3)

(define y (lambda (n) ...))
```

(The same is true with the shorthand form of **define** – it merely provides a way of defining a function with fewer keystrokes.) Consequently, if either **x** or **y** is evaluated, a first-class object is returned, which can be used in any number of ways. For instance, in Scheme the same technique can be used for passing variables and functions as arguments; namely, either one can be passed by simply coding the identifier in the proper argument position.

The call-by-value technique for passing arguments stipulates that (1) all arguments are evaluated, and (2) the resulting values are passed to the called function. In the case of **x** and **y**, and a function call such as

```
... (z x y) ...
```

z would be called with the values **3** and **(lambda (n) ...)**, respectively. That is, **x** evaluates to a constant value and **y** evaluates to a procedure, both of which would presumably be used by **z**. The main point is that passing **y** requires no special consideration, since it evaluates to an executable procedure.

12.3 Functions as Arguments

Suppose that we have some standard or frequent operation that is to be applied to several sets of data, e.g.,

1. squaring numbers
2. cubing numbers
3. computing cross-products
4. calculating each salesperson's commission
5. calculating wages for hourly workers
6. determining each employee's Christmas bonus.

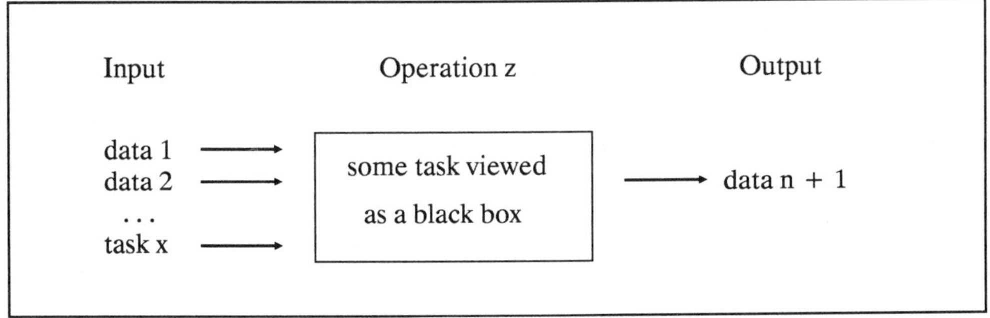

Figure 12.1 The Abstraction Process

In computer science we say that each of these routine operations can be abstracted as a procedure. That is, once we have written the code to calculate hourly wages, we can abstract away from the low-level details of the calculations treating the entire operation as a single task.

In mathematics, functions provide a similar abstraction mechanism, such that a function, say, $f(x,y)$, can be viewed as a *black box* which produces some output, given input x and y, e.g., hourly pay rate and hours worked. The process of codifying a task like wage calculation as a black box operation is called *procedure abstraction*.

The beauty of Scheme is that the language fully supports procedure abstraction. That is, consider a large, complex programming project that logically can be broken down into many separate tasks where some tasks require other tasks as input; i.e., one task is a parameter of another. Figure 12.1 illustrates the abstraction process. Even though task x is viewed, logically speaking, as input to operation z, many languages force us to call task x, quite arbitrarily, from some point inside operation z – back door programming, if you will.

Scheme, on the other hand, by treating procedures (operations) as first-class objects, allows us to code the project in a manner that parallels its logical organization. Thus the translation, or mapping, of a large-scale, real world operation to computer algorithm(s) is more straightforward. This in turn enhances the long-term utility of the software, primarily by increasing the feasibility of software update operations. This kind of straightforward mapping of complex tasks to computer algorithm(s) is especially useful for AI programming projects, which typically are quite complex.

As a straightforward example of procedure passing in Scheme, consider a basic mathematical operation such as summation, which permeates engineering and statistical applications. Suppose we think of summation as operation z in Figure 12.1 and squaring numbers as task x. In this case, the data would be a set of numbers, provided either directly or indirectly. Consider the following code:

```
;;;;     sums.s      ;;;;;;;;;;;;;;;;;;;;;;;;;;;;;;;;;;;;;;;;;;;;

(define (square x) (* x x))                     ;task x
```

```
(define (cube x) (* x x x))                      ;task y

;;;;;;;;;;;;;;;;;;;;;;;;;;;;;;;;;;;;;;;;;;;;;;;;;;;;;;;;;;;;;;
;; SUMMATION sums values over an interval, after applying
;; a formula to each integer in the interval.
;;;;;;;;;;;;;;;;;;;;;;;;;;;;;;;;;;;;;;;;;;;;;;;;;;;;;;;;;;;;;;

(define (summation formula start stop)           ;operation z
  (do ((i start (+ i 1))                         ;see Fig. 12.1
       (sum 0 (+ (formula i) sum)))
      ((> i stop) sum)))
```

Procedure **summation** takes some task, say, task *x*, as input, plus data in the form of start and stop values and computes the sum of squares of integers between **start** and **stop** inclusive.

Note that our code completely mirrors the mathematical task; no artificial mechanisms are needed to communicate the **formula** to **summation**. Moreover, if task *x* changes slightly, or is replaced by some other task, say, task *y*, and operation *z* remains the same, no changes are required in **summation**. Languages not allowing procedure passing would require that a procedure call inside **summation** be changed, say, from **square** to **cube**.

So far we've addressed the coding process per se. However, using the previous code is equally straightforward, as demonstrated by the following dialog with Scheme.

```
[1] (load "sums.s")
OK
[2] (square 3)
9
[3] (cube 3)
27
[4] (summation square 1 3)
14
[5] (summation cube 1 3)
36
[6] (exit)
```

As another example, consider operations (4) and (5) given earlier: computing wages for employees, where some are based on commission and some on hours worked. The following Scheme code provides a simple demonstration of one form of abstraction.

```
;;;;     paycheck.s     ;;;;;;;;;;;;;;;;;;;;;;;;;;;;;;;;;;;;;;;;

;;;;;;;;;;;;;;;;;;;;;;;;;;;;;;;;;;;;;;;;;;;;;;;;;;;;;;;;;;;;
;; COMMISSION provides one formula for calculating pay.
;;;;;;;;;;;;;;;;;;;;;;;;;;;;;;;;;;;;;;;;;;;;;;;;;;;;;;;;;;;;
```

```
(define commission
  (lambda (sales commission-rate)
    (* sales commission-rate)))


;;;;;;;;;;;;;;;;;;;;;;;;;;;;;;;;;;;;;;;;;;;;;;;;;;;;;;;;;;;;;;;
;; HOURLY-WAGES provides another formula for
;; calculating pay.
;;;;;;;;;;;;;;;;;;;;;;;;;;;;;;;;;;;;;;;;;;;;;;;;;;;;;;;;;;;;;;;

(define hourly-wages
  (lambda (no-hours hourly-rate)
    (if (<= no-hours 40)
        (* no-hours hourly-rate)           ;regular pay only
        (+ (* 40 hourly-rate)              ;regular pay plus
           (* (- no-hours 40)              ;"time and a half"
              hourly-rate
              1.5)))))


;;;;;;;;;;;;;;;;;;;;;;;;;;;;;;;;;;;;;;;;;;;;;;;;;;;;;;;;;;;;;;;;;;;;;;;;;;;
;; CALC-PAY performs payroll calculations based on the
;; formulas provided by functions such as COMMISSION
;; and HOURLY-WAGES.
;;;;;;;;;;;;;;;;;;;;;;;;;;;;;;;;;;;;;;;;;;;;;;;;;;;;;;;;;;;;;;;;;;;;;;;;;;;

(define calc-pay
  (lambda (formula base rate)
    (formula base rate)))
```

The previous example used the shorthand version of **define**, whereas this example formally codes the functions in terms of the **lambda** syntactic form. Although we've already emphasized that they are equivalent, in terms of defining functions, it's important to emphasize that the focus at this point is on passing functions as arguments, and not on how those functions have been defined.

Suppose that **calc-pay** represents some "real" program that is used on a regular basis. If new procedures are developed for calculating pay, for either existing or new job classifications, no changes are required to **calc-pay** – new pay-calculation rules are simply coded as procedures and passed to **calc-pay**.

Moreover, Scheme's handling of procedures as first-class objects provides a language-level tool for implementing what is often called *object-oriented programming*, in particular, *message passing* schemes. That is, we can view **commission** and **hourly-wages** as *methods* that prescribe certain actions. Methods can be attached to the appropriate objects, in this case, employees. Subsequently, instead of applying the formula directly, a program such as **calc-pay** could send a message initiating wage calculation to an object, e.g., the object named "Bill Jones", in which case the appropriate method would be used.

Getting back to the procedure-oriented approach, at prompts [4] and [5] each *method* for calculating an employee's wages is passed to **calc-pay** in turn.

```
[1] (load "paycheck.s")
OK
[2] (commission 100 .04)
4.
[3] (hourly-wages 50 10)
550.
[4] (calc-pay commission 100 .04)
4.
[5] (calc-pay hourly-wages 50 10)
550.
[6] (exit)
```

12.4 Using lambda for Anonymous Functions

Up to this point in our discussion of **lambda** we've been concerned with its usage as a syntactic device for defining functions, i.e., purely as a syntactic form. This is analogous to a Pascal programmer's usage of the keyword **function** in

```
function Double(X: integer): integer;
begin
  Double := X * 2;
end;
```

except that we aren't confined to a particular data type:

```
(define double (lambda (x) (* x 2)))
```

However, **lambda** has more utility than suggested by our examples so far. For example, we can use **lambda** to define temporary, or *anonymous*, functions. Basically, there are three situations where anonymous functions may be useful:

1. when local variables are needed
2. as a component of certain syntactic forms and functions
3. as a description of some procedural task.

In comparison, however, anonymous functions are more useful in the latter two cases. We address each of these, after a brief discussion of **lambda**.

Formally, **lambda** is called a syntactic, or special, form; i.e., it is part of the syntax of the Scheme language, much like **let**, **do**, **begin**, and others. In particular, it's used to specify function definitions. When Scheme encounters a **lambda** form, it creates and returns a procedure; for convenience, we informally refer to the latter as a *lambda function*, i.e., a function "created" by a **lambda** form.

We may or may not assign the returned function to an identifier; if we do not, it is called an *anonymous* function. Anonymous functions are easily illustrated at the top-level REP loop.

```
[1] (lambda (n) (* n n))        ;returns a procedure
#<PROCEDURE>
[2] ((lambda (n) (* n n)) 2)    ;form:   "(<function> <arg>)"
4
[3] (load "sums.s")
OK
[4] (summation (lambda (n) (* n n)) 1 3)
14
[5] ((lambda (proc n) (* 2 (proc n))) (lambda (n) (* n n)) 3)
18
[6] (exit)
```

At prompt [1] Scheme evaluates the **lambda** *syntax* and returns a procedure. The rules of expression evaluation in Scheme require that (1) all items within an expression are evaluated, and (2) the first item (if it isn't a keyword) should evaluate to a function that can be applied to the following arguments. The number of arguments supplied should be consistent with the requirements of the function specified in the first position of the expression. At prompt [2] the first item evaluates to a function that squares an number. The second (last) item is the number to be squared. In this case, 2 squared returns 4.

A function can be named or anonymous. At prompt [4] the function **summation** (discussed earlier) is called with an anonymous function as its first argument, instead of **square**. At prompt [5] **lambda** forms are provided as the first and second arguments. The function returned by the first **lambda** form is evaluated, with the function returned by the second **lambda** as the first argument and the constant 3 as the second argument:

```
                                                          Third
                                                          Item
               First Item                  Second Item     |
      <---------------------------->   <---------------->  v

[5] ((lambda (proc n) (* 2 (proc n))) (lambda (n) (* n n)) 3)

18  <-- returned value
```

Again, a function doesn't need a name to be treated as a first-class object.

12.4.1 Anonymous Functions and Local Variables

The utility of the **let** syntactic form has been demonstrated in previous chapters. However, **let** is provided as a programmer convenience; it isn't necessary, since local variable bindings can be established with **lambda**. **let** is an example of a binding construct that is provided through syntactic extension of core constructs.

The relationship between **lambda** and **let** can be seen by examining a variation of our earlier **greeting** program.

```
;;;;     local.s     ;;;;;;;;;;;;;;;;;;;;;;;;;;;;;;;;;;;;;;;;;;;;;

;;;;;;;;;;;;;;;;;;;;;;;;;;;;;;;;;;;;;;;;;;;;;;;;;;;;;;;;;;;;;;;;;;;;
;; HI prompts for and reads the user's name (in symbol
;; form--first character lowercase), and then greets the user.
;;;;;;;;;;;;;;;;;;;;;;;;;;;;;;;;;;;;;;;;;;;;;;;;;;;;;;;;;;;;;;;;;;;;

(define hi (lambda ()
  (display "Your (first) name please:  ")
  ((lambda (name)
    (display "Hi ")
    (display name)
    (display "!"))
    (read))))                           ;bind result of read to name

;;;;;;;;;;;;;;;;;;;;;;;;;;;;;;;;;;;;;;;;;;;;;;;;;;;;;;;;;;;;;;;;;;;;
;;(define hi (lambda ()
;;  (display "Your (first) name please:  ")
;;  (let ((name (read)))                ;bind result of read to name
;;    (display "Hi ")
;;    (display name)
;;    (display "!"))))
```

hi has been rewritten to use a **lambda** instead of a **let**, as in an earlier example. The **let** version is also provided in comment form for comparison purposes. We've abandoned any use of the shorthand method for defining functions, as its usage in this context is confusing at best. In this case, **hi** is defined to be a function which has a lambda function (our terminology) as its function body.

Given this particular design of **hi**, in order to greet the user with interleaved prompting, there must be a local variable, **name**, to hold the user's name (temporarily). The nested function body, i.e., the lambda function, serves as a mechanism for binding values to **name**, which is merely a parameter of the anonymous function. Hence, the initial binding is established via procedure call.

Another point concerns the practice of establishing a function solely for the purpose of using its parameters as local variables. This is legitimate in **hi** because of the call-by-value philosophy of Scheme, and because the anonymous function is local to **hi**.

Even though the use of **lambda** for establishing local variables is legitimate, such code is inherently more cumbersome and less readable than equivalent code written with **let**—this is precisely the motivation behind Scheme's provision for **let** and our preference for **let** in earlier examples. A comparison between **lambda** and **let** is provided here for completeness.

12.4.2 Anonymous Functions and Scheme Mapping Functions

Scheme provides three functions that are useful for list processing operations in situations where some function must be applied to the elements of a list. The respective essential syntactic forms are:

```
(apply <function> <list>)

(map <function> <list>)

(for-each <function> <list>)
```

(Please see your documentation for extensions to these functions.) The first function, **apply**, is useful primarily for the case where a function expects *n* arguments, say, (+ <arg>...), but the arguments have been collected/built in list form by some previous operation, e.g., (1 2 3). **apply** takes the elements in **<list>** and supplies them as arguments to **<function>**, eliminating the need for cdr recursion. The following dialog with Scheme illustrates **apply**.

```
[1] (apply * '(1 2 3 4))
24
[2] (apply (lambda (n) (* n n)) '(3))
9
[3] (apply max '(-3 0 3))
3
[4] _
```

At prompts [1] and [3] Scheme built-in functions are applied to the respective lists; the number of elements in each list must be compatible with the legal argument count for the function.

Suppose you are building a function that for whatever reason must apply some basic, non-built-in operation to a list containing the required data (function arguments), e.g., squaring a number. In this case, an anonymous function (prompt [2]) may be preferable to a standalone function. We've mentioned the possibility of name conflicts among standalone function definitions in large programming projects. Note that by defining an anonymous function to handle basic tasks such as squaring a number, as opposed to defining and referencing a standalone function, you can reduce the potential for function name conflicts. As an example, consider the case where a number squaring function named **square** is later redefined (inadvertently) to calculate the area of a square.

The other two functions listed previously are for mapping operations, in the sense that they take a **<function>** and apply (map) it to each element of **<list>**:

```
[4] (map round '(1.2 1.5 1.9))
(1 2 2)
[5] (map (lambda (n) (* n n)) '(1 2 3))
(1 4 9)
[6] (apply + (map (lambda (n) (* n n)) '(1 2 3)))
14
[7] (for-each round '(1.2 1.5 1.9))
#T
[8] (for-each display '(1.2 #\newline 1.5 #\newline 1.9))
1.2
1.5
1.9#T
[9] (define a-string "abcde")
A-STRING
[10] (for-each (lambda (i) (format "~a~%" (string-ref a-string
       i)))
       '(0 1 2 3 4))
a
b
c
d
e
#T
[11] (exit)
```

map and **for-each** differ in two ways:

1. **map** returns the result of each function application, collected in list form, whereas, **for-each** is executed for its side effect(s) only.

2. **for-each** guarantees that the elements are processed in left-to-right sequential form; **map** does not.

Thus, at prompt [7] the use of **for-each** to **round** each number in the list is futile, as the side effect operations are thrown away – the value returned by **for-each** is implementation-specific. **for-each** is more useful when the primary intent is to iterate over a list applying some function for its side effect only; e.g., prompts [8] and [10] where each element of the list is to be printed.

The utility of an anonymous function is demonstrated at prompt [10]. The goal is to print each character in the string **a-string**. In order to reference/extract each character in **a-string** an index variable must be established. An anonymous function with one parameter is used to take advantage of the guaranteed, sequential processing provided by **for-each** – the string index values are simply specified in **<list>**. Each element of **<list>** is systematically bound to **i** and used by the anonymous function to print each character in **a-string**. (**format** is a user-defined function given as a utility in an earlier chapter.)

apply, **map**, and **for-each** are frequently confused by programmers new to LISP. For this reason, we use each of these in various redefinitions of the **summation** program given earlier in this chapter – some are preferable to others, but they nevertheless illustrate and contrast these three functions.

```
;;;;     map.s     ;;;;;;;;;;;;;;;;;;;;;;;;;;;;;;;;;;;;;;;;;;;;;;;;;;;;;;;;;;;;;

;;;;;;;;;;;;;;;;;;;;;;;;;;;;;;;;;;;;;;;;;;;;;;;;;;;;;;;;;;;;;;;;;;;;;;;
;; Three illustrations of Scheme mapping functions.
;;;;;;;;;;;;;;;;;;;;;;;;;;;;;;;;;;;;;;;;;;;;;;;;;;;;;;;;;;;;;;;;;;;;;;;

;;;;;;;;;;;;;;;;;;;;;;;;;;;;;;;;;;;;;;;;;;;;;;;;;;;;;;;;;;;;;;;;;;;;;;;;;;;;;;;
;; SUMMATION-1 builds a list from START to STOP inclusive,
;; and then uses APPLY to sum the elements of the list.
;; FORMULA is applied to each list element during the
;; list-building stage.
;;;;;;;;;;;;;;;;;;;;;;;;;;;;;;;;;;;;;;;;;;;;;;;;;;;;;;;;;;;;;;;;;;;;;;;;;;;;;;;

(define (summation-1 formula start stop)
(apply +
(let make-list ((i start) (result-list ()))
           (if (> i stop)
               result-list
               (make-list (+ i 1)
                          (cons (formula i) result-list))))))


;;;;;;;;;;;;;;;;;;;;;;;;;;;;;;;;;;;;;;;;;;;;;;;;;;;;;;;;;;;;;;;;;;;;;;;;;;;;;;;
;; SUMMATION-2 builds a list from START to STOP inclusive,
;; and then uses APPLY to sum the elements of the list.
;; FORMULA is applied to each list element in an inter-
;; mediate stage by using MAP.
;;;;;;;;;;;;;;;;;;;;;;;;;;;;;;;;;;;;;;;;;;;;;;;;;;;;;;;;;;;;;;;;;;;;;;;;;;;;;;;

(define (summation-2 formula start stop)
  (apply +
         (map formula
              (let make-list ((i start) (result-list ()))
                (if (> i stop)
                    result-list
                    (make-list (+ i 1)
```

```
(cons i result-list)))))))


;;;;;;;;;;;;;;;;;;;;;;;;;;;;;;;;;;;;;;;;;;;;;;;;;;;;;;;;;;;;;;;;
;; SUMMATION-3 builds a list from START to STOP inclusive,
;; and then uses FOR-EACH to sum the elements of the list.
;; Since FOR-EACH can be used for its side effect(s) only,
;; i.e., its returned value is unspecified, SET! is used
;; capture the sum.
;;;;;;;;;;;;;;;;;;;;;;;;;;;;;;;;;;;;;;;;;;;;;;;;;;;;;;;;;;;;;;;;

(define (summation-3 formula start stop)
  (let ((sum 0))
    (for-each (lambda (j)
                (set! sum (+ sum (formula j))))
              (let make-list ((i start) (result-list ()))
                (if (> i stop)
                    result-list
                    (make-list (+ i 1)
                               (cons i result-list)))))
    sum))
```

In each of the preceding summation examples, a named **let** is used to cons together a list of integers from start to stop; although it makes no difference here, the consing action creates the list in reverse order.

summation-1 simply applies the **+** operator to the list returned by the named **let**. Note that although a named **let** is a syntactic form, it returns a list, and thus can appear as an argument in the function **apply**. In **summation-1** the passed function is bound to **formula** and applied to **i** in the named **let** before the consing operation.

summation-2 is slightly different, and somewhat inferior to **summation-1**. In order to illustrate the **map** function, the named **let** builds a "raw" list of integer values between **start** and **stop**. That is, **formula** is not applied when the first list is built; instead **map** applies **formula** to the list in the next phase, necessitating two list processing sequences. (You may recall that we used **map** earlier in the example of a four-function calculator.)

summation-3 is the most inferior implementation of the three. In order to capture the result of each application of **formula** to a list element, a local variable **sum** is established by **let** syntax and then modified by a **set!** operation. The two-stage operation of first applying **formula** and then performing the **set!** modification requires an anonymous function. As we've mentioned, code that uses a **set!** can usually be replaced by something more straightforward; in this case, both **summation-1** and **summation-2** are more readable. However, the objective in **summation-3** is to illustrate **for-each**. By definition, **for-each** is executed for side effects only; i.e., its returned value is unspecified. Thus, having used **for-each** to implement the mapping operation, **set!** provides the most straightforward way of capturing the returned value.

12.4.3 Anonymous Functions and Procedural Tasks

Much of science and engineering is concerned with uncovering rules or procedures that describe natural events, e.g., dynamics, and developing techniques for applying these rules, e.g. bridge building. Computers are valuable in engineering applications because they provide assistance in the application of rules, which typically are expressed as mathematical formulas.

Scheme is an ideal language for these applications because (engineering) rules/procedures can easily be expressed as Scheme procedures, either named or anonymous. As a further example of anonymous functions, and as an example of Scheme's support for mathematical applications, we consider the task of finding roots of equations. This is a central and routine task in engineering, mathematics, statistics, and the social sciences. For example, exploratory analysis of a new questionnaire designed to measure public opinion on some issue typically requires statistical analysis, which involves solving for the roots of various equations.

As a specific approach to finding roots we consider Newton's method, primarily because it is one of the most popular and it is easily extended to multivariable situations. (Readers interested in a more mathematical application of Scheme than is presented in this text are encouraged to see Abelson and Sussman (1985). Our discussion of Newton's method is similar to their discussion and to that presented in introductory calculus texts. However, Abelson and Sussman (1985) presents many other mathematical applications using Scheme, e.g., series approximation.)

Recall that Newton's method of root finding states that if we have an estimate for a root of some (differentiable) function, say, in equation form: $f(x) = x + 1 = 0$, we can improve our estimate by taking

new-estimate = old-estimate - [f(old-estimate) / f'(old-estimate)]

where f' is the derivative

$$f'(x) = [f(x + dx) - f(x)] / dx$$

and dx is some small increment in x.

For our purposes, we are primarily concerned with using Scheme to implement such rules/procedures, and thus are less interested in the formulas per se.

In this example we can again take advantage of Scheme's first-class procedures. In particular, both of the preceding formulas involve passing functions as arguments; that is, the formulas can be applied for any function, f, (within certain limits, of course, beyond the scope of this text). The usage of f in the preceding equations is analogous to our earlier example for hourly- and commission-based wages. In addition, however, this application involves a function that returns a function, namely, we need a function, **derivative**, that takes some function f and returns another function f', the derivative.

Anonymous functions are useful in this application as well. First of all, we can use a **lambda** form to return the derivative. Secondly, if we have some function $f(x) = x + 1$, we would like to be able to provide this function as input to our root-finding program without formally binding it to some identifier, much like with the previous mapping functions – anonymous functions are ideal for communicating such a function to our root finder.

The following code implements Newton's method.

```
;;;;    roots.s    ;;;;;;;;;;;;;;;;;;;;;;;;;;;;;;;;;;;;;;;;;;

;;;;;;;;;;;;;;;;;;;;;;;;;;;;;;;;;;;;;;;;;;;;;;;;;;;;;;;;;;;
;; ROOTS uses Newton's root finding method to estimate
;; the roots of a differentiable function.
;; Example usage:  (roots (lambda (x) (+ x 1)) 0)
;;                 estimates the function f(x) = x + 1,
;;                 using 0 as the initial estimate.
;;;;;;;;;;;;;;;;;;;;;;;;;;;;;;;;;;;;;;;;;;;;;;;;;;;;;;;;;;;

(define (roots function estimate)
  (cond
    ((test-epsilon function estimate)
     estimate)
    (else
      (roots function (next-estimate function estimate)))))


;;;;;;;;;;;;;;;;;;;;;;;;;;;;;;;;;;;;;;
;; TEST-EPSILON tests convergence.
;;;;;;;;;;;;;;;;;;;;;;;;;;;;;;;;;;;;;;

(define (test-epsilon function estimate)
  (let ((epsilon .001))
    (< (abs (function estimate)) epsilon)))


;;;;;;;;;;;;;;;;;;;;;;;;;;;;;;;;;;;;;;;;;
;; NEXT-ESTIMATE uses Newton's method
;; for estimating roots.
;;
;;                      f(old-x)
;; new-x = old-x - -----------
;;                      f'(old-x)
;;;;;;;;;;;;;;;;;;;;;;;;;;;;;;;;;;;;;;;;;

(define (next-estimate function estimate)
  (- estimate
     (/ (function estimate)
        ((derivative function) estimate))))
```

```
;;;;;;;;;;;;;;;;;;;;;;;;;;;;;;;;;
;; DERIVATIVE uses the formula:
;;
;;             f(x + dx) - f(x)
;; f'(x) =  -------------------
;;                  dx
;;;;;;;;;;;;;;;;;;;;;;;;;;;;;;;;;

(define (derivative function)
  (let ((dx .001))
    (lambda (x)                          ;return an anonymous
      (/ (- (function (+ x dx))          ;function as the
            (function x))                ;derivative
         dx))))
```

The driver function, **roots**, accepts two arguments: a function and an initial estimate for a root. **roots** calls **test-epsilon** to determine whether the difference between the new and old estimates of the root is large enough to warrant further iteration. If not, the **estimate** of the root is returned and the program terminates; otherwise, **roots** continues the iteration by calling itself recursively after calculating a new estimate. (Up to this point, our implementation of Newton's method is similar to a FORTRAN implementation, except that the latter must omit the recursion.)

next-estimate mirrors the preceding formula. Of particular note is the call to **derivative**. The function for which we seek a root is passed as an argument; **derivative** returns a *function* which is the derivative of the passed function. The returned function is used in the calculation of a new estimate.

Next, consider **derivative**, which is the first example we've had of returning a function. It uses a **let** to set up a logical constant for the increment **dx**. The **let** body consists of a **lambda** form which evaluates to a function and is then returned. In essence, **derivative** uses one function as a model for building another function, which can later be executed. Note that this is an example of Scheme code *producing* Scheme code.

The truly fantastic thing about using Scheme for this type of application is the similarity between the application and the Scheme implementation. Contrived techniques are not needed for mapping the mathematical procedures of the application to Scheme procedures. Moreover, this carries over to the actual application. In the following dialog, the user merely has to express the function for which roots are sought in lambda form. This is particularly nice for a sophisticated user working with functions such as $f(x) = x^5 + 1$ with a varying number of terms. For a naive user, a simple shell program could be written to prompt for the function's coefficients.

```
[1] (load "roots.s")
OK
[2] (roots (lambda (x) (+ x 1)) 0) ;f(x) = x + 1, 1st est. = 0
-1.00000000000011
[3] (roots (lambda (x) (+ x 1)) 1) ;f(x) = x + 1, 1st est. = 1
```

```
-1.00000000000022
[4] (roots (lambda (x) (- (* x x) (* x 2) 3)) 1)
3.00000060090009
[5] (roots (lambda (x) (- (* x x) (* x 2) 3)) -1)
-1
[6] (roots (lambda (x) (- (* x x) (* x 2) 3)) -2)
-1.00000850632091
[7] (exit)
```

At prompts [2] and [3] we find the root for $f(x) = x + 1$, namely, -1. At prompts [4] through [6] we try for the roots of $f(x) = x^2 - 2x - 3$. Since it's quadratic, we try positive and negative start values—just experimenting. At prompt [4] it converges to 3 and at prompt [6] it converges to -1, which are the equation's actual roots. The guess at prompt [5] was lucky.

At this point, you may want to review the discussion of **letrec** and mutual recursion in Chapter 7. Recall that **lambda** forms were used to implement a function that tests numbers for even or odd status.

Exercises

1. Define your own version of standard Scheme's **for-each**. Assume that only one list is provided as an argument, i.e., the standard Scheme essential procedure. Thus, there are only two parameters: the procedure to be applied and the list to which it is applied.

2. Modify Exercise 1 to support multiple lists as arguments following the first argument, which represents the passed procedure.

3. Common LISP provides a mapping function named **every** that stops the application of functions to arguments as soon as a function application returns Boolean false. That is, it will return non-false, only if *every* function application is non-false. Develop a variation of **for-each** (the essential version mentioned in Exercise 1) that mimics Common LISP's **every**.

4. Rewrite **summation** from this chapter so that if only two arguments are present (start and stop values) a default procedure, **square**, is substituted for **formula**. This modification is primarily an exercise in handling a variable number of arguments where something other than the last argument(s) is optional. Consider the second **lambda** form from Chapter 11.

5. Show the value returned for each of the following:

```
a. (+ 3 4)
b. (lambda (i j) (+ i j))
```

```
c. ((lambda (i j) (+ i j)) 3 4)
d. (map (lambda (i) (* i i)) '(1 2 3 4))
e. (for-each (lambda (i) (* i i)) '(1 2 3 4))
```

6. We've used an internal **define** on numerous occasions to define a function local to another function. Use a **let** in conjunction with a **lambda** form to define a function local to the **let**, where the **let** encompasses any references to the local function. E.g., rewrite **fact** from Chapter 6 so that **tr-fact** is established by a **let** and a **lambda** form.

7. It should be clear at this point that **lambda** provides a syntactic mechanism for describing procedures or tasks. Develop a function, **build-function**, that, given the coefficients of any simple equation (in list form), uses **lambda** to build a formula definition as a Scheme function, which is then returned for use by the calling function. Examples of simple equations, valid arguments to the function, and the respective returned values are:

$f(x) = -x + 4$	(-1 4)	(lambda (x) (+ (- x) 4))
$f(x) = x^2 + 2x - 1$	(1 2 -1)	(lambda (x) (+ (* x x) (* x 2) (- 1)))

8. This exercise requires simple algebra only. The example programs **summation** and **calc-pay** demonstrate the procedure passing technique needed for this exercise.

A common programming exercise in FORTRAN textbooks is the approximation of square roots using Newton's method of successive approximations. Newton's method states that, given a guess, **old-guess**, for the square root of a number, **x**, we can compute a better guess, **new-guess**, by averaging together **old-guess** and **(x / old-guess)**. Or, iteratively,

$$guess_{i+1} = (guess_i + x / guess_i) / 2$$

Develop a function, **approx**, for performing approximations via iteration that accepts two functions as arguments. The first function should be the formula for calculating an improved approximation and the second function should be the formula that encodes the criteria for terminating the approximation (for deciding when the estimate is close enough). In addition to accepting two function arguments, **approx** should accept the data that is to be approximated as the third argument.

For example, to estimate square roots by Newton's method you could code the following:

```
(approx newton-sqrt close-enough? 2)
```

where **newton-sqrt** performs the iterative improvement described above, **close-enough?** determines when to stop the iterative improvement, and 2 is the number for which you seek the square root. One way to implement **close-enough?** is to compare the third parameter of **approx** to the square of the (estimated) square root. If these two values differ by no more than, say, 0.001, **close-enough?** should return Boolean true.

Chapter 13

Internal Organization and Equivalence Predicates

13.1 Introduction

In this chapter we address two loosely related topics. First, we consider memory organization and destructive modification of data structures; second, we investigate equivalence predicates. The discussion is by no means exhaustive; the interested reader is encouraged to explore the documentation for standard Scheme in addition to that provided by specific Scheme implementations.

13.2 Memory Organization

For the most part, low-level details concerning how to implement Scheme are not prescribed by standard Scheme, which primarily addresses those aspects of implementation that affect operation. However, low-level implementation decisions can affect operational-level decisions, i.e., program design. This is especially true for those predicates that test certain aspects of internal memory organization. As an example, consider the *equivalence predicates* (discussed later) which are used to compare objects with respect to level (degree) of equality; e.g., two objects may be internally identical or just outwardly equal, i.e., evaluate to the same printed value. The relationship between memory organization and equivalence predicates dictates a closer examination of certain aspects of Scheme internal data structures.

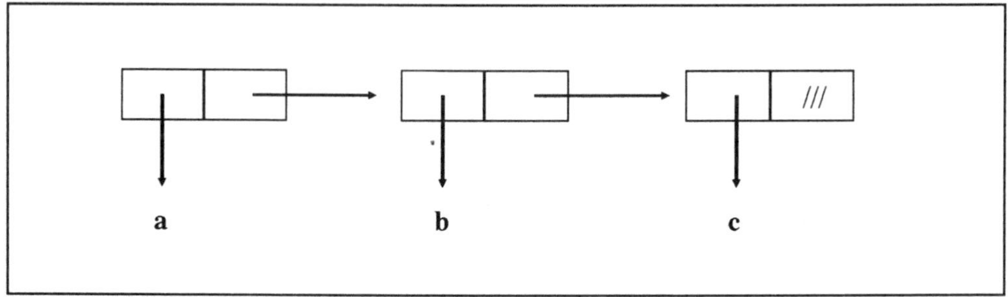

Figure 13.1 Box-and-arrow Notation

Scheme represents lists internally in binary tree form – in much the same way that a programmer would represent a tree using languages such as C and Pascal. However, in contrast to more traditional languages, Scheme (like other LISPs) is designed to support symbolic processing. Primarily, this means that symbol manipulation should be as efficient as possible. For example, older LISP dialects store each newly-created symbol in a structure known as a object list, or *oblist*. An oblist is essentially just a symbol table. Modern LISPs, such as Common LISP, may have, in effect, multiple symbol tables called *packages*. Earlier, we investigated Scheme environments and lexical scoping; in essence, Scheme must maintain multiple name spaces based on lexical environment. Regardless of the details, which vary considerably from implementation to implementation and dialect to dialect, the main idea is that for an expression such as

```
[10] (define x '(a b c))
```

a list must be built containing three symbols: **a**, **b**, and **c**. The new list is constructed by linking pointers to the symbol table entries for each of these symbols; symbols that don't currently exist must be added to the symbol table prior to list formation. Each symbol table entry contains specific information, such as the symbol's printed representation, plus other information beyond the scope of this text.

(For convenience, we take a simplistic view of internal organization. In particular, the symbol table may actually contain very little symbol information; that is, each entry may simply contain pointers to other memory locations where the information associated with each symbol is stored. The level of indirection used in a particular LISP implementation is a matter of software-developer prerogative.)

Again, the exact details are implementation- and dialect-specific. However, abstract representations are convenient and sufficient for our discussion here. First, the so-called *box-and-arrow notation* is given in Figure 13.1 for the list **(a b c)**. A list is built internally by linking *cons cells*. A cons cell is a data structure composed of two components; the left half is called the car component and the right half is called the cdr component – cons cells contain pointers only, either valid memory pointers or a special null pointer. For the preceding list, the car component is a pointer to the symbol table entry for that particular element of the list and the cdr component is a pointer to the cons cell representing the next element in the list. The cons cell for the last ele-

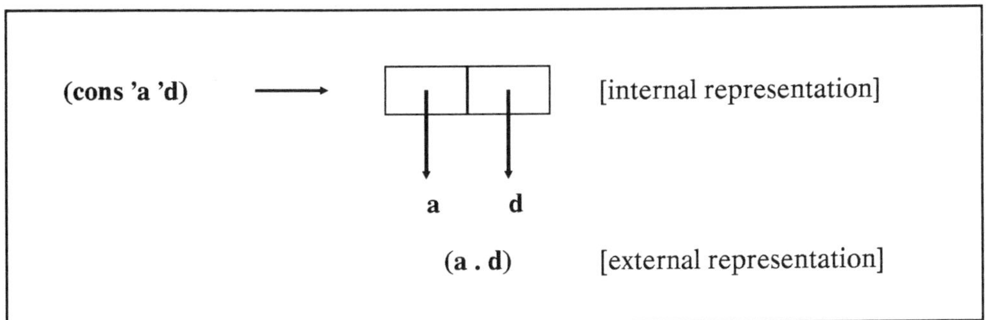

Figure 13.2 A cons Cell

ment of the list has a null pointer in its cdr component, represented in Figure 13.1 by "///".

You may recall from our earlier discussion of dotted pairs that when two atoms are consed together a dotted pair is formed, as shown in Figure 13.2. Earlier we focused on the external representation only. Here, we can see that a dotted pair is simply one cons cell with two valid pointers, in this case, pointers to the symbols **a** and **d**.

On the other hand, proper lists are composed of cons cells with car pointers to elements, which may be nested lists, and with a final null cdr pointer signaling end-of-list. Figure 13.3 presents an alternate, hypothetical representation of internal data structures that may convey the pointer idea more clearly. Typically, the symbol table is organized as a hash table of sorts to facilitate efficient symbol processing. In Figure 13.3 we've pictured two different lists in memory, both composed of the symbols **a**, **b**, and **c**. **x** and **z** point to one of the lists, beginning at location 2000. **y** points to the other list beginning at position 2010. Note that the symbols **a**, **b**, and **c** are only represented once in the symbol table. Figure 13.3 is also explained via a subsequent Scheme dialog.

Scheme, in at least one sense, can be viewed as a higher level language than other LISP dialects. Namely, Scheme provides fewer facilities for destructive modification of data structures (objects). Although it's true that Scheme provides **set!**, **string-set!**, **string-fill!**, **set-car!**, **set-cdr!**, etc., their effects are rather localized, i.e., confined to one data structure. On the other hand, older LISPs, as well as Common LISP, provide facilities for more extensive, and hence potentially dangerous, pointer surgery in memory, such as making the last element of one list point to the first element of another list. Some Scheme implementations supplement standard Scheme with additional language constructs for pair/list modification; e.g., **append!**, which "hooks" together lists by modifying the last element of each list to point to the beginning of the next list.

Traditionally, destructive modification of data structures has been promoted for reasons of efficiency. It is more efficient to build a new list from two existing lists by a simple pointer reconnection, than it is to copy all elements from both lists to a newly-allocated list. The problem with the former approach is unanticipated side effects. For example, if **x** is some list and if at some point **z** is **define**d to be the same list as **x**, a

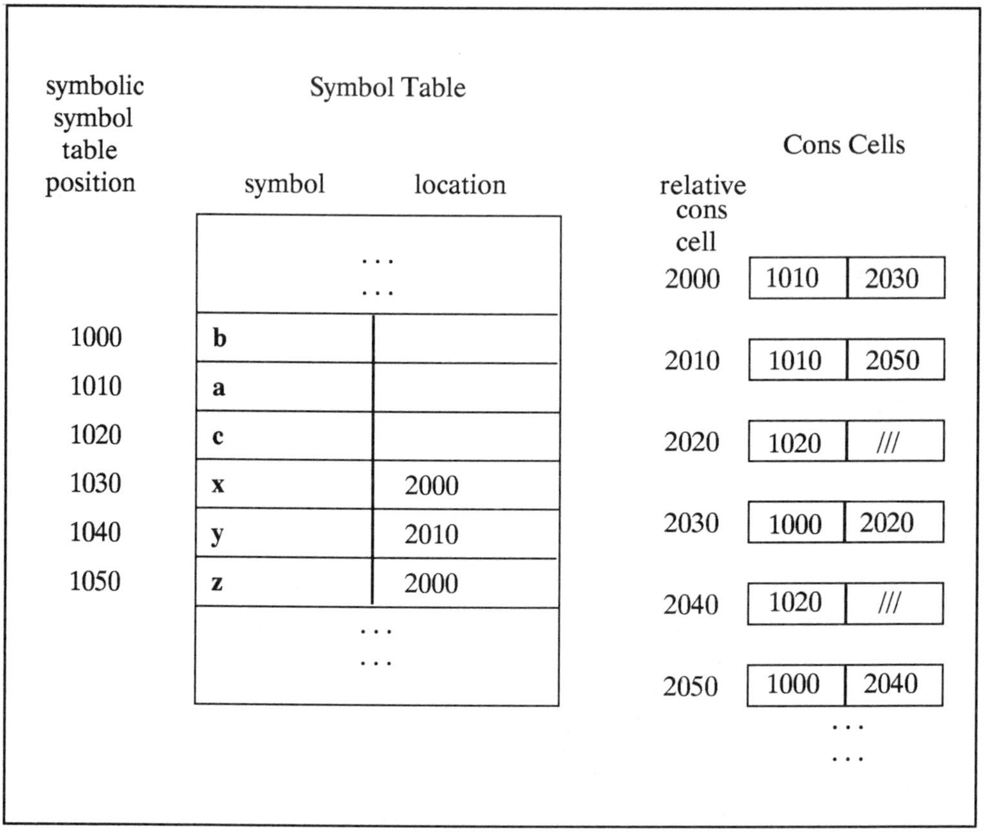

Symbol Table

symbolic symbol table position	symbol	location
	. . .	
1000	**b**	
1010	**a**	
1020	**c**	
1030	**x**	2000
1040	**y**	2010
1050	**z**	2000
	. . .	

Cons Cells

relative cons cell		
2000	1010	2030
2010	1010	2050
2020	1020	///
2030	1000	2020
2040	1020	///
2050	1000	2040
	. . .	

Figure 13.3 A Hypothetical Internal Organization

destructive operation such as "hooking" list **w** onto the end of **x** would have the side effect of changing **z**, which may or may not be appropriate in a given situation.

At this point we reconsider some of the preceding information via a Scheme dialog.

```
[1] (define x '(a b c))
X
[2] (define y '(a b c))       ;y is a different list,
Y
[3] (define z x)              ;but z is the same as x
Z
[4] (define w '(1 2 3))
W
[5] x                         ;initially, x, y, and z have
(A B C)                       ;the same printed form
[6] y
```

```
(A B C)
[7] z
(A B C)
[8] w
(1 2 3)
[9] (define combo (append x w)) ;build a new list with append
COMBO
[10] combo
(A B C 1 2 3)
[11] x                          ;x, w, and z remain unchanged
(A B C)
[12] w
(1 2 3)
[13] z
(A B C)
[14] (append! x w)              ;destructively modify x such
(A B C 1 2 3)                   ;that end of x points to begin-
[15] x                          ;ning of w
(A B C 1 2 3)
[16] w
(1 2 3)
[17] z
(A B C 1 2 3)                   ;z has been changed also
[18] y
(A B C)
[19] (set-car! w 10)            ;a change to w is a change to x
(10 2 3)
[20] x
(A B C 10 2 3)
[21] w
(10 2 3)
[22] z
(A B C 10 2 3)
[23] y
(A B C)
[24] (define p (cons 'a 'd))    ;p is just a cons cell
P                               ;as pictured above
[25] p
(A . D)
[26] (exit)
```

You may want to compare this Scheme dialog to Figure 13.3. At prompt [9] **combo** is defined to be a new list, built from the elements of **x** and **w**. Even though the symbols occur only once in the symbol table, it is convenient to think of **append** as a copy operation; i.e., copies are made of the lists **x** and **w** and then appended together. The new list is a copy in the sense that destructive modifications to either **x** or **w** have no side effects with respect to **combo**.

At prompt [14] the destructive function **append!** is used to append **x** and **w** by changing the last cons cell of **x** to point to the first cons cell of **w**; note that **append!** is not part of standard Scheme. Thus, at prompts [15] and [17] it is clear that *both* **x** and **z** have new values. A Scheme programmer must be careful when using a define operation such as the one at prompt [3] and a destructive modification such as **append!**; in particular, you must decide whether you want to create a new data structure, independent of a previous one, or whether you want an additional identifier/synonym for an existing data structure.

Prompts [19] through [23] further illustrate that the **append!** at prompt [14] establishes a permanent relationship among **x** and **w**, and indirectly between **z** and **w**, due to the definition at prompt [3]. Prompts [24] and [25] simply illustrate the dotted pair from Figure 13.2.

Due to the potential for unanticipated side effects, it is generally a good idea to avoid destructive modification of data structures. Broadly speaking, the use of language constructs that operate by pointer modification instead of creating new cons cells may be more efficient, but this practice leads to code that is less easily updated/modified. Systems programming applications, such as compiler writing projects, are good examples of situations where such destructive data modification may be justified. Scheme's provision of rather limited capabilities for destructive modification of data structures can be viewed as a compromise between efficiency and code maintainability.

13.3 Equivalence Predicates

In this section we investigate in more detail the Scheme predicates for testing equivalence of data structures. In the previous chapters we used **equal?**, plus several others that are data type-specific, such as **char=?**, **=**, etc. Here, we are primarily interested in the relationship between such predicates and internal memory organization, and how implementation differences can lead to lack of portability among Scheme systems.

In general, there will be some differences among implementations with respect to how equivalence predicates handle data structures, especially lists, numeric constants, characters, and/or strings. The Scheme standard provides some latitude in the treatment of literals, e.g., the empty string, and in the relationship between false and the empty list. Rather than present a formal investigation of equivalence predicates, we examine their behavior under PC Scheme; you will want to make similar investigations with your Scheme system. *The investigation here is not exhaustive; consult your documentation and the Scheme standard for a more complete treatment.*

First, consider the following interaction with Scheme:

```
[1] (define x '(a b c))
X
[2] (define y '(a b c))
```

```
Y
[3] (define z x)
Z
[4] (eq? x x)
#T
[5] (eq? x y)
()
[6] (eq? x z)
#T
[7] _
```

As before, we set up two physically different lists, **x** and **y**, and we define **z** to be the same as **x**. The equivalence predicate **eq?** is the most discriminating; it tests whether or not its arguments are (physically) identical. The operation of **eq?** with respect to list data structures is predictable, given our discussion of memory organization in Figure 13.3. Lists **x** and **y** are different, even though they contain pointers to the same elements, and thus are not **eq?**. On the other hand, lists **x** and **z** are by definition **eq?**.

The same idea applies with other data structures as well. For example, the following two procedures, although they perform the same task, are not identical; i.e., the symbols **square** and **sqr** do not reference the same structure.

```
[7] (define square (lambda (n) (* n n)))
SQUARE
[8] (define sqr (lambda (n) (* n n)))
SQR
[9] (define sqr-2 sqr)
SQR-2
[10] (eq? square sqr)
()
[11] (eq? sqr-2 sqr)
#T
[12] _
```

Since **sqr-2** is defined as an alternate identifier for **sqr** at prompt [9], **sqr** and **sqr-2** are **eq?**.

Based on our discussion of symbol table organization, the symbol **a** should be **eq?** to itself:

```
[12] (eq? 'a 'a)
#T
[13] _
```

Moreover, two arguments that evaluate to the same symbol, say, **a**, should be **eq?**:

```
[13] (eq? 'a (car x))
#T
```

```
[14] _
```

Next, two different symbols can't possibly be identical:

```
[14] (eq? 'a 'b)
()
[15] _
```

Neither are two different, single-element lists built from the same symbol:

```
[15] (eq? '(a) '(a))
()
[16] _
```

The following illustrates how PC Scheme handles characters, strings, the empty list, and false, respectively.

```
[16] (eq? #\a #\a)
#T
[17] (eq? "a" "a")
()
[18] (eq? '() '())
#T
[19] (eq? () ())
#T
[20] _
```

Lastly, PC Scheme recognizes two references to the same addition procedure.

```
[20] (eq? + +)
#T
[21] (exit)
```

eq? is the most efficient equivalence predicate, in the sense that it involves a pointer comparison only. However, if you are only interested in whether or not two structures have the same printed representation, it may be unwise to substitute **eq?** for **equal?**, just because you know that the stronger condition holds.

So far, we've examined the behavior of **eq?** under PC Scheme. With respect to portability of Scheme code, note that the results for the following comparisons are unspecified by standard Scheme.

```
[1] (eq? '(a) '(a))                    ;list comparison
()
[2] (eq? "a" "a")                      ;string comparison
()
[3] (eq? "" "")                        ;null string comparison
```

```
()
[4] (eq? 1 1)                      ;numeric constant comparison
#T
[5] (eq? #\a #\a)                  ;character comparison
#T
[6] (let ((x (+ 2 3))) (eq? x x)) ;expression comparison
#T
[7] (exit)
```

How are these handled by your Scheme implementation?

You must be careful when using **eq?**, since Scheme programs with such comparisons may behave differently from one implementation to another. Primarily, indiscriminant use of **eq?** can lead to portability problems among Scheme systems.

It's important to realize that such issues of portability arise for good reason, not just because Scheme designers can't decide on how **eq?** should operate. That is, **eq?** is inherently a rather low-level function – it essentially tests physical equivalence of data structures. If standard Scheme is to allow designers of Scheme systems some latitude with respect to low-level implementation details, such issues cannot be transparent to the programmer.

An alternate equivalence predicate **eqv?** addresses some of these portability problems. According to standard Scheme, **eqv?** should return true for three of the six preceding comparisons, namely, null string, numeric, and character constant comparisons:

```
[1] (eqv? "" "")
#T
[2] (eqv? 1 1)
#T
[3] (eqv? #\a #\a)
#T
[4] (exit)
```

You should get the same response with your Scheme implementation.

At this point, we further illustrate the behavior of **eqv?** under PC Scheme.

```
[1] (define x '(a b c))
X
[2] (define y '(a b c))
Y
[3] (define z x)
Z
[4] (eqv? x y)
()
[5] (eqv? x z)
#T
[6] (let* ((sqr (lambda (n) (* n n)))
```

```
            (square (lambda (n) (* n n)))
            (sqr-2 sqr))
        (list (eqv? sqr square) (eqv? sqr sqr-2) (eqv? sqr sqr)))
(() #T #T)
[7] (eqv? 1 1.0)
#T
[8] (eqv? '(a) '(a))
()
[9] (eqv? '() #f)
#T
[10] (eqv? 'anything #t)
()
[11] (exit)
```

The third and least discriminating equivalence predicate is **equal?**. It is the most costly in terms of computing efficiency, as it may be necessary to recursively compare the contents of, say, lists, strings, etc. A general rule of thumb is that **equal?** succeeds for objects that have the same printed representation:

```
[1] (define x '(a b c))
X
[2] (define y '(a b c))
Y
[3] (define z '(a b c))
Z
[4] (define w (cons (car x) (cdr y)))
W
[5] w
(A B C)
[6] (define square (lambda (n) (* n n)))
SQUARE
[7] (define sqr (lambda (n) (* n n)))
SQR
[8] (equal? x y)
#T
[9] (equal? x z)
#T
[10] (equal? x w)
#T
[11] (equal? square sqr)
()
[12] (eq? 1 1.0)
()
[13] (eqv? 1 1.0)
#T
[14] (equal? 1 1.0)
```

```
()
[15] (= 1 1.0)
#T
[16] (equal? '(a) '(a))
#T
[17] (equal? #\a #\a)
#T
[18] (equal? #\a 97)
()
[19] (equal? (char->integer #\a) 97)
#T
[20] (exit)
```

Note the result at prompt [11]. According to the Scheme standard, it is in general impossible to determine operational equivalence of procedures.

As a final comment, recall that Scheme provides several data type-specific predicates for testing equivalence of objects. It is recommended that those predicates be used, where possible, for code readability, portability, and maintainability.

Exercises

1. Draw box-and-arrrow notation for the following:

```
a. (define list-1 '(1 2))
b. (define list-2 '(1 2 (3 4) 5))
c. (define list-3 '())
d. (define list-4 '(1 . (2 . (3 . (4 . ())))))
e. (define list-5 '(1 . (2 . (3 . 4))))
```

2. Suppose that a Scheme symbol table contains entries for the following symbols: **apple, pear, banana, orange, grapefruit, lime, tomato, potato, squash, tennis, fruit, vegetable,** and **sport**. Show the hypothetical pointer relationships via a diagram similar to that in Figure 13.3, given the following definitions:

```
(define fruit '(apple banana grapefruit lime orange pear))
(define vegetable '(tomato potato squash))
(define sport '(squash tennis))
```

Place the symbols in the symbol table in an arbitrary order. Use symbolic (relative) memory addresses.

3. Develop a function named **dpn** that prints the dotted pair notation representation of its argument. It should handle dotted pairs, improper lists, and proper lists.

4. Provide box-and-arrow notation to describe each of the data structures that results from the dialog at prompts [1] through [18] in Section 13.2.

5. Systematically test how your Scheme system handles **equal?**, **eqv?**, and **eq?** for lists, strings, and numbers. Outline the performance of these predicates in a two-dimensional table with the three predicates across the top forming columns and several examples of data comparisons down the margin forming rows. You may want to keep such a table, or a more extensive version with your documentation.

Chapter 14

Association Lists and Vectors

14.1 Introduction

Sometimes it is convenient to store information in tabular form for subsequent retrieval. There are two broad approaches to retrieval, or access, of such information: (1) sequential, and (2) direct. In the former case, a table is scanned sequentially from beginning to end in search of the desired information; in the latter case, a mechanism is employed that allows immediate retrieval of the desired table element, typically by position; i.e., offset into the table, without need for sequential scanning. In Scheme, association lists are provided for the former type of access and vectors for the latter.

14.2 Association Lists

Association lists provide a convenient mechanism for simple table lookup operations where each element of a table contains a key, plus some associated data. For example, suppose it is necessary during numeric computations with simple integer values to print an integer's word representation, as opposed to its digit representation – say, when an integer is between zero and ten.

In this case, we could establish a table such as

Key	Data
0	"zero"
1	"one"
2	"two"
...	...
10	"ten"

where the first table entry has two components: a key in integer form and its associated data, i.e., word representation. (Actually, this situation is so simple that the key is unnecessary, since the key value and table offset are identical; however, the present representation is convenient for illustrating association lists.)

Depending on the programming language, the *logical* table representation could be *physically* implemented in a variety of ways. For example, several languages provide aggregate data structures called arrays. An array would be inadequate for representing the preceding table for those languages where array elements must all be of the same data type. Many languages, e.g., C, Pascal, PL/I, and so on, provide an aggregate data structure called a "record," or "structure," that can contain multiple data items of differing data types. In this case, a Pascal programmer could implement the table as an array of records. However, a Pascal program would then have to be written to search the array iteratively for an element that matched the key.

Scheme, on the other hand, supplements the standard list data structure (which we've been using all along) with three sequential access functions for performing the table look-up operations:

1. **assoc** – based on **equal?**
2. **assq** – based on **eq?**
3. **assv** – based on **eqv?**

Each of the table look-up functions is based on the syntax:

```
(<association> <key> <alist>)
```

where **<association>** is one of the preceding functions, **<key>** is the search key, and **<alist>** is an association list.

As an example of simple association list retrieval consider the following Scheme dialog.

```
[1] (define a-list '((a 1) (b 2) (c 3)))
A-LIST
[2] (assoc 'b a-list)
(B 2)
[3] (cadr (assoc 'b a-list))
2
[4] (exit)
```

In this example we've used **assoc**, which searches an association list for a key value using the **equal?** equivalence predicate. At prompt [2] the association list from prompt [1] is searched for a sublist containing the key "b" as the first element. The entire sublist is returned; subsequently, the key can be discarded by simple list processing operations.

assoc is the most commonly used of the association list functions; the others operate similarly. Also, as with many Scheme functions, **<alist>** may be a pair, not just a proper list, even though the latter is more common.

An association list is nothing more than a nested list, i.e., a list of sublists, where the first element in each sublist is taken to be the key and the remaining elements constitute the associated data. The latter may be in any form, i.e., as sublist elements 2 through n:

```
(irish-setter large red long-haired sporting)
```

in a (further) nested list:

```
(irish-setter (large red long-haired sporting))
```

etc. A complete association list of selected dog information would be

```
((irish-setter large red long-haired sporting)
 (newfoundland giant black long-haired working)
 (norwegian-elkhound medium gray medium-haired hound))
```

Getting back to the integer conversion example, we could implement the table as the following association list:

```
((0 "zero")
 (1 "one")
 (2 "two")
 (3 "three")
 ...
 ...

 (9 "nine")
 (10 "ten"))
```

In this manner, we could provide a function, **convert**, for performing the “conversion” to word representation:

```
;;;;     assoc.s     ;;;;;;;;;;;;;;;;;;;;;;;;;;;;;;;;;;;;;;;;;;;;;;;;

;;;;;;;;;;;;;;;;;;;;;;;;;;;;;;;;;;;;;;;;;;;;;;;;;;;;;;;;;;;;
;; CONVERT converts an integer to word form.
;; The legal range is zero to ten.
;;;;;;;;;;;;;;;;;;;;;;;;;;;;;;;;;;;;;;;;;;;;;;;;;;;;;;;;;;;;

(define (convert integer)
  (if (and (> integer -1)
           (< integer 11))
      (let ((integer-table '((0 "zero")
                             (1 "one")
                             (2 "two")
```

```
                                (3 "three")
                                (4 "four")
                                (5 "five")
                                (6 "six")
                                (7 "seven")
                                (8 "eight")
                                (9 "nine")
                                (10 "ten"))))
        (cadr (assoc integer integer-table)))
      "illegal data"))
```

convert works as follows.

```
[1] (convert 5)
"five"
[2] (convert 11)
"illegal data"
[3] (convert 0)
"zero"
[4] (convert 10)
"ten"
[5] (exit)
```

This example brings to mind several issues that commonly arise in situations where association lists could be used. First, the association list functions do their work by sequentially scanning the association list. If the application is one involving many sublists, there could be some performance problems due to the sequential nature of the search. For example, you probably would not want to use a simple association list to implement a large, internal database of employee information:

```
(define employee-database
  '(("bill smith" "engineering" 28000 ...) ;; approx.
    ...                                    ;; 1000
    ...                                    ;; employees
    ("mary brown" "accounting" 31000 ...)));;
```

It is important to note that slowness of sequential search is not a Scheme deficiency. Sequential search is the most primitive computer science search technique, and consequently, complex applications may require a more sophisticated technique. However, for those applications where the search space is reasonably small, sequential search may be adequate; Scheme's built-in support for sequential search makes it especially convenient.

Another issue that arises is the use of association lists versus case constructs, e.g., **case** and **cond**. For example, **convert** could perhaps have been coded more easily using **case**. This is actually a special case of the bigger issue of data and procedure abstraction. In this case, should we view the selection of "five", given an argument value 5 to

convert, as a matter of alternative action within a procedure, or as a table look-up operation?

Of course real decisions on such issues are a matter of application; no one would argue that the employee database above should be hard-coded into the source code in the form of a **case** structure. Instead, the employee database should exist independent of the procedures that are built to access it – this is the idea of separation of data and procedure. In addition, it typically would be defined globally, as opposed to being local to the **let**, possibly in an external database (file).

The digit-to-word conversion example is so straightforward and simple that either approach is adequate. However, there are some fairly simple examples where, in our opinion, the use of association lists is inappropriate and leads to "difficult" code. The following is an *inferior* recoding of the **change** program from an earlier chapter using an association list.

```
;;;;     assoc.s     ;;;;;;;;;;;;;;;;;;;;;;;;;;;;;;;;;;;;;;;;;;;

;;;;;;;;;;;;;;;;;;;;;;;;;;;;;;;;;
;; CHANGE makes change at the
;; neighborhood laundromat.
;;;;;;;;;;;;;;;;;;;;;;;;;;;;;;;;;

(define (change money-tendered)
  (display (cadr
    (cond
      ((assoc money-tendered
         '((dollar "quarter quarter quarter dime dime nickel")
           (half-dollar "quarter dime dime nickel")
           (quarter "dime dime nickel")
           (dime "nickel nickel"))))
      (else
        '(error
"insert dollars, half-dollars, quarters, and dimes only"))))))
```

In our opinion, this type of coding appears all too often in LISP code, especially with older LISP dialects. The nesting of the association list within the function call to **assoc**, within the **cond** within the **cadr**, and so on, makes this implementation of **change** almost opaque, and greatly inferior to the earlier version which used a **case**. It is for this reason that association lists have been presented here primarily as a mechanism for implementing table look-up operations.

A third issue that arises with association lists is somewhat related to the first. Namely, it is possible to use association lists to implement "mini-tables" of information for which sequential retrieval time is insignificant. In this manner, data abstraction is promoted by storing/hiding small amounts of information in data structures; functions can be built for systematically storing and retrieving selected data.

To be more specific, even though the sequential search nature of **assoc** makes association lists inappropriate for implementing large tables, they are sometimes appropriate for implementing an approach to programming and data management that has become popular in recent years. Specifically, the enormity of the task of managing large bodies of data that are common in database and AI applications has led to the development of so-called object-oriented programming techniques and object-oriented data models.

Object-oriented programming constructs have been incorporated into several AI languages, e.g., Flavors (Weinreb et al., 1983), LOOPS (Bobrow and Stefik, 1983), and Smalltalk (originally developed at Xerox PARC; see Goldberg and Robson [1983]). In the database arena, the entity-relationship data model proposes that data management can be accomplished by recognizing the existence of entities (in essence, objects) and relationships among entities (Chen, 1976).

Regardless of the environment, object-oriented paradigms of many forms/varieties have been proposed for data management. In general, object-oriented models are based on the idea that data is more easily managed by storing pertinent data (and procedures) with each object, in a manner that facilitates hierarchical classification of information. There is much debate at present with respect to what constitutes object-oriented programming; our intention here is to present what must be considered an overly-simple example – merely collecting information about objects in an association list – primarily to illustrate how association lists can be used to implement higher-level data structures.

First, consider a traditional database application for employee information, similar to that presented previously, whereby information associated with each employee, e.g., department, salary, and so on, is collected in a rectangular format. The preceding database example employs the practice of associating attributes (information) with a specific entity:

```
("bill smith" "engineering" 28000 ...)
```

That is, each sublist in the association list represents a *specific* individual. The knowledge that Bill Smith is an employee in the Engineering department is *implicit*; i.e., each employee's department is specified second in the list.

In contrast, it is possible to develop separate categorizations that promote hierarchical relationships and classifications. An example of a more object-oriented approach can be given by an example based on storing canine information. The following definition establishes (and encapsulates) a specific body of information about Irish Setters in general, as opposed to information about a particular Irish Setter.

```
(define irish-setter '((size large)
                       (color red)
                       (hair long-haired)
                       (category sporting)))
```

In this case, the attributes are *explicit* – **size** is repeated within each definition of a dog breed. (There are many arguments for and against both explicit and implicit codings of attributes, all of which are beyond the scope of this text – we are purely interested in how association lists may be used to implement such structures.)

Having established such a definition, we can employ it directly as a "scalar" value:

```
(define old-red '(irish-setter ...))
```

The main point here is that it is quite easy to define *access functions* for manipulating these data structures. For example, we could define a function for retrieving an Irish Setter's color:

```
(define (irish-setter-color)
  (cadr (assoc 'color irish-setter)))
```

Typically, a more general function is preferable:

```
(define (canine-color dog-breed)
  (cadr (assoc 'color dog-breed)))
```

In some cases, you would prefer even more generalization:

```
(define (canine-attribute dog-attr dog-breed)
  (cadr (assoc dog-attr dog-breed)))
```

Note that although we've represented attributes and attribute values as symbols, we could just as well use alternate data types, e.g., strings. The above access functions provide the following response.

```
[1] (load "assoc.s")
OK
[2] (irish-setter-color)
RED
[3] (canine-color irish-setter)
RED
[4] (canine-color newfoundland)
BLACK
[5] (canine-attribute 'color irish-setter)
RED
[6] (canine-attribute 'size newfoundland)
GIANT
[7] (exit)
```

In any case, it is apparent that the sequential nature of the retrieval functions for association lists is adequate and quite convenient for these types of applications. We will make use of association lists in a database application in a later chapter.

14.3 Vectors and Vector Functions

Vectors are provided as a separate data type in Scheme, along with several functions for their manipulation. In this section we discuss vectors and vector functions per se; in the next section we provide several simple vector applications.

In Scheme, vectors are externally represented much like lists:

```
#(1 (a b) "bill smith")
```

Vectors are distinguished from lists by the presence of a "#" immediately before the opening parenthesis; i.e., vectors begin with "#(" and end with ")". Vectors elements may be heterogeneous with respect to data type. The preceding vector has an integer as its first element, a list as its second element, and a string as its third element.

Vectors differ from lists primarily in that elements are (integer) indexed internally by Scheme for efficient retrieval. Thus, even though Scheme provides functions for retrieval of the nth element of both lists and vectors, only for vectors would such a retrieval be efficient for large *n*.

The following Scheme session informally presents the vector functions provided by standard Scheme.

```
[1] (vector? 'victor)          ;type checking predicate
()
[2] (vector 1 2 3)             ;returns a vector of the
#(1 2 3)                       ;specified elements
[3] (make-vector 5)            ;returns a vector of specified
#(() () () () ())              ;length--contents unspecified
[4] (make-vector 5 'a)         ;returns a vector of specified
#(A A A A A)                   ;length--each element initialized
[5] (define v '#(0 #\1 "2" three (four)))
V
[6] v
#(0 #\1 "2" THREE (FOUR))
[7] (vector-length v)           ;returns a vector's length
5
[8] (vector-ref v 1)            ;extracts element--zero-based
#\1
[9] (vector-ref v 4)
(FOUR)
[10] (vector-set! v 4 'four)    ;destructively modifies the
#(0 #\1 "2" THREE FOUR)         ;nth element of a vector
[11] (vector->list v)           ;converts a vector to a list
(0 #\1 "2" THREE FOUR)
[12] (list->vector '(a b c))    ;converts a list to a vector
#(A B C)
[13] (list->vector (vector->list v))
```

```
#(0 #\1 "2" THREE FOUR)
[14] (exit)
```

14.4 Examples Using Vectors

In this section we provide three examples involving vectors. Each example is quite straightforward; in a later chapter we will provide a more extensive application of vectors.

Our first example illustrates sequential processing of every element in a vector. **vector-max** is a simple function that finds the maximum value of the elements in a vector. There is little error checking; each element must be numeric, otherwise, an error occurs.

```
;;;;     vector.s      ;;;;;;;;;;;;;;;;;;;;;;;;;;;;;;;;;;;;;;;;;;

;;;;;;;;;;;;;;;;;;;;;;;;;;;;;;;;;;;;;;;;;;;;;;;;;;;;;;;;;;;;
;; VECTOR-MAX finds the largest element in a vector of
;; numbers.  There is no error checking for data type.
;;;;;;;;;;;;;;;;;;;;;;;;;;;;;;;;;;;;;;;;;;;;;;;;;;;;;;;;;;;;

(define (vector-max v)
  (if (> (vector-length v) 0)
      (do ((i 0 (+ i 1))
           (max (vector-ref v 0)))
          ((= i (vector-length v)) max)
          (if (> (vector-ref v i) max)
              (set! max (vector-ref v i))))))
```

vector-max produces the following output.

```
[1] (load "vector.s")
OK
[2] (vector-max #(1 2 3))
3
[3] (vector-max #(3 2 1))
3
[4] (vector-max #(-100 20 3.2 -25 30))
30
[5] (exit)
```

Note that in this function we really haven't taken advantage of the capability for direct access of individual vector elements afforded by Scheme vectors. That is, we've merely accessed each element in the vector sequentially—element by element, beginning to end. The point is that although vectors offer the greatest (relative) performance advantage when used to implement data structures for which we need direct, sometimes called random, access to individual elements, it is still possible to process the entire vector sequentially.

The second example, a simple bubble sort for numeric data, illustrates direct processing of vector elements. (Later, we will discuss how to write a function that sorts a data structure, regardless of data type.)

```
;;;;     bubble.s     ;;;;;;;;;;;;;;;;;;;;;;;;;;;;;;;;;;;;;;;;

;;;;;;;;;;;;;;;;;;;;;;;;;;;;;;;;;;;;;;;;;;;;;;;;;;;;;;;;;;
;; BUBBLE! sorts a vector of numbers using a primitive
;; bubble sorting technique, i.e., it always performs
;; every cycle.  The sorting is done destructively.
;;;;;;;;;;;;;;;;;;;;;;;;;;;;;;;;;;;;;;;;;;;;;;;;;;;;;;;;;;

(define (bubble! vec)
  (let ((temp ())
        (last-pos (- (vector-length vec) 1)))
    (do ((i 0 (+ i 1)))
        ((= i last-pos) vec)
        (do ((j 0 (+ j 1)))
            ((= j (- last-pos i)) "")    ;nothing to return
            (if (> (vector-ref vec j) (vector-ref vec (+ j 1)))
                (begin
                  (set! temp (vector-ref vec j))
                  (vector-set! vec j (vector-ref vec (+ j 1)))
                  (vector-set! vec (+ j 1) temp)))))))
```

In order to avoid creating a second vector, **bubble!** sorts a vector's elements "in place." We assume that most readers are familiar with this type of primitive bubble sort. In particular, the algorithm used here compares adjacent elements and exchanges them if they are out of order, assuming an ascending-order sort. **vector-set!** is used to perform exchanges of vector elements, in conjunction with **set!** and the temporary variable **temp**.

bubble! cannot detect when a vector is sorted. For example, if the input to **bubble!** is already sorted, it still (mechanically) performs each sort cycle. (As an exercise, you may want to modify **bubble!** so that it terminates the sorting process after the first cycle where the vector is sorted.)

The output from **bubble!** is

```
[1] (load "bubble.s")
OK
[2] (bubble! #(3 2 1))
#(1 2 3)
[3] (bubble! #(20 -10 32 -4 17 82 -5 5 -5 0 100 0))
#(-10 -5 -5 -4 0 0 5 17 20 32 82 100)
[4] (define vec #(-4 -3 -2 -9 22 34 9 20 -11))
```

```
VEC
[5] vec
#(-4 -3 -2 -9 22 34 9 20 -11)
[6] (bubble! vec)
#(-11 -9 -4 -3 -2 9 20 22 34)
[7] vec
#(-11 -9 -4 -3 -2 9 20 22 34)
[8] (exit)
```

The third example illustrates processing of nested vectors. **vector-sum** sums every element in a vector, including elements of nested vectors. Note that we cannot perform car-cdr processing of vectors, as we did with lists; instead, a more iterative approach is required.

```
;;;;     vector.s     ;;;;;;;;;;;;;;;;;;;;;;;;;;;;;;;;;;;;;;;;;;;;;

;;;;;;;;;;;;;;;;;;;;;;;;;;;;;;;;;;;;;;;;;;;;;;;;;;;;;;;;;;;;;;;;;;;
;; VECTOR-SUM returns the sum of the elements in a vector.
;; There is no error checking for non-numeric elements.
;; Nested vectors are processed also.
;;;;;;;;;;;;;;;;;;;;;;;;;;;;;;;;;;;;;;;;;;;;;;;;;;;;;;;;;;;;;;;;;;;

(define (vector-sum v)
  (let sum-loop ((pos 0) (sum 0) (vec v))
    (cond
      ((= pos (vector-length vec))
       sum)
      ((vector? (vector-ref vec pos))
       (sum-loop (+ pos 1)
                 (+ sum (sum-loop 0 0 (vector-ref vec pos)))
                 vec))
      (else
        (sum-loop
          (+ pos 1) (+ sum (vector-ref vec pos)) vec)))))
```

In this implementation we use a named **let** to increment **pos** and **sum**. If a particular element is a vector, the named **let** is called recursively in the second parameter, where the sum is accumulated. Otherwise, each element is simply accumulated into **sum**. The third parameter is required due to the potential for recursive processing of a nested vector – the nested vector becomes the new **vec**. **vector-sum** works as follows:

```
[1] (load "vector.s")
OK
[2] (vector-sum #(1 2 3))
6
[3] (vector-sum #())
```

```
0
[4] (vector-sum #(1 4 -5 #(3 -3 #(3 4) 4 -4) 1 1))
9
[5] (vector-sum #(1 1 #() 1 1))
4
[6] (exit)
```

Exercises

1. Show the value returned by each of the following:

```
a. (assoc 'd '((a 1) (b 2) (c 3)))
b. (assoc 'b '((a 1) (b 2) (b 3)))
c. (assoc 'b '(((a) 1) ((b) 2) ((c) 3)))
```

2. Develop a Scheme mini-database of canine information, where each dog's "record" is kept in a top-level data structure similar to the following:

```
(<dog-breed> <size> <color> <hair-length> <group>)
```

Develop access functions such as

```
(define (canine-attribute dog-attr dog-breed)
  (cadr (assoc dog-attr dog-breed)))
```

plus functions for insertion, deletion, and modification of attributes. Surround these functions with a menu-based driver program that prompts the user for database activity. Note that by defining each dog breed at the top level you are essentially using Scheme's automatic symbol table look-up capabilities to organize the canine database and to assist in storage and retrieval.

3. If you don't like dogs, do Exercise 2 for an album library instead, e.g.,

```
(<album-title> <album-artist> <album-price> <music-type>)
```

4. Show the value returned by each of the following:

```
a. (vector? '(1 2 3))
b. (vector? '#(1 2 "scheme" 4))
c. (make-vector 5)
d. (make-vector 5 #\space)
e. (vector-ref 5 '#(1 2 3 4 5))
f. (vector-ref 2 '#(1 2 3 4 5))
```

5. Describe the advantages and disadvantages of vectors versus lists.

6. Is it possible to use cdr recursion to process a vector?

7. Provide a pseudocode algorithm for **bubble!**.

8. Modify **bubble!** so that it can terminate the sorting operation after the first cycle for which no exchanges are required. Basically, this requires the setting and resetting of a flag variable during and at the beginning of each cycle, respectively, if any exchanges are made during that cycle.

9. Implement Exercise 2 within a Scheme vector. That is, each "doggy record" is stored as an element in a vector. Note that this requires you to establish a vector of arbitrary size initially, and also to search the vector. Be content with a linear, **do**-based, sequential search of the vector when necessary.

10. Implement **vector-sum** from this chapter using a **do** instead of a named **let**. What advantages do you see for named **let** in comparison to **do** for nested iteration?

Chapter 15

Eval, Quasiquote, and Macros

15.1 Introduction

This chapter addresses: (1) the expression evaluation process in more detail, and (2) macros. Complete and partial evaluation of expressions is of general interest to Scheme programmers, in addition to being a basic part of macro programming. Consequently, expression evaluation is dealt with first.

The discussion of macros is introductory and optional, primarily because macros are not formally addressed by standard Scheme. The optional nature of the material covering macros is discussed in a later section.

15.2 eval

Throughout this text our programs have made use of Scheme's facility for implicit, in essence automatic, evaluation of expressions. On occasion, we've found it necessary to use **quote** to prevent evaluation of an expression, e.g.,

```
(define x '(a b c))
```

In this case, we want the list to be taken literally, *not* as an expression to be evaluated where **a** is some function with **b** and **c** as arguments.

One of the principal tasks of the Scheme listener is to conduct a read-*eval*-print, or REP, loop. An expression typed at the top level, and additionally any expressions that are passed as arguments during function calls, are processed by a built-in Scheme function named **eval**.

Moreover, **eval** can be called directly at the top level, or from any function:

```
[1] (define x 'a)
X
[2] (define y 'b)
Y
[3] (define a 1)
A
[4] (define b 2)
B
[5] x
A
[6] 'x
X
[7] (eval x)
1
[8] (eval 'x)
A
[9] (define list-1 '(x y))
LIST-1
[10] list-1
(X Y)
[11] (eval list-1)

[ERROR encountered!] Attempt to call a non-procedural object
(A Y)

[Inspect] Quit
[12] (map eval list-1)
(A B)
[13] (eval (list '+ a b))
3
[14] (exit)
```

At prompts [1] and [3] **x** is given the value **a**; then **a** is given the value 1. Note that it's possible to define **a** as an identifier, even after **a** has been assigned to **x**. At prompt [5] the normal evaluation component of read-eval-print evaluates **x** returning **a**. At prompt [7] **eval** is used to force an additional round of evaluation. Following the standard rules for expression evaluation, the Scheme listener recognizes **eval** as a function and **x** as its argument. First, the argument to **eval** is automatically evaluated, since it isn't quoted; hence, **x** evaluates to **a**. Subsequently, the function **eval** is applied to the result, **a**, returning "1". At prompt [8] **quote** prevents the automatic evaluation of the argument **x**. Subsequently, **eval** is applied to **x** returning **a**.

Suppose that it is necessary to evaluate each element of a list in an element-by-element fashion. You cannot just apply **eval** to the list, since **eval** assumes that the list represents an expression, i.e., the first element is taken as a function. For example, at prompt [10] the read-eval-print evaluation of **list-1** returns the actual list. However, at prompt [11] the **eval** causes further evaluation of this list, producing an error. An error occurs because Scheme attempts to process the list as an expression, i.e., evaluating the list as a function plus one argument. In this case, **a** is not a function, and thus cannot be applied to **b**. Element-by-element evaluation of a list can be accomplished by applying (mapping) **eval** to each element of the list; see prompt [12].

Prompt [13] provides a simple illustration that Scheme can be used to build Scheme code, which can then be evaluated by **eval**. Thus, Scheme programs can build other Scheme programs and use **eval** to execute them "on the fly."

As a final example of **eval**, consider the following program that implements a primitive top-level, infix-based interpreter.

```
;;;;     lispeval.s     ;;;;;;;;;;;;;;;;;;;;;;;;;;;;;;;;;;;;;;;;

;;;;;;;;;;;;;;;;;;;;;;;;;;;;;;;;;;;;;;;;;;;;;;;;;;;;;;;;;;;;;;;;;;;;;;
;; LISP-EVAL illustrates expression evaluation with EVAL.
;;;;;;;;;;;;;;;;;;;;;;;;;;;;;;;;;;;;;;;;;;;;;;;;;;;;;;;;;;;;;;;;;;;;;;

(define (lisp-eval)
  (define (display-prompt)
    (newline)
    (display "LISP EVALUATOR [enter (end) to exit] ==> "))

  (display-prompt)
  (do ((eval-list (read) (read)))
      ((equal? (car eval-list) 'end)
       (newline) (display "END LISP-EVAL"))
      (display (eval eval-list))
      (newline)
      (display-prompt)))
```

The interpreter loop is implemented with **do**. **read** is used to assign to **eval-list** each expression that is read from the console – for the first and subsequent interpreter cycles. **re-order-exp** is used to put the components of the expression in prefix order so that **eval** can perform a normal Scheme expression evaluation; subsequently, **display** prints the results:

```
[1] (load "lispeval.s")
OK
[2] (lisp-eval-infix)

LISP EVALUATOR [enter (end) to exit] ==> (1 + 2)
3

LISP EVALUATOR [enter (end) to exit] ==> (20 / 2)
10

LISP EVALUATOR [enter (end) to exit] ==> (end)
```

```
END LISP-EVAL
[3] (exit)
```

15.3 quasiquote

Suppose that you are building executable Scheme code programmatically, e.g., by using **list** to put together a list that can be processed by **eval**. Consider an example where, for whatever reason, it is convenient to build a list of symbols for subsequent output at the console:

```
(the sum of x and y is z)
```

(We assume that this list is built during some intermediate level of processing.) In this example, **x**, **y**, and **z** are variables and all other symbols are to be taken literally. Thus, we need to instruct Scheme to replace selectively three of the symbols (identifiers) with their current values.

Let's try doing this with **quote**. First, we simulate the existence of a Scheme environment with the preceding variables already defined:

```
[1] (define x 3)
X
[2] (define y 4)
Y
[3] (define z (+ x y))
Z
[4] _
```

If we **quote** the entire list, *nothing* gets evaluated:

```
[4] '(the sum of x and y is z)
(THE SUM OF X AND Y IS Z)
[5] _
```

We can use **list** to build a list, but we must instruct Scheme regarding which symbols are literals:

```
[5] (list 'the 'sum 'of x 'and y 'is z)
(THE SUM OF 3 AND 4 IS 7)
[6] _
```

Including the quotes isn't too difficult, since the list is short, and 38 percent of the symbols are not quoted. However, a real application could require hundreds of quotes.

For situations such as this Scheme provides a syntactic form **quasiquote**, sometimes called "backquote," which is convenient for controlling partial quoting. **quasiquote** comes in two forms:

1. **quasiquote** plus "," (comma – or **unquote**)
2. **quasiquote** plus ",@" (comma-at-sign – or **unquote-splicing**)

Each special form has an abbreviation:

1. (quasiquote <template>) <–> '<template>
2. (unquote <expression>) <–> ,<expression>
3. (unquote-splicing <expression>) <–> ,@<expression>

quasiquote signals the occurrence of a template which may contain either **unquote** or **unquote-splicing**. **quasiquote** prohibits evaluation just like **quote**, except that within the bounds of a **quasiquote** both **unquote** and **unquote-splicing** temporarily turn on evaluation for the expression that follows. In the case of **unquote-splicing**, the expression that follows must evaluate to a list; the result is then entered into the **<template>** *without* the opening and closing parentheses, i.e., it is *spliced* in.

Consider the following formulation of the previous list using **quasiquote** (the "back" quote character on a traditional keyboard) and **unquote** (comma).

```
[6] '(the sum of ,x and ,y is ,z)
(THE SUM OF 3 AND 4 IS 7)
[7] _
```

In this case, partial evaluation takes place within the list for each expression following an **unquote**; here, each expression is just an identifier.

A common error is to misinterpret the need for **list**:

```
[7] (eval '(list + ,(+ x y) 2 1))
(#<PROCEDURE +> 7 2 1)
[8] _
```

At prompt [7] we attempt to formulate the list "(+ ?? 2 1)" where "??" is the result of an expression evaluation. Note that the expression evaluation is called for by the **unquote**. **eval** is used to cause the list to be built by **list** – which isn't quite right.

Actually, for this type of list building, **list** isn't necessary:

```
[8] (eval '(+ ,(+ x y) 2 1))
10
[9] _
```

That is, the use of **quasiquote** with the desired expression (plus **unquote**) is sufficient.

The following output further illustrates the control over evaluation that **quasiquote** provides.

```
[9] '(define w (+ x y))
(DEFINE W (+ X Y))
[10] '(define w ,(+ x y))
(DEFINE W 7)
[11] (define sq-definition '(define sq (lambda (n) (* n n))))
SQ-DEFINITION
[12] sq-definition
(DEFINE SQ (LAMBDA (N) (* N N)))
[13] (eval sq-definition)
SQ
[14] (sq 4)
16
[15] _
```

Prompts [9] through [15] illustrate a very powerful feature of Scheme. Namely, we can "store" an *inactive* procedure definition under an identifier name, and more importantly, programmatically activate it (specifically, its definition) at some point in the future. Note that this activation of definitions is similar to the task performed by the **load** primitive in most Scheme implementations.

This facility for embedding a definition inside a list allows the programmer to write specialized functions that accept simple data values and then build (more) complex data structures behind the scenes—the essence of data abstraction. Using these facilities of Scheme, we can develop a **system** of procedures for building data structures from data values, called *data constructors*, and procedures for retrieving data from the high-level data structures, called *data selectors*. (See the exercises.)

Finally, **unquote-slicing** is useful for splicing lists into the middle of a list:

```
[15] (define healthy-lunch '(burger and fries))
HEALTHY-LUNCH
[16] healthy-lunch
(BURGER AND FRIES)
[17] '(for lunch we could have a ,healthy-lunch)
(FOR LUNCH WE COULD HAVE A (BURGER AND FRIES))
[18] '(for lunch we could have a ,@healthy-lunch)
(FOR LUNCH WE COULD HAVE A BURGER AND FRIES)
[19] (exit)
```

15.4 Macros [OPTIONAL]

In this section we provide a brief introduction to macros. Although standard Scheme does not specifically address macros, most Scheme implementations do provide macro facilities. Traditionally, macro facilities have been provided by most LISP dialects—this may explain in large part the inclusion of macros in current Scheme implementations.

It is important to note that significant extension of the Scheme language, i.e., the creation of syntactic extensions, by using the macro facilities of a particular Scheme implementation, may lead to Scheme code that is nonportable – code that cannot easily be rendered portable – primarily due to differences in how macros are implemented in various Scheme systems, in conjunction with Scheme's lexically scoped nature.

For this reason, discussion of macros in Scheme will be confined to this section. If you have no interest in macro programming, or if you are primarily interested in standard Scheme, you may prefer to skip this section entirely. If you are interested in macros in general, or PC Scheme macros in particular, you may want to continue with the present chapter.

Note that confining our discussion of macros to this section makes it possible for later chapters to remain primarily independent of specific Scheme implementations.

15.4.1 Macro Programming

In general, macros provide a method of shorthand coding. That is, a macro is simply a body of code (written once) that can be substituted into a program on demand. In this section we explore macros somewhat "theoretically."

There are two primary uses for macros:

1. extending a language's functionality
2. improving code readability.

Consider the first use. So far in this text we've extended Scheme by providing function definitions. For example, standard Scheme provides no function for squaring a number; however, defining **square**, as we did in earlier chapters, is quite straightforward.

In general, language extension via function definition, especially for simple extensions, can have a negative impact on the overall efficiency of a large Scheme program. Squaring, say, **radius**, by calling a function such as **square** involves considerable run-time overhead, chiefly associated with lexical environment management and argument/parameter passing. All of this is required just so we can write

```
(square radius)
```

instead of

```
(* radius radius)
```

Note that from the code readability point of view the former expression is "higher level" than the latter – it tells us more about the logical intent of our code.

Consider the second use. In the preceding chapter we defined a function, **canine-color**, which would retrieve the color of a particular breed of dog:

```
(define (canine-color dog-breed)
  (cadr (assoc 'color dog-breed)))
```

We did so because littering a Scheme program with code such as

```
(cadr (assoc 'color dog-breed))
```

leads to code that is almost impossible to update/modify later in the life cycle of the program.

Both uses are related of course. In both cases the function definitions make the code more readable and more easily updated. However, in the case of defining functions for language extension, the motivation for doing so extends beyond a single programming project. On the other hand, functions such as **canine-color** are typically useful for a single project—code readability is the sole motivation behind defining the function.

Macros may be preferable to functions for these uses primarily due to the potential savings in run-time overhead, especially if functions such as **canine-color** are called many times in the course of executing a program. Note that this point is entirely theoretical. In practice, whether or not macros are more efficient than functions depends on the particular Scheme system, i.e., how well it implements macros. Parenthetically, macros offer a secondary advantage over functions, namely, delayed evaluation of arguments. Each of these points is addressed in the following section with respect to PC Scheme.

15.4.2 PC Scheme Macros

A good way to illustrate macros is by way of comparison with functions:

```
[1] (define add3 (lambda (n) (+ n 3)))            ;a function
ADD3
[2] (macro plus3 (lambda (exp) '(+ ,(cadr exp) 3))) ;a macro
PLUS3
[3] (add3 4)                         ;same
7                                    ;outward
[4] (plus3 4)                        ;effect
7
[5] (exit)
```

add3 and **plus3** are function and macro implementations of the same task, respectively. Macros are defined in PC Scheme by the syntax

```
(macro <macro-name> <syntax-expander>)
```

It is important to note that **<macro-name>** is not defined to be the function **<syntax-expander>** – **<macro-name>** is a macro, not a function. Instead, **<syntax-expander>** is the function that PC Scheme creates to handle the macro expansion, i.e., the process of replacing the macro (the shorthand) by its expansion (the longhand). Thus, **<syntax-expander>** is the mechanism by which the programmer specifies the code that replaces the macro reference. A function is required because macro expansion may be quite involved; specifically, macros may have parameters.

Consider **plus3**:

```
(macro plus3
  (lambda (exp)
    '(+ ,(cadr exp) 3)))
```

Scheme passes a single argument to **<syntax-expander>**, which is bound to the expression involving the macro reference, e.g., "(plus3 4)" is bound to **exp**. The programmer must specify replacement code in **<syntax-expander>**; i.e., the syntax that is to replace the macro reference. This is typically done by using **eval, quote, quasiquote**, and so on to build a Scheme expression in the manner described earlier. In **plus3**,

```
'(+ ,(cadr exp) 3)))
```

specifies that a list is to be built with the addition operator as the first element and the integer 3 as the third element. The second element is determined by evaluating the passed argument, e.g., "(plus3 4)", which is bound to **exp**. Note that the **unquote** within the **quasiquote** turns on evaluation temporarily; in this case, **(cadr exp)** evaluates to the second item in "(plus3 4)", or integer 4. Thus,

(plus3 4)   – expands to – >   (+ 4 3)

As you can see at prompt [4], two processes are involved during macro expansion:

1. code expansion: (plus3 4)   – expands to – >   (+ 4 3)

2. code evaluation: (+ 4 3)   – evaluates to – >   7

Let's consider a slightly more extensive example. The programming language PL/I has the function **repeat** which repeats a particular character a specified number of times, forming a string. Scheme's version of this is **make-string**; for demonstration purposes only, we can define a "roundabout" version of **make-string** named **repeat**.

```
;;;;     repeat.s     ;;;;;;;;;;;;;;;;;;;;;;;;;;;;;;;;;;;;;;;;

;;;;;;;;;;;;;;;;;;;;;;;;;;;;;;;;;;;;;;;;;;;;;;;;;;;;;;;;;;;;;
;; REPEAT-CH implements a version of the repeat function, as
;; found in languages such as PL/I, as a PC Scheme macro.
;; REPEAT-CH repeats a character n times to form a string.
;; For demo only--same as Scheme make-string function.
;;;;;;;;;;;;;;;;;;;;;;;;;;;;;;;;;;;;;;;;;;;;;;;;;;;;;;;;;;;;;

(macro repeat-ch
  (lambda (exp)
```

```
    '(let ((str-char (make-string 1 ,(cadr exp))))
       (do ((i 1 (+ i 1))
            (str "" (string-append str str-char)))
           ((> i ,(caddr exp)) str)))))


;;;;;;;;;;;;;;;;;;;;;;;;;;;;;;;;;;;;;;;;;;;;;;;;;;;;;;;;;;;;;;;;
;; REPEAT-CHAR implements a version of the repeat function, as
;; found in languages such as PL/I, as a Scheme function.
;; REPEAT-CHAR repeats a character n times to form a string.
;; For demo only--same as Scheme make-string function.
;;;;;;;;;;;;;;;;;;;;;;;;;;;;;;;;;;;;;;;;;;;;;;;;;;;;;;;;;;;;;;;;

(define (repeat-char char n)
  (let ((str-char (make-string 1 char)))
    (do ((i 1 (+ i 1))
         (str "" (string-append str str-char)))
        ((> i n) str))))
```

Again, for comparison, we provide both macro and function versions of **repeat**, as we are more accustomed to defining functions. After defining both of the above with your Scheme try the following, but with a fairly large repetition factor.

```
[1] (load "repeat.s")
OK
[2] (make-string 50 #\a)
"aaaaaaaaaaaaaaaaaaaaaaaaaaaaaaaaaaaaaaaaaaaaaaaaaa"
[3] (repeat-ch #\a 50)
"aaaaaaaaaaaaaaaaaaaaaaaaaaaaaaaaaaaaaaaaaaaaaaaaaa"
[4] (repeat-char #\a 50)
"aaaaaaaaaaaaaaaaaaaaaaaaaaaaaaaaaaaaaaaaaaaaaaaaaa"
[5] (exit)
```

Which one executes more efficiently with your Scheme system?

The same comments given for the add3/plus3 example apply here also. Note the use of **unquote** to substitute the proper argument values; compare the macro definition with prompts [3] and [4].

Another point is that within **<syntax-expander>** the task is merely to build the proper expression. In particular, it isn't necessary to use **quasiquote**; for example, as discussed in an earlier section, you could use various combinations of **quote, list,** and/or **eval,** depending on the Scheme code to be produced.

As another example, the following code represents the "beginnings" of a primitive database system of canine information.

```
;;;;     dogs.s     ;;;;;;;;;;;;;;;;;;;;;;;;;;;;;;;;;;;;;;;;;;;;;;;
```

```
;;;;;;;;;;;;;;;;;;;;;;;;;;;;;;;;;;;;;;;;;;;;;;;;;;;;;;;;;;;;;;
;; This file defines several access "functions" for a
;; simple database of dog information.  Each breed of
;; dog is maintained in an association list; each
;; association list is globally defined.
;; Example:  (define newfoundland '((size giant)
;;                                  (color black)
;;                                  (hair long-haired)
;;                                  (category working)))
;;;;;;;;;;;;;;;;;;;;;;;;;;;;;;;;;;;;;;;;;;;;;;;;;;;;;;;;;;;;;;

(macro dog-size (lambda (exp)     ;;e.g. (dog-size collie)
  '(cadr (assoc 'size ,(cadr exp)))))

(macro dog-color (lambda (exp)    ;;e.g. (dog-color collie)
  '(cadr (assoc 'color ,(cadr exp)))))

(macro dog-hair (lambda (exp)     ;;e.g. (dog-hair collie)
  '(cadr (assoc 'hair ,(cadr exp)))))

(macro dog-category (lambda (exp) ;;e.g. (dog-category collie)
  '(cadr (assoc 'category ,(cadr exp)))))

(macro dog-attr (lambda (exp)     ;;e.g. (dog-attr size collie)
  '(cadr (assoc ',(cadr exp) ,(caddr exp)))))


;;;;;;;;;;;;;;;;;;;;;;;;;;;;;;;;;;;;;;;;;;;;;;;;;;;
;; DOG-CHAR is the function version of DOG-ATTR.
;; Example usage:  (dog-char 'size collie)
;;;;;;;;;;;;;;;;;;;;;;;;;;;;;;;;;;;;;;;;;;;;;;;;;;;

(define dog-char
  (lambda (attribute dog-breed)
    (cadr (assoc attribute dog-breed))))
```

It's obvious that for a complex kennel-club application, the use of the preceding macros would be superior to direct usage of combinations of **cadr** and **assoc**. However, the main reason for this example is to illustrate another utility provided by macros. Consider **dog-attr** and **dog-char** (char = characteristics). If we use a function definition to encode retrieval of dog attributes, such as **dog-char**, Scheme automatically evaluates the arguments before binding them to the corresponding parameters of **dog-char**. The net effect is that (when using **dog-char**), **quote** must be applied to the attribute argument to prevent evaluation, since **attribute** represents a symbol and **dog-breed** represents a variable.

The programmer can't get around this in the definition of **dog-char**, because the evaluation of "color" in the expression **(dog-char 'color newfoundland)** takes place before the function call, if the **quote** is omitted. On the other hand, macros are expanded first, giving the programmer the opportunity to override argument evaluations, as in **dog-attr** above – in this case, by putting a **quote** in the syntax generated at macro expansion time. This point is illustrated by the following Scheme session.

```
[1] (load "dogs.s")
OK
[2] (define newfoundland '((size giant)
(color black)
(hair long-haired)
(category working)))
NEWFOUNDLAND
[3] (dog-size newfoundland)
GIANT
[4] (dog-color newfoundland)
BLACK
[5] (dog-hair newfoundland)
LONG-HAIRED
[6] (dog-category newfoundland)
WORKING
[7] (dog-char size newfoundland)

[VM ERROR encountered!] Variable not defined in current
environment
SIZE

[Inspect] Quit
[8] (dog-char 'size newfoundland)
GIANT
[9] (dog-attr size newfoundland)
GIANT
[10] (exit)
```

In other words, with macros the programmer can write code that *hides* the fact that the first argument is a symbol, whereas the second argument is a variable in the underlying representation of the dog database. This type of information-hiding is mandatory in real applications.

The last point we address in our introduction to macros is the potential for identifier name conflicts. This problem is common with macro processing, regardless of LISP dialect or implementation. We illustrate name conflict by way of **bad-iterate** and **iterate**, which are largely motivated by an example in the PC Scheme documentation (Texas Instruments, 1987). Consider the following Scheme session.

```
[1] (load "iterate.s")
```

```
OK
[2] (define i 20)
I
[3] i
20
[4] (bad-iterate (set! i (- i 1)) 5)   ;begin bus trip to
                                       ;never-never land
[VM ERROR encountered!] User keyboard interrupt
()

[Inspect] Quit
[5] (iterate (set! i (- i 1)) 5)
()
[6] i
15
[7] (exit)
```

Before looking at the functions, try to figure out what happens at prompt [4]. Both **bad-iterate** and **iterate** take two arguments – the Scheme code specified by the first argument is repeatedly executed, as many times as specified by the second argument.

bad-iterate is instructed to perform an update to **i**, specifically a decrement operation, five times; **i** is defined global to the expression involving **bad-iterate**. Thus, **i** should be reduced to 15. The problem is that **bad-iterate** is written with a **do**, which inadvertently uses **i** as a local variable:

```
;;;;     iterate.s     ;;;;;;;;;;;;;;;;;;;;;;;;;;;;;;;;;;;;;;;;;;

;;;;;;;;;;;;;;;;;;;;;;;;;;;;;;;;;;;;;;;;;;;;;;;;;;;;;;;;;;;;
;; These macros illustrate a potential scope problem
;; during macro definition.
;; Example usage:   (iterate (display #\a) 5)
;; See PC Scheme manual for a more-extensive examp.
;;;;;;;;;;;;;;;;;;;;;;;;;;;;;;;;;;;;;;;;;;;;;;;;;;;;;;;;;;;;


(macro bad-iterate
  (lambda (exp)
    '(do ((i ,(caddr exp) (- i 1)))
         ((zero? i) ())
         ,(cadr exp))))   ;; if the body uses i, it will be
                          ;; the i local to the do
```

In this example, the body of the **do** is expanded to

```
(set! i (- i 1))
```

Thus, **set!** operates on the local **i**, which is initialized to 5, not the global **i**. Of course, the hair-raising aspect of this error is that "by chance" the local **i** is initialized to an odd value, such that it is decremented "around" the termination test for **i** equal to 0.

This kind of error can be avoided by writing macros that use **let** and/or **lambda** to isolate the interaction of global and local variables:

```
(macro iterate
  (lambda (exp)
    '(let ((function-appl (lambda () ,(cadr exp)))
           (n ,(caddr exp)))
       (do ((i n (- i 1)))
           ((zero? i) ())
           (function-appl)))))
```

Why does this work, since **function-appl** still occurs local to the **do** which contains an **i**? It works properly because Scheme is lexically scoped—the **lambda** function incorporating the **set!** operation is defined in the **let**, before the **do** is established with its local **i**. Hence, **function-appl** is defined with a reference to the global **i**—the **do**'s **i** doesn't yet exist. In this respect, Scheme is statically scoped. That is, when a function is defined, references to global identifiers are resolved immediately. Consequently, destructive identifier references, such as with **set!**, are applied to the correct identifiers.

It should be clear that macros, notwithstanding their obvious utility, are a potential source of coding problems and must be used with considerable care and respect.

Exercises

1. Given the following definitions, show the returned values for each expression.

```
(define x 1)
(define y 2)
(define x2 x)
(define y2 y)
(define z (+ x y))
```

```
a. x
b. (eval x)
c. x2
d. (eval x2)
e. z
f. (eval z)
g. (+ x2 y2)
h. (+ (eval x2) (eval y2))
i. (list x2 y2)
j. (eval (list '+ (eval x2) (eval y2)))
```

2. Given the definitions from Exercise 1, show the returned values for each expression.

```
a. (list x 'plus y 'is (+ x y))
b. '(,x plus ,y is ,(+ x y))
c. '(x plus y is (+ x y))
d. '(,x plus ,y is ,(+ x y))
e. (eval '(list + 1 2 3))
f. (let ((favorite-flavor '(peaches and cream)))
     '(her favorite flavor is ,@favorite-flavor))
```

3. Discuss the principal advantages of macros over functions, including when and where macros would be preferable.

4. Provide macro alternatives to the following function definitions:

```
a. (define (times x y) (* x y))
b. (define reciprocal (lambda (n) (if (number? n)
                                      (if (not (= n 0))
                                          (/ 1 n)))))
c. (define first (lambda (lst) (car lst)))
```

5. Provide a macro version of the following functions from Chapter 8:

a. string-index
b. str-insert
c. str-delete

6. Procedure abstraction is the practice of hiding the low-level details of particular tasks inside procedures, such that we need only address the task abstractly at a later date; i.e., when we need to perform that task, we simply supply the correct arguments to the appropriate function, and it performs the required task for us.

Data abstraction is the practice of organizing data in a manner that facilitates abstract views, or operations, on that data. As a simple example, consider the process of setting up an employee record in memory. An abstract view of **employee** is simply the set of attributes associated with each employee. A more specific (less abstract) view of employee would consider things such as organization of the collection of attributes, maximum number of attributes that can be associated with each **employee**, and so on.

For this exercise, set up a system of data constructor and data selector procedures that can be used to manage a simple employee database, existing at the Scheme top level. That is, if Bill Smith is added to the database, he should be defined by the top-level identifier **bill**, where **bill** is one of the data items (arguments) passed to the data constructor procedure. More specific details about Bill would be stored behind the scenes. This should include Bill's full name, department, manager, etc. (Use string variables where appropriate.) You should use an association list or a vector (or a combination of the two) as the implementation data structure for each employee.

Also, at least one item/field in your data structure for an employee should be a compound data item. For example, in this chapter we developed a specific definition for the Newfoundland breed of dogs. If, say, Bruno, were a Newfoundland, then **newfoundland** could be "attached" to **bruno**, the doggy database entry for Bruno. In a similar manner, you could develop top-level definitions for, say, insurance plans, or departments.

Next, write data selector procedures for retrieving relevant information for each employee. Make your own decisions about whether or not to employ macros. Don't be concerned over the existence of top-level definitions. In a later chapter, we'll develop a more structured, menu-driven database system with encapsulated procedures and data structures. At this point, your main interest should be developing some facility with the Scheme features discussed in this chapter.

If employee databases remind you of work (and you'd rather not be so reminded), substitute an alternative database subject, e.g., dogs, cats, fish, fast cars...

Chapter 16

Additional Control Structures

16.1 Introduction

This chapter provides an overview of some programming constructs that are mostly unique to the Scheme dialect of LISP. First, Scheme's facility for control of process continuation is discussed. And second, **delay** and **force** are introduced as a means of implementing lazy evaluation. Examples are given for each.

16.2 Scheme Continuations

Suppose you could suspend a computation temporarily. The unfinished part of that computation is called its *continuation*. Thus, a continuation represents the future of a computation.

Consider the evaluation of a typical Scheme expression. Such an evaluation is likely to involve several intermediate operations (expression evaluations). Hence, the *continuation* of the outer evaluation is typically contingent on the evaluation of an inner expression. As an example, consider the arithmetic expression

```
(+ 4 (* 2 3))
```

In this case, the continuation of the addition operation is contingent on the multiplication operation. In particular, the innermost expression evaluation must return a value of 6 before the outer expression evaluation can continue, ultimately producing a value of 10.

Most programming languages handle such process continuations strictly behind the scenes. Scheme, on the other hand, allows the programmer to manipulate the continuation of any process; **call-with-current-continuation** is a Scheme function that captures the continuation of a process in the form of a function. Most Scheme implementations provide **call/cc** as an abbreviation for **call-with-current-continuation**. The following Scheme session illustrates **call/cc** with respect to the preceding paragraph; subsequent paragraphs discuss **call/cc** in more detail.

```
[1] (+ 4 (* 2 3))
10
[2] (call/cc (lambda (k) (+ 4 (* 2 3))))
10
[3] (call/cc (lambda (k) (+ 4 (* 2 (k 11) 3))))
11
[4] (call/cc (lambda (k) (display "first") (k 'dummy)
       (display "second")))
firstDUMMY
[5] (exit)
```

call/cc operates as follows. When **call/cc** is invoked in the following context,

```
     ...
     ...

(call/cc <proc>)
     ...
```

it gathers together all data structures necessary to continue the current computation, in the form of a function, and passes the newly-created function as an argument to **<proc>**. **<proc>** must be a function of one parameter. Within **<proc>**, the programmer can use the passed continuation just like any other parameter. For example, since it is a function, it can be executed. Or, since Scheme functions are first-class data objects, the continuation can be assigned to some identifier, even a top-level identifier.

Typically, **<proc>** is a lambda function:

```
(call/cc (lambda (escape) ...
```

In this example, the current continuation is passed as **escape**; there is nothing special about the name:

```
(call/cc (lambda (escape) ...   or

(call/cc (lambda (k) ...        or

(call/cc (lambda (return) ...   etc.
```

However, **call/cc** has considerably more utility. In general,

```
(call/cc (lambda (<escape-proc>) ...
```

creates and passes the current continuation as an escape procedure, such that if **<escape-proc>** is later invoked:

```
     ...
     ...

(<escape-proc> <value>)
     ...
```

<escape-proc> ignores the continuation that is presently in effect, returning **<value>** to the continuation that was in effect when **<escape-proc>** was created. Note that lexical scoping rules apply to the parameter name.

We can illustrate continuations with some examples. First, consider the process of capturing a continuation. The following code illustrates how to capture the remainder of a looping operation.

```
;;;;     callcc.s     ;;;;;;;;;;;;;;;;;;;;;;;;;;;;;;;;;;;;;;;;

;;;;;;;;;;;;;;;;;;;;;;;;;;;;;;;;;;;;;;;;;;;;;;;;;;;;;;;;;;;;;;;;
;; This example illustrates a continuation by capturing the
;; remainder of a looping operation in a top-level identifier.
;;;;;;;;;;;;;;;;;;;;;;;;;;;;;;;;;;;;;;;;;;;;;;;;;;;;;;;;;;;;;;;;

(define whats-next #f)           ;; the continuation of the
                                 ;; looping operation
(define (one-to-ten)
  (do ((i 1 (+ i 1)))
      ((> i 10) (display "-- end --"))
      (display i)
      (newline)
      (if (= i 5)
          (call/cc (lambda (esc)           ;; continuation passed
            (set! whats-next esc))))))    ;; as parameter (esc)
```

The **do** loop prints the integers 1 through 10. In addition, if **i** is equal to five, the continuation of the entire looping process is captured and passed as **esc**. The only operation inside the lambda function is the assignment of the passed function to the top-level variable **whats-next**.

Note that the capturing of the continuation is supplemental to the incrementing and printing of **i**'s value. Afterwards, **whats-next** can be executed; however, by the preceding rules, it must be passed a value, in this case, a dummy value:

```
[1] (load "callcc.s")
OK
```

```
[2] whats-next
()
[3] (one-to-ten)
1
2
3
4
5
6
7
8
9
10
-- end --
[4] (whats-next 'anything)
6
7
8
9
10
-- end --
[5] _
```

At prompt [2] **whats-next** evaluates to false as expected, since **one-to-ten** hasn't been invoked. At prompt [3] **one-to-ten** is invoked, printing the expected output. However, when **i** is equal to 5, the remainder of the looping operation is assigned to **whats-next**; note that **call/cc** is invoked subsequent to the **display** that prints **i**'s value for each cycle. Thus, when **whats-next** is invoked at prompt [4], the first integer printed is 6. Since we are only interested in capturing the continuation in this example, the value passed to **whats-next** is immaterial.

As another example of capturing a continuation consider the following:

```
;;;;    callcc.s    ;;;;;;;;;;;;;;;;;;;;;;;;;;;;;;;;;;;;;;;;;;;;;

;;;;;;;;;;;;;;;;;;;;;;;;;;;;;;;;;;;;;;;;;;;;;;;;;;;;;;;;;;;;;;;;;
;; This example illustrates a continuation by capturing the
;; remainder of a recursive process.
;;;;;;;;;;;;;;;;;;;;;;;;;;;;;;;;;;;;;;;;;;;;;;;;;;;;;;;;;;;;;;;;;

(define continue #f)          ;; the continuation of factorial

(define (factorial n)
  (if (= n 4)
      (call/cc (lambda (k)
        (set! continue k))))  ;; capture continuation if n = 4
  (display n)
```

```
  (newline)
  (if (zero? n)
      1
      (* n (factorial (- n 1)))))
```

Here we've captured the remainder of a recursive process. Even though the continuation is captured in the middle of the recursive execution, executing the continuation produces the same result as does the original invocation of **factorial.** That is, everything necessary to complete the continuation is packaged as part of the escape procedure:

```
[5] continue
()
[6] (factorial 3)
3
2
1
0
6
[7] continue
()
[8] (factorial 5)
5
4
3
2
1
0
120
[9] (continue 'anyvalue)
4
3
2
1
0
120
[10] (exit)
```

continue is false at prompt [5]. At prompt [6] **factorial** is invoked with an argument of 3, which means that the continuation is never established; hence, at prompt [7] **continue** is still false. At prompt [8] an argument of 5 is provided to **factorial** and thus the continuation is captured when **n** equals 4. Executing **continue** at prompt [9], again, the argument is immaterial, invokes the remainder of the recursive process printing 4,3...0, plus the correct final value of 120.

Having illustrated the capturing of a continuation, let's address the use of the escape procedure for controlling program flow. A common example is error trapping, i.e., interrupting execution and returning some value.

Consider **p-l-length**, a function that determines the length of a *proper* list, and which "dies gracefully" when given an improper argument:

```
[1] (load "l-length.s")
OK
[2] (p-l-length ())
0
[3] (p-l-length '(a b c d))
4
[4] (p-l-length '(a b c . d))
()
[5] (p-l-length '(a b c . (d e)))
5
[6] (exit)
```

In this case, we choose to have **p-l-length** return false if the list is improper, and to return the actual length otherwise. Thus, a non-false value indicates both the list length and that the list was a proper one. **p-l-length** is implemented with **call/cc** as follows.

```
;;;;     l-length.s     ;;;;;;;;;;;;;;;;;;;;;;;;;;;;;;;;;;;;;;;;

;;;;;;;;;;;;;;;;;;;;;;;;;;;;;;;;;;;;;;;;;;;;;;;;;;;;;;
;; P-L-LENGTH determines the length of a list
;; using CALL/CC to abort if the list is improper.
;;;;;;;;;;;;;;;;;;;;;;;;;;;;;;;;;;;;;;;;;;;;;;;;;;;;;;

(define (p-l-length lst)
  (call-with-current-continuation
    (lambda (exit)
      (let loop ((len 0) (lst lst))
        (cond
          ((null? lst) len)
          ((pair? lst) (loop (+ len 1) (cdr lst)))
          (else
            (exit #f)))))))    ;; call the escape procedure
```

In **p-l-length** the continuation is the entire function. That is, we capture the continuation of **p-l-length** immediately after it is invoked, and the scope of the **call/cc** includes the named **let**, which is used to implement cdr processing of the list. In the event that the remainder of the list is not a pair, the escape procedure **exit** is called, returning false to the pending continuation; since nothing else remains to be done in **p-l-length**, **p-l-length** simply returns false.

At this point you should contemplate the global/local usage of escape procedures in the previous examples. In the last example **exit** is used locally, whereas in the previous examples the escape procedures were stored globally.

As a final example of continuations, we illustrate perhaps their most common usage – implementation of non-local exits. In many cases, it is convenient to terminate program execution from within a loop, or even from within nested procedure calls. That is, if **a** calls **b** and **b** calls **c** and **c** calls **d**, there may be conditions under which it is necessary to escape from, say, **d**, and return immediately to, say, **a**. **call/cc** can be used to perform such a structured, non-local exit.

The following example presents a simple, menu-driven program for performing basic mathematical calculations. In order to illustrate the preceding idea, it is written so that the driver function implements a main menu and calls subordinate functions for each possible task. Further, these subordinate functions call another function – hence, providing multiple, nested procedures.

```
;;;;     mathmenu.s       ;;;;;;;;;;;;;;;;;;;;;;;;;;;;;;;;;;;;;;;;;;;;;

;;;;;;;;;;;;;;;;;;;;;;;;;;;;;;;;;;;;;;;;;;;;;;;;;;;;;;;;;;;;;;;;;;;;;;;
;; MATH-MENU illustrates escape/error operations in Scheme.
;;;;;;;;;;;;;;;;;;;;;;;;;;;;;;;;;;;;;;;;;;;;;;;;;;;;;;;;;;;;;;;;;;;;;;;

(define (math-menu)
  (letrec
      ;;;;;;;;;;;;;;;;;;;;;;;;;;;;;;;;;;;;;;;;;;;;;;;;;;;;;;;;;;;;;;;;;;;
      ;; ESCAPE is the escape procedure--initially, given
      ;; a dummy value.
      ;;;;;;;;;;;;;;;;;;;;;;;;;;;;;;;;;;;;;;;;;;;;;;;;;;;;;;;;;;;;;;;;;;;

      ((escape #f)

      ;;;;;;;;;;;;;;;;;;;;;;;;;;;;;;;;;;;;;;;;;;;;;;;;;;;;;
      ;; Four simple menu choices--immediately
      ;; subordinate to MATH-LOOP
      ;;;;;;;;;;;;;;;;;;;;;;;;;;;;;;;;;;;;;;;;;;;;;;;;;;;;;

      (add (lambda ()
        (format "~%The sum is:   ~a~%"
                (+ (get-number) (get-number)))))

      (subtract (lambda ()
        (format "~%The difference is:   ~a~%"
                (- (get-number) (get-number)))))

      (multiply (lambda ()
        (format "~%The product is:   ~a~%"
                (* (get-number) (get-number)))))
```

```
(divide (lambda ()
  (format "~%The quotient is:  ~a~%"
          (/ (get-number) (get-number)))))

;;;;;;;;;;;;;;;;;;;;;;;;;;;;;;;;;;;;;;;;;;;;;;;;;;;;;
;; GET-NUMBER prompts for and reads one number.
;; It also provides an escape to the main menu.
;;;;;;;;;;;;;;;;;;;;;;;;;;;;;;;;;;;;;;;;;;;;;;;;;;;;;

(get-number (lambda ()
  (let read-loop ()
    (format
      "~%*** READ MENU ***~%~%Choose function: ~%~%")
    (format
      "r -- read a number~%e -- escape to main menu~%")
    (case (read)
      ((r) (format "Enter a number: ") (read))

      ((e) (escape 'dummy))        ;;escape from innermost
                                   ;;operation
      (else
        (format "~%*** invalid choice ***~%")
        (read-loop))))))

;;;;;;;;;;;;;;;;;;;;;;;;;;;;;;;;;;;;;;;;;;;;;;
;; MATH-LOOP drives the menu iteratively.
;;;;;;;;;;;;;;;;;;;;;;;;;;;;;;;;;;;;;;;;;;;;;;

(math-loop (lambda ()
  (do ((option ()))
      ((equal? option 'e) (display #\newline))
      (call/cc (lambda (k)            ;;set up return point
        (set! escape k)               ;;assign escape proc

        (format
          "~%*** MATH MENU ***~%~%Choose function: ~%~%")
        (format
          "a -- add~%s -- subtract~%m -- multiply~%")
        (format
          "d -- divide~%e -- exit~%")
        (set! option (read))
        (case option
          ((a) (add))
          ((s) (subtract))
          ((m) (multiply))
```

```
                ((d) (divide))
                ((e) (format "~%END OF PROGRAM~%"))
                (else
                  (format "~%*** invalid choice ***~%")))))))))

    (math-loop)))        ;;letrec body
```

It is undesirable in a program that could have some real utility to have multiple, top-level identifiers floating around, simply to hold escape procedures. (Our simple program **math-menu** is a skeleton of a more realistic program.) Thus, in **math-menu** all identifiers and associated functions are contained within **math-menu**.

In order to define the escape procedure **escape** at the same level as the other procedures, we need a way of accommodating mutually-recursive procedures. Recall that **letrec** provides a mechanism for such definitions. **math-menu** consists entirely of a **letrec**. The identifier **escape** is established first in the **letrec**; note that the assigned value is immaterial. Next, four simple functions are defined, each of which calls the function **get-number**, which is defined at the same level.

The idea behind **get-number** is that, for the purposes of our example, the user may want to escape from the current calculation, all the way back to the main menu. Thus, **get-number** provides a mini menu with two choices: read the number, and escape. The escape operation is implemented by calling **escape** (again, the argument is immaterial). Note that at the time of **get-number**'s *definition*, **escape** has not been defined as an escape procedure.

However, consider **math-loop**, the driver function for the main menu. The entire operation is implemented via a **do**, such that program termination occurs when the user enters the symbol **e**. In every other case, the menu is presented, the chosen **option** is read, and the proper function invoked, with the exception of illegal options. In particular, note that **call/cc** is used to capture as the current continuation the entire main menu operation, such that any subsequent escape will return the user to the main menu. This is easily accomplished by assigning the passed continuation, which is passed as **k**, to **escape**. Recall that during the nested procedure invocations **escape** may be called as an escape procedure to return to the main menu.

The following Scheme dialog illustrates **math-menu**'s overall operation:

```
[1] (load "mathmenu.s")
OK
[2] (math-menu)

*** MATH MENU ***

Choose function:

a -- add
s -- subtract
m -- multiply
d -- divide
```

```
e -- exit
a

*** READ MENU ***

Choose function:

r -- read a number
e -- escape to main menu
r
Enter a number:  3

*** READ MENU ***

Choose function:

r -- read a number
e -- escape to main menu
r
Enter a number:  4

The sum is:  7

*** MATH MENU ***

Choose function:

a -- add
s -- subtract
m -- multiply
d -- divide
e -- exit
m

*** READ MENU ***

Choose function:

r -- read a number
e -- escape to main menu
r
Enter a number:  4

*** READ MENU ***

Choose function:
```

```
r -- read a number
e -- escape to main menu
e                                 ; <--- escape to main menu

*** MATH MENU ***

Choose function:

a -- add
s -- subtract
m -- multiply
d -- divide
e -- exit
e

END OF PROGRAM

[3] (exit)
```

For convenience **math-menu** makes use of **format**, which we discussed earlier. However, it is straightforward to replace **format** by your own print function. Again, **math-menu** is intended to serve only as an example for a real application involving multiple nesting levels, say, 20 levels deep. In practice, this type of procedure nesting commonly arises in AI and systems programming applications, e.g., (search) tree traversal and compiler routines.

The access to process continuations that Scheme provides is a major language feature that perhaps distinguishes Scheme from other languages; it can be at the same time both rewarding and humbling.

16.3 delay and force

delay and **force** are provided as tools for implementing *lazy evaluation*. Lazy evaluation is the process whereby an expression is not evaluated until needed; it is a component of some, but not all (not even most) computer languages. The basic idea with lazy evaluation is that there may be some computation, possibly space or time inefficient, that is actually used only occasionally; i.e., say, only one out of four times that a program is executed. **delay** provides a mechanism for isolating and postponing such computations, whereas **force** is used to initiate them. Thus, employing lazy evaluation where possible in a program can lead to a considerable increase in space and/or time efficiency over the life of a software product. By providing **delay** and **force**, Scheme gives the programmer *direct* control over lazy evaluation.

In essence, **delay** returns a *delayed object*, or *promise*, responsible for the evaluation of **<exp>**, *if* evaluation is ever called for:

```
(delay <exp>)
```

A promise is much like a procedure of no parameters with a body composed of **<exp>**. Evaluation of a promise is requested with **force**:

```
(force <promise>)
```

The first time a promise is passed to **force**, the promise evaluates its body and remembers, or memorizes, the resulting value. Subsequently, an invocation of **force** against the same promise returns the same value. That is, the first returned value is cached, eliminating any future recomputation.

delay is a syntactic form, whereas **force** is a function. (If you read the material on macros, it should be clear why **delay** cannot be implemented as a procedure; namely, arguments are always evaluated with procedures, which would defeat the purpose of **delay**, as we will see in the following.)

The next Scheme session illustrates a straightforward usage of **delay** and **force**.

```
[1] (define x 5)
X
[2] (define y (delay (+ x 2)))                    ;y is a promise
Y
[3] x
5
[4] y
#(|#!DELAYED-OBJECT| #<PROCEDURE %DELAY>)         ;verify that y
[5] (set! x 10)                                   ;is a promise
10
[6] y
#(|#!DELAYED-OBJECT| #<PROCEDURE %DELAY>)
[7] (force y)
12
[8] x
10
[9] y
#(|#!DELAYED-OBJECT| #<PROCEDURE %DELAY>)
[10] (set! x 15)
15
[11] (force y)
12
[12] (exit)
```

At prompt [1] **x** is defined, as a normal variable, and given the value 5. At prompt [2] **y** is defined/assigned a promise to evaluate the expression "(+ x 2)". This action has no impact on **x** (e.g., prompt [3]). Prompt [4] verifies that **y** is a promise (delayed object). Prompts [5] through [7] illustrate that a promise evaluates an expression using the identifier values that are active at the time of the **force**, not at the time the promise was created by the **delay**. Lastly, prompts [10] and [11] illustrate the caching aspect of **delay** and **force**.

Lazy evaluation is particularly convenient for two purposes:

1. memorizing initial values for expression evaluations
2. postponing operations that impact space or time utilization.

We can illustrate both with a program that mimics a simple (computer) memory management operation.

Suppose we have a *potential* need for a large table in some application; i.e., depending on run-time factors, it may or may not be required for a particular execution of the application. In this case, it may be desirable to delay, and potentially to avoid, allocation of memory for the table in question. You can view this application from either a systems or applications programming perspective, e.g., an implementation of, say, overlays, or a large table holding personnel information, respectively. (In the example, we work with a table of 20 elements for convenience; imagine a 512K table.)

Given that the table in question may or may not be needed, it is desirable to write Scheme code that, when the table is first referenced, can dynamically detect that it doesn't exist; and create the table. Moreover, subsequent references to the same table should not cause it to be recreated, possibly destroying its current contents. The situation described here is one form of a process called *autoloading*. That is, if a referenced identifier (variable or procedure) is not available, it is dynamically loaded from some predefined location, say, a computer disk. This process should be transparent to the application.

The following program illustrates how this form of autoloading can be implemented in Scheme.

```
;;;;     autoload.s     ;;;;;;;;;;;;;;;;;;;;;;;;;;;;;;;;;;;;;;;;

;;;;;;;;;;;;;;;;;;;;;;;;;;;;;;;;;;;;;;;;;;;;;;;;;;;;;;;;;;;;;
;; A simple illustration of the use of delay and force
;; to implement lazy evaluation and "memorizing."
;;;;;;
;; PARTITION-1 is a memory partition in a virtual machine
;; implemented as a Scheme vector.
;;;;;;;;;;;;;;;;;;;;;;;;;;;;;;;;;;;;;;;;;;;;;;;;;;;;;;;;;;;;;


(define partition-1 #f)              ;; don't load it initially

(define auto-partition-1                            ;; a promise
  (delay (set! partition-1 (make-vector 20))))

(define autoload (lambda (id)
  (cond
```

```
    ((equal? id 'partition-1)
     (force auto-partition-1) (eval id))
;   ...
;   other identifiers
;   ...
    (else
      #f))))
```

In the preceding program, **autoload** is a function that "insulates" any usage of an autoload identifier from the issue of whether or not it is currently (properly) defined. First, **partition-1** is defined to be false, indicating that the table hasn't been allocated. Next, a promise, **auto-partition-1**, is defined that can be activated to cause the allocation. When **autoload** is invoked for a particular identifier, if that identifier matches one specified in the **cond**, **force** is used to activate, i.e., initialize, the identifier. And, if the identifier has already been initialized, **force** simply returns the same identifier.

This example provides further evidence of the power afforded by treating procedures as first-class objects, especially in conjunction with **eval**. Make sure you are clear on the evaluation process that takes place for the parameter **id** in **autoload**, the use of **equal?** in the **cond**, and the reason that "(eval id)" is necessary. Hint: In some cases, we need to reference the data structure per se, and in some cases, we need to reference its name. The following Scheme session should help clarify the need for **eval**.

```
[1] (load "autoload.s")
OK
[2] partition-1
()
[3] (vector-set! (autoload 'partition-1) 4 'hello)
#(() () () () HELLO () () () () ())
[4] partition-1
#(() () () () HELLO () () () () ())
[5] (vector-set! (autoload 'partition-1) 5 'there)
#(() () () () HELLO THERE () () () ())
[6] (vector-set! (autoload 'partition-1) 4 'hi)
#(() () () () HI THERE () () () ())
[7] partition-1
#(() () () () HI THERE () () () ())
[8] (exit)
```

At prompt [2] **partition-1** is false. At prompt [3] **vector-set!** references the vector **partition-1** via **auto-load**, assigning the symbol **hello** to the fourth element. (Note the quoted argument.) Prompt [4] verifies that **partition-1** has been created and modified. Prompt [5] illustrates a second modification to the vector, and additionally, the memorizing aspect of **force**. Note that memorizing the identifier **partition-1** does not mean that it cannot be modified, merely that it is not redefined by the **make-vector** operation – **force** never forgets a promise.

The preceding implementation is unnecessarily pedestrian and, in general, limited to the extent that the **cond** in **autoload** must provide a clause for every autoload identifier. It is possible to write a shorter, more elegant, and more general version that is only slightly more convoluted in its use of **eval**. See the exercises.

Exercises

1. Show the returned value for each of the following:

```
a. (call/cc (lambda (c) (+ 3 4)))
b. (call/cc (lambda (c) (* 3 4 (c 5))))
c. (call/cc (lambda (c)
      (display "print this")
      (c "return this")))
d. (let ((x 4))
      (call/cc (lambda (x) (/ 30 (* 3 (x 5))))))
e. (* 10 (call/cc (lambda (k) (+ 3 (k 7)))))
```

2. Develop a function that sums the elements of a list. **call/cc** should be used to provide graceful termination of the function in the event that an element of the list is not a number.

3. Many computer applications require the ability to temporarily interrupt program execution, for whatever reason, and then optionally restart the program. Develop a program that prints the integers from 1 to 10,000 on the screen, one number per line. The screen printing operation is the primary computing task. Define another arbitrary function to represent a secondary computing task, say, printing the integers from 1 to 10 across the screen. The program for the primary task should include a mechanism for temporarily suspending execution, i.e., discontinuing the integer printing operation, so that the secondary task can be executed.

The restart mechanism for the primary task should allow the primary task to be restarted regardless of whether or not the secondary task is executed. You can use continuations to implement the restart mechanism. However, you must also include a mechanism for detecting suspension of the primary task, i.e., a breakpoint command. One way of handling this is to include code in the primary task that polls the keyboard for a specific keystroke after each integer is printed to the screen.

4. Show the returned value for each of the following expressions:

```
a. (define a 2)
b. (define d (delay (* a 10)))
c. a
d. d
e. (set! a (delay (* a 5)))
```

```
f. (force a)
g. a
h. d
i. (force a)
```

5. Show the returned value for each of the following expressions:

```
a. (force (delay (* 3 4)))
b. (let ((d (delay (+ 2 3))))
     (list (force d) (force d) (eval (force d)) d))
```

6. Modify the autoload example from this chapter in the manner suggested at the end of the chapter. That is, modify **autoload** so that it works for any identifier with the same status as **partition-1**.

7. **delay** and **force** can be used to implement a data structure called a *stream*. A stream is a sequence of data objects of any type, e.g., integers, reals, strings. See Abelson and Sussman (1985) for an extensive treatment of streams, or the standard Scheme documentation (Rees and Clinger, 1986) for a brief treatment.

Consider the following definition of a stream which is similar to the one provided in the standard Scheme documentation.

```
;;;;      stream.s      ;;;;;;;;;;;;;;;;;;;;;;;;;;;;;;;;;;;;;;;;;;;;

;;;;;;;;;;;;;;;;;;;;;;;;;;;;;;;;;;;;;;;;;;;;;;;;;
;; POSITIVE-INTEGER-STREAM produces a stream of
;; positive integers on demand.
;;;;;;;;;;;;;;;;;;;;;;;;;;;;;;;;;;;;;;;;;;;;;;;;;

(define positive-integer-stream
  (letrec ((next
             (lambda (n)
               (cons n (delay (next (+ n 1)))))))
    (next 1)))


;;;;;;;;;;;;;;;;;;;;;;;;;;;;;;;;;;;;;;;;;
;; HEAD returns the head of a stream.
;;;;;;;;;;;;;;;;;;;;;;;;;;;;;;;;;;;;;;;;;

(define head car)

;;;;;;;;;;;;;;;;;;;;;;;;;;;;;;;;;;;;;;;;;;;;
;; TAIL forces additional computation of
;; the stream.
;;;;;;;;;;;;;;;;;;;;;;;;;;;;;;;;;;;;;;;;;;;;
```

```
(define tail
  (lambda (stream)
    (force (cdr stream))))
```

A **letrec** is used to create a stream in the form of a pair:

```
(<number> . <promise>)
```

where the car component is an integer and the cdr component is a promise to compute additional elements of the stream. Subsequent elements in the stream are produced on demand by calling **tail** which forces the computation. In this manner, no more of the stream need be generated than is required for a particular application.

Streams have many utilities that are beyond the scope of this text. As an exercise, and to make sure you understand this particular implementation of a stream, write the function **one-to-n** that prints the positive integers between 1 and **n**, where **n** is a parameter. Of course, the point here is to use the stream to produce the integers – don't use a **do**. The stream may be set up either internal or external to **one-to-n**. Preferably, **one-to-n** should have only one parameter, **n**. That is, the use of a stream to implement **one-to-n** should remain transparent.

Chapter 17

Scheme Programming Examples

17.1 Introduction

In this chapter we present examples that are on average more extensive than in previous chapters. For clarity, each example is given in a separate section. The examples vary considerably with respect to topic and length. In some cases an example is provided primarily to illustrate a specific feature of Scheme; in others, the focus is more on the topic and its implementation using Scheme.

17.2 Latent Typing

In this text we've dealt informally with Scheme's method for determining the (data) type of identifiers, i.e., integer, real, continuation, procedure, etc. In this section, we explore Scheme's latent typing in more detail and provide a specific example of the power it provides.

Formally, Scheme employs what is generally called *latent typing*. That is, Scheme builds executable code that must determine the type of an identifier at run-time. In contrast, languages that employ strong, compile-time typing, e.g., Pascal, build code that assumes a particular data type. For example, consider the following function written in Pascal.

```
function Square(N: integer): integer;
  begin
    Square := N * N;
  end;
```

In Pascal, each parameter is listed along with its data type in parentheses following the function name, e.g.,

```
function <function-name>(<parm>:<type>...): <function-type>
```

In addition, the data type of the value returned by the function must be specified also.

Let's consider the significance of such typing. For the preceding example the implication is that we may need sibling functions—a "square" function for each type of number to be squared. In particular, for **Square** the function call

```
Square(3.01)
```

will fail due to a type mismatch, integer versus real. On the other hand, if it's known that **Square** will always be called with an integer argument and always return an integer result, this approach allows the compiler to produce very efficient code. A somewhat unrelated point is that this type of strong typing leads to inconsistencies between Pascal primitives and user-defined functions; i.e., some operators (functions) accept multiple data types, others do not.

The main point is that trade-offs are involved in choosing one language over another. As Scheme programmers, we are free to write a simple function for squaring a number, without having to deal with the issue of data type. The price we pay for this freedom is the presence of run-time code for accommodating various data types, even though we may never do anything other than square integers.

There are, however, other important advantages to latent typing beyond simple numerical applications. Specifically, latent typing in conjunction with type-checking predicates, e.g., **integer?**, **real?**, and so on, and other type-sensitive predicates, e.g., **=**, **char=?**, **string=?**, etc., allows the programmer to write generalized procedures that are impossible in many other languages.

As an example, we can develop a sort routine that works with integers, strings, and characters. Consider **g-bubble!**.

```
;;;;     bubble.s     ;;;;;;;;;;;;;;;;;;;;;;;;;;;;;;;;;;;;;;;;

;;;;;;;;;;;;;;;;;;;;;;;;;;;;;;;;;;;;;;;;;;;;;;;;;;;;;;
;; G-BUBBLE! sorts a vector using a primitive
;; bubble sorting technique, i.e., it always performs
;; every cycle.  The sorting is done destructively.
;; Also, several data types are accommodated.
;;;;;;;;;;;;;;;;;;;;;;;;;;;;;;;;;;;;;;;;;;;;;;;;;;;;;;

(define (g-bubble! vec)
  (let ((proper-order?
          (cond
            ((char? (vector-ref vec 0))
             char<?)
            ((string? (vector-ref vec 0))
```

```
            string<?)
          (else
            <))))

  (let ((temp ())
        (last-pos (- (vector-length vec) 1)))
    (do ((i 0 (+ i 1)))
        ((= i last-pos) vec)
        (do ((j 0 (+ j 1)))
            ((= j (- last-pos i)) "")    ;nothing to return
            (if (not (proper-order?
                         (vector-ref vec j)
                         (vector-ref vec (+ j 1))))
                (begin
                  (set! temp (vector-ref vec j))
                  (vector-set!
                    vec j (vector-ref vec (+ j 1)))
                  (vector-set! vec (+ j 1) temp))))))))
```

g-bubble! is a variation on **bubble!**, which was discussed in a previous chapter. Again, the vector data structure is used to implement a primitive bubble sort. (This sorting application is used simply as a vehicle for discussing latent typing; we are not concerned with the efficiency of a bubble sort at this point.)

g-bubble! illustrates that Scheme's flexibility with respect to latent typing allows the programmer to build powerful applications with a minimal amount of coding. In developing a sort routine, the typical obstacles to writing a generalized program, with respect to programming languages, are:

1. fixed size data structures
2. fixed typing of data structures
3. inflexibility of programming language operators

In the case of (1), run-time checking of data structures extends to size as well as type. Hence, in

```
(define (g-bubble! vec) ...
```

the parameter **vec** can represent a vector of any length. **g-bubble!** merely has to determine a vector's length at run-time using **vector-length**. Note that for simplicity in our code, we have not included error checking for an empty vector.

Cases (2) and (3) are interrelated with respect to Scheme of course. First, the function definition requires no specification of **vec**'s type, and second, Scheme predicates can be used to determine the proper operator:

```
...
...

(let ((proper-order?
        (cond
          ((char? (vector-ref vec 0))
           char<?)
          ((string? (vector-ref vec 0))
           string<?)
          (else
            <))))
...
...
```

Our approach in this example is to define a predicate for testing sort order. There are many ways to set up the sort predicate; here, we equate **proper-order?** to the Scheme primitive **char<?**, **string<?**, or **<**, depending on data type. Perhaps a more elegant approach would be to formally define a function that determines the proper sort predicate, returning the predicate as a function; we take this approach in a later section on sorting. Another alternative would be to set up the sort function with a parameter representing the sort predicate – requiring the user to pass an extra parameter.

In any case, the power behind Scheme's first-class procedures is evident. That is, with no hassles whatsoever, we can assign one procedure to another, either inside the sort procedure or via argument/parameter passing.

17.3 Representing Trees in Scheme

As with other programming languages, Scheme provides several methods for representing high-level data structures such as stacks and trees. For example, in Scheme, trees could be represented using:

1. vectors – each vector element representing a tree node
2. association lists – each sublist representing a tree node
3. nested lists – each nesting level representing a subtree.

In this section we investigate implementation method (3); methods (1) and (2) are left as exercises.

We mentioned earlier that the common list data structure, a fundamental component of all list processing languages, is internally represented as a binary tree. That particular usage of trees is of no particular concern at this point. The use of trees by Scheme to implement list structures should not be confused with a programmer's use of Scheme lists for a particular application, say, to represent a canine database – even when that application involves trees.

Consider the binary tree in Figure 17.1. A common method of representing such a tree is with nested lists, such that each nesting level represents a subtree:

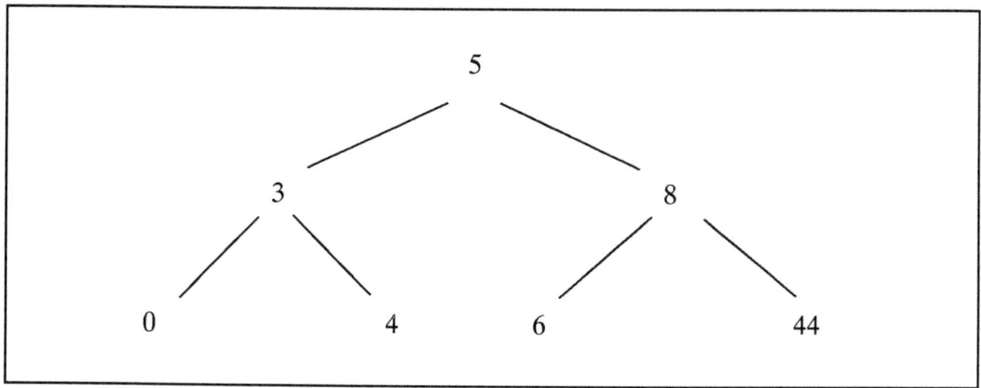

Figure 17.1 A Binary Tree

'(5 (3 (0 () ()) (4 () ())) (8 (6 () ()) (44 () ())))))

If the parentheses appear overwhelming, note that we don't normally need to work directly with the tree in this form. That is, we can easily write Scheme functions for all tree management operations, including tree creation—thus parenthesis balancing is performed automatically by our routines.

Consider the nested parentheses and their relationship to the above tree:

```
'(5
   (3                   ;;left subtree of 5
     (0 () ())          ;;
     (4 () ()))         ;;
;;
   (8                   ;;right subtree of 5
     (6 () ())          ;;
     (44 () ()))))      ;;
```

In our version we've represented nodes in the form:

```
(<node-value> <left-subtree> <right-subtree>)
```

where **<node-value>** is the information to be stored in the node, e.g., a atom, list, or vector, and **<left-subtree>** and **<right-subtree>** represent additional nodes, in a recursive manner. For terminal nodes we've used "nil", i.e., "()" (Scheme's representation of false), to signify absence of a child node, i.e., to terminate the recursion.

This form of nested representation with lists is convenient for developing tree manipulation/access functions. For example, the left and right subtrees of a given node can be retrieved with the following functions, respectively.

```
;;;;     trees.s     ;;;;;;;;;;;;;;;;;;;;;;;;;;;;;;;;;;;;;;;;;;;;;;
```

```
;;;;;;;;;;;;;;;;;;;;;;;;;;;;;;;;;;;
;; Common tree access functions.
;;;;;;;;;;;;;;;;;;;;;;;;;;;;;;;;;;;

(define (left-subtree tree)
  (cadr tree))

(define (right-subtree tree)
  (caddr tree))
```

Also, the "data" component of a node is simply the **car** of the node:

```
(define (current-node tree)
  (car tree))
```

Lastly, we can build a new node with **list**:

```
(define (build-node node left-tree right-tree)
  (list node left-tree right-tree))
```

An important point is that our functions, in conjunction with our tree representation (even with this simple approach), are useful for promoting data and procedure abstraction. According to modern programming philosophy, it is important to provide mnemonically meaningful identifiers for these simple operations, either in the form of functions or macros. This approach allows the programmer to abstract away from the lower-level details of list structures and list manipulation functions. With this abstraction mechanism, the programmer can concentrate on the higher level tree data structure and associated functions. As further evidence of our abstraction mechanism, consider the following code which allows us to build a tree, simply by specifying a list as an argument to **build-tree**.

```
;;;;    trees.s    ;;;;;;;;;;;;;;;;;;;;;;;;;;;;;;;;;;;;;;;;;;;;

;;;;;;;;;;;;;;;;;;;;;;;;;;;;;;;;;;;;;;;;;;;;;;;;;;;;;;;;;;;;;;;;;;;;;;
;; BUILD-TREE builds a binary tree from each element of a list
;; by repeatedly calling INSERT-TREE to build up the tree.
;; There is no attempt to maintain a balanced tree.
;;;;;;;;;;;;;;;;;;;;;;;;;;;;;;;;;;;;;;;;;;;;;;;;;;;;;;;;;;;;;;;;;;;;;;

(define (build-tree lst)
  (let build-loop ((lst lst) (bin-tree '()))
    (if (null? lst)
        bin-tree
        (build-loop (cdr lst)
                    (insert-tree (car lst) bin-tree)))))
```

```
;;;;;;;;;;;;;;;;;;;;;;;;;;;;;;;;;;;;;;;;;;;;;;;;;;;;;
;; INSERT-TREE adds a new node to a binary tree.
;;;;;;;;;;;;;;;;;;;;;;;;;;;;;;;;;;;;;;;;;;;;;;;;;;;;;

(define (insert-tree element tree)
  (cond
    ((null? tree)
     (build-node element '() '()))
    ((< element (current-node tree))
     (build-node (current-node tree)
                 (insert-tree element (left-subtree tree))
                 (right-subtree tree)))
    ((> element (current-node tree))
     (build-node (current-node tree)
                 (left-subtree tree)
                 (insert-tree element (right-subtree tree))))
    ((= element (current-node tree))
     (build-node (current-node tree)
                 (insert-tree element (left-subtree tree))
(right-subtree tree)))))
```

build-tree takes a list as an argument and uses cdr recursion to iterate over the list, calling **insert-tree** to insert each new node into the tree.

In our case, we've chosen to build an ordered tree – ordered in the sense that for each subtree node its left subtree represents nodes with data values that are less than or equal to its data value, and its right subtree represents nodes with data values that are greater than its data value. Although this ordering is totally arbitrary, it has proven useful in many computer science applications.

In general, there are many uses for binary trees in computer applications, especially in AI, database, and systems programming. Regardless of the application, a common task is to traverse a tree, in an application-specific manner, processing data stored at each node. By taking advantage of the recursive nature of our implementation of trees, it is easy to develop tree traversal functions. The following functions perform traditional preorder, postorder, and inorder traversal, respectively. A fourth function, **visit**, is a place-holder for a data processing task associated with each tree node. The previous example tree is also defined.

```
;;;;    trees.s    ;;;;;;;;;;;;;;;;;;;;;;;;;;;;;;;;;;;;;;;;

;;;;;;;;;;;;;;;;;;;;;;;;;;;;;;;;;;;;;;;;;;;;;;;;;;;;;;
;; This file contains data and program structures
;; associated with binary tree representations.
;;;;;;;;;;;;;;;;;;;;;;;;;;;;;;;;;;;;;;;;;;;;;;;;;;;;;;
```

```
;;;;;;;;;;;;;;;;;;;;;;;;;;;;;;;;;;;;;;;;;;;;;;;;;;;;;;;;;;;;;;;;;
;; NUMBER-TREE is a binary tree represented in list form.
;;;;;;;;;;;;;;;;;;;;;;;;;;;;;;;;;;;;;;;;;;;;;;;;;;;;;;;;;;;;;;;;;

(define number-tree
  '(5 (3 (0 () ()) (4 () ()))
      (8 (6 () ()) (44 () ()))))


;;;;;;;;;;;;;;;;;;;;;;;;;;;;;;;;;;;;;;;;;;;;;;;;;;;;;;;;;;;;;;;;;
;; PRE-ORDER-TRAVERSAL performs a preorder traversal of a
;; binary tree; each node's data is printed during the
;; traversal.
;;;;;;;;;;;;;;;;;;;;;;;;;;;;;;;;;;;;;;;;;;;;;;;;;;;;;;;;;;;;;;;;;

(define (pre-order-traversal tree)
  (if (null? tree)
      #t
      (begin
        (visit tree)
        (pre-order-traversal (left-subtree tree))
        (pre-order-traversal (right-subtree tree)))))


;;;;;;;;;;;;;;;;;;;;;;;;;;;;;;;;;;;;;;;;;;;;;;;;;;;;;;;;;;;;;;;;;;
;; POST-ORDER-TRAVERSAL performs a postorder traversal of a
;; binary tree; each node's data is printed during the
;; traversal.
;;;;;;;;;;;;;;;;;;;;;;;;;;;;;;;;;;;;;;;;;;;;;;;;;;;;;;;;;;;;;;;;;;

(define (post-order-traversal tree)
  (if (null? tree)
      #t
      (begin
        (post-order-traversal (left-subtree tree))
        (post-order-traversal (right-subtree tree))
        (visit tree))))


;;;;;;;;;;;;;;;;;;;;;;;;;;;;;;;;;;;;;;;;;;;;;;;;;;;;;;;;;;;;;;;;
;; IN-ORDER-TRAVERSAL performs an inorder traversal of a
;; binary tree; each node's data is printed during the
;; traversal.
;;;;;;;;;;;;;;;;;;;;;;;;;;;;;;;;;;;;;;;;;;;;;;;;;;;;;;;;;;;;;;;;
```

```
(define (in-order-traversal tree)
  (if (null? tree)
      #t
      (begin
        (in-order-traversal (left-subtree tree))
        (visit tree)
        (in-order-traversal (right-subtree tree)))))


;;;;;;;;;;;;;;;;;;;;;;;;;;;;;;;;;;;;;;;;;;;;;;;;;;;;;
;; VISIT represents a function that processes data
;; stored in each tree node.
;;;;;;;;;;;;;;;;;;;;;;;;;;;;;;;;;;;;;;;;;;;;;;;;;;;;;

(define (visit tree)
  (display (current-node tree))
  (display #\newline))
```

As you probably recall, a preorder traversal dictates that for a given node the subtree root is visited before visiting subordinate subtrees. Likewise, in a postorder traversal of a tree each subtree is visited before the subtree root; and in an inorder traversal the subtree root is visited between visits to left and right subtrees.

The following Scheme session illustrates these functions.

```
[1] (load "trees.s")
OK
[2] number-tree
(5 (3 (0 () ()) (4 () ())) (8 (6 () ()) (44 () ())))
[3] (current-node number-tree)
5
[4] (left-subtree number-tree)
(3 (0 () ()) (4 () ()))
[5] (right-subtree number-tree)
(8 (6 () ()) (44 () ()))
[6] (left-subtree (left-subtree number-tree))
(0 () ())
[7] (build-tree '(5 3 8))
(5 (3 () ()) (8 () ()))
[8] (build-tree '(5 8 3))
(5 (3 () ()) (8 () ()))
[9] number-tree
(5 (3 (0 () ()) (4 () ())) (8 (6 () ()) (44 () ())))
[10] (build-tree '(5 3 4 0 8 6 44))
(5 (3 (0 () ()) (4 () ())) (8 (6 () ()) (44 () ())))
[11] (build-tree '(0 3 4 5 6 8 44))
(0 () (3 () (4 () (5 () (6 () (8 () (44 () ())))))))
```

```
[12] (pre-order-traversal number-tree)
5
3
0
4
8
6
44
#T
[13] (post-order-traversal number-tree)
0
4
3
6
44
8
5
[14] (in-order-traversal number-tree)
0
3
4
5
6
8
44
#T
[15] (exit)
```

As you may also recall, an inorder traversal of an ordered tree (that is, ordered in the manner described previously) produces the data in sorted order (see prompt [14]). We will use this feature in the next section in a sorting application. Other applications of trees are left as exercises.

17.4 Sorting with Scheme

In this section the focus is partly sorting and partly the interaction between a particular language, Scheme, and a specific use of that language. That is, we aren't so much interested in sorting per se, as we are in the issues that arise in using Scheme to develop applications; sorting does, however, provide a mechanism for exploring selected Scheme programming issues.

Earlier we used sorting functions to illustrate two features of Scheme: vectors and latent typing. In both cases, a simple bubble sort served our purposes quite well. More pertinent questions at this point include:

Sort Cycle	Unsorted List	Sorted List
Initial	(1 8 4 9 2)	()
1	(1 8 4 9 2)	(1)
2	(1 8 4 9 2)	(1 8)
3	(1 8 4 9 2)	(1 4 8)
4	(1 8 4 9 2)	(1 4 8 9)
5	(1 8 4 9 2)	(1 2 4 8 9)

Figure 17.2 Linear Insertion Sort

1. Are some sorting techniques more appropriate than others?
2. Are some data structures more appropriate than others?
3. How does accommodating multiple data types impact sorting efficiency?

Although we can by no means provide an exhaustive treatment of these questions in this section, it is reasonable to provide several sort functions that partially address such issues. Moreover, it is impossible to say which sorting technique is best, and in conjunction with which data structure – this of course depends on many things such as the application, the "unsortedness" of the data on average, and the cost/benefit ratio of programmer time versus sort routine development time. Ultimately, the programmer must decide on a sorting technique, often based on experience. The following routines raise several points; you are encouraged to explore these issues in more detail using a particular Scheme system.

Having already explored the bubble sort, we now consider another common sorting technique, the insertion sort, illustrated in Figure 17.2. An insertion sort can be implemented with either lists or vectors; in describing the algorithm we arbitrarily choose a list representation. Initially, an unsorted list is provided as an argument to an insertion sort routine, i.e., the input list. The sorted, or output, list is built up one element at a time by cycling through the input list. Each cycle examines the next element in the input list and *inserts* it in the output list in the proper position.

Subsequent to cycle 1 (where an element is inserted into an empty list), an insertion can occur: (1) before the first element in the output list, (2) at the end of the output list, or (3) between output list elements. The most straightforward way to perform such insertions is by **cons** and **append** operations, e.g., for case (3), consing the current input list element onto the sublist that represents the second "half" of the new output list, and then appending this list to the sublist for the first "half" of output list.

Scheme, however, does not provide a function for splitting a list in this manner; hence, it's necessary to iterate over the list using cdr recursion to build up the first sublist by extracting elements from the second sublist. The following code illustrates.

```
;;;;    ins-sort.s    ;;;;;;;;;;;;;;;;;;;;;;;;;;;;;;;;;;;;;;;;;;

;;;;;;;;;;;;;;;;;;;;;;;;;;;;;;;;;;;;;;;;;;;;;;;
;; INS-SORT performs a simple insertion sort.
;;;;;;;;;;;;;;;;;;;;;;;;;;;;;;;;;;;;;;;;;;;;;;;

(define (ins-sort lst)

;;;;;;;;;;;;;;;;;;;;;;;;;;;;;;;;;;;;;;;;;;;;;;;;;;;;;;;;;;;;;;;;
;; INSERT-ELEMENT inserts an element into a list in the
;; specified position.
;;;;;;;;;;;;;;;;;;;;;;;;;;;;;;;;;;;;;;;;;;;;;;;;;;;;;;;;;;;;;;;;

(define (insert-element new-element lst)
  (let ((proper-order?                          ;ordering operator
          (cond
            ((char? new-element)                ;characters
             char<?)
            ((string? new-element)              ;strings
             string<?)
            (else                               ;else--assume
              <))))                             ;      numeric

    (let insert-loop ((new-list '()) (old-list lst))
      (cond
        ((null? old-list)
         (append new-list (list new-element)))
        ((proper-order? new-element (car old-list))
         (append new-list (cons new-element old-list)))
        (else
          (insert-loop (append new-list (list (car old-list)))
                       (cdr old-list)))))))

;;;;    end internal definitions    ;;;;;;;;;;;;;;;;;;;;;;;;;;;

  (let get-next ((unsorted-list lst) (sorted-list '()))
    (cond
      ((null? unsorted-list)
       sorted-list)
      (else
```

```
        (get-next
          (cdr unsorted-list)
          (insert-element (car unsorted-list) sorted-list))))))
```

ins-sort uses cdr recursion to iterate over each element of the unsorted list; this occurs in the named **let**, **get-next**. Each element is stripped from the input list and passed to **insert-element** where it is inserted into the output list in the proper position. In **insert-element** a **cond** is used to test for insertion at the end of the sorted list or insertion in the "middle" of the sorted list; the **else** clause is used to transfer elements from the incoming sorted list to the outgoing sorted list.

From a performance perspective, we can see intuitively that a simple, linear insertion sort isn't going to be very efficient due to the constant consing action. On the other hand, it may be adequate in many circumstances, and it requires very little in the way of programmer development time.

An alternative approach would be to implement the insertion sort with vectors:

```
;;;;    i-sort.s    ;;;;;;;;;;;;;;;;;;;;;;;;;;;;;;;;;;;;;;;;;;;;;

;;;;;;;;;;;;;;;;;;;;;;;;;;;;;;;;;;;;;;;;;;;;;;;;;;;;;;;
;; I-SORT performs a simple insertion sort.
;;;;;;;;;;;;;;;;;;;;;;;;;;;;;;;;;;;;;;;;;;;;;;;;;;;;;;;;

(define (i-sort in-vec)

  ;;;;;;;;;;;;;;;;;;;;;;;;;;;;;;;;;;;;;;;;;;;;;;;;;;;;;;;;;;;;;;;
  ;; FIND-POS searches a vector for an insertion point.
  ;;;;;;;;;;;;;;;;;;;;;;;;;;;;;;;;;;;;;;;;;;;;;;;;;;;;;;;;;;;;;;;
  (define (find-pos element vec last-pos order-predicate)
    (let find-loop ((i 0))
      (cond
        ((= i last-pos) i)
        ((order-predicate element (vector-ref vec i)) i)
        (else (find-loop (+ i 1))))))

  ;;;;;;;;;;;;;;;;;;;;;;;;;;;;;;;;;;;;;;;;;;;;;;;;;;;;;;;;;;;;;;;;;;;
  ;; DETERMINE-ORDER-PREDICATE returns the proper ordering
  ;; predicate.
  ;;;;;;;;;;;;;;;;;;;;;;;;;;;;;;;;;;;;;;;;;;;;;;;;;;;;;;;;;;;;;;;;;;;
  (define (determine-order-predicate element)
    (cond
      ((char? element) char<?)
      ((string? element) string<?)
      (else <)))

;;;;    end internal definitions    ;;;;;;;;;;;;;;;;;;;;;;;;;;;;;;
```

```
  (do ((n 0 (+ n 1))
       (out-vec (make-vector (vector-length in-vec))))
      ((= n (vector-length in-vec)) out-vec)
      (do ((j n (- j 1)))                              ;;loop to
          ((= j (find-pos (vector-ref in-vec n)        ;;shuffle
                          out-vec                      ;;elements
                          n                            ;;forward
                          (determine-order-predicate
                            (vector-ref in-vec 0)))))
           (vector-set! out-vec j (vector-ref in-vec n)))
          (vector-set! out-vec
                       j
                       (vector-ref out-vec (- j 1))))))
```

The main focus of **i-sort** is a straightforward implementation of an insertion sort using Scheme vectors. We've followed the standard algorithm found in data structures textbooks; namely, insertion of a new element in the vector is performed after the appropriate elements have been copied forward one position (refer to Figure 17.2). **find-pos** is used to find the point of insertion of the next element. Subsequently, a **do** is used to perform the iteration required to move the elements forward.

Of secondary importance is the code provided to allow multiple data types. Again, the intent here is not an exhaustive comparison of sorting techniques. With this in mind, we've used a different approach for handling multiple data types – purely for illustration. In previous sorting routines, we've defined an ordering predicate internal to the sorting routine and assigned it the proper Scheme predicate, e.g., **char=?**, **string=?**, etc. In this case, we've set up a separate function, **determine-order-predicate**, in order to illustrate a function returning a function.

For the Scheme system used in this text, **i-sort** is considerably slower than any sorting routines we've used so far. You may find it interesting to experiment with list versus vector implementations using your Scheme system. One important consideration is how many times the call to **determine-order-predicate** is made within the nested **dos**, i.e., how extensive is the optimization?

As a final example of sorting, let's consider a binary tree sort, which is a generalization of insertion sort, i.e., a non-linear insertion sort. At this point we consider a simple binary tree sort using the binary tree structure and algorithms discussed earlier.

A binary tree structure is typically used for storage and retrieval of individual data items. For example, in a database application each record can be stored as a node in a binary tree and new records can be inserted periodically. In this case, retrieval of data for an individual record is quite efficient, since each advance from one tree node to a child node reduces the search space considerably (depending on balance characteristics of the tree).

On the other hand, a binary tree sort application is not as cost effective as a database application – in a relative sense. Specifically, each time the data is sorted, (1) a binary tree must be built, and (2) traversed to retrieve items in sorted order. That is, the advantage afforded by a binary tree sort, in comparison to a linear insertion sort, occurs during tree building and not during data retrieval, since every item in the tree must be retrieved. On average, assuming that the unsorted data is in random order, insertion of data elements into a binary tree will be faster than insertion into an ordered linear list. Thus, a binary tree sort achieves a performance advantage over a linear insertion sort largely because it is more efficient to build and connect nodes than to append and cons together lists.

The following binary tree sort program, **b-sort**, makes use of the Scheme code for binary trees from an earlier section. (For convenience, we've included all the necessary routines from our earlier coverage of trees.)

```
;;;;    b-sort.s    ;;;;;;;;;;;;;;;;;;;;;;;;;;;;;;;;;;;;;;;;;;

;;;;;;;;;;;;;;;;;;;;;;;;;;;;;;;;;;;;;;;;;;;;;;;;;;;;;
;; B-SORT performs a binary tree sort using list
;; data structures.
;;;;;;;;;;;;;;;;;;;;;;;;;;;;;;;;;;;;;;;;;;;;;;;;;;;;;

(define (b-sort lst)

  ;;;;;;;;;;;;;;;;;;;;;;;;;;;;;;;;;;;;;;;;;;;;;;;;;;;;;;;;;;;
  ;; BUILD-LIST performs an inorder traversal of a binary
  ;; tree; for each node visited a new element is added to
  ;; SORTED-LIST.
  ;;;;;;;;;;;;;;;;;;;;;;;;;;;;;;;;;;;;;;;;;;;;;;;;;;;;;;;;;;;

  (define (build-list tree)
    (let ((sorted-list '()))
      (let traverse ((tree tree))
        (if (null? tree)
            sorted-list
            (begin
              (traverse (left-subtree tree))
              (set! sorted-list
                    (append sorted-list
                            (list (current-node tree))))
              (traverse (right-subtree tree)))))))

  ;;;;;;;;;;;;;;;;;;;;;;;;;;;;;;;;;;;;;;;;;;;;;;;;;;;;;;;;;;;;;;;;
  ;; BUILD-TREE builds a binary tree from each element of a list
  ;; by repeatedly calling INSERT-TREE to build up the tree.
  ;;;;;;;;;;;;;;;;;;;;;;;;;;;;;;;;;;;;;;;;;;;;;;;;;;;;;;;;;;;;;;;;

  (define (build-tree lst)
    (let build-loop ((lst lst) (bin-tree '()))
      (if (null? lst)
          bin-tree
          (build-loop (cdr lst)
```

```
                         (insert-tree (car lst) bin-tree)))))

;;;;;;;;;;;;;;;;;;;;;;;;;;;;;;;;;;;;;;;;;;;;;;;;;;;;;;;;;;;;;;;;;;;;
;; INSERT-TREE adds a new node to a binary tree.  There is no
;; balancing; the worst-case scenario is a degenerate tree.
;;;;;;;;;;;;;;;;;;;;;;;;;;;;;;;;;;;;;;;;;;;;;;;;;;;;;;;;;;;;;;;;;;;;

(define (insert-tree element tree)
  (cond
    ((null? tree)
     (build-node element '() '()))
    ((< element (current-node tree))
     (build-node (current-node tree)
                 (insert-tree element (left-subtree tree))
                 (right-subtree tree)))
((> element (current-node tree))
     (build-node (current-node tree)
                 (left-subtree tree)
                 (insert-tree element (right-subtree tree))))
    ((= element (current-node tree))
     (build-node (current-node tree)
                 (insert-tree element (left-subtree tree))
                 (right-subtree tree)))))

;;;;;;;;;;;;;;;;;;;;;;;;;;;;;;;;;;;;
;; Common tree access functions.
;;;;;;;;;;;;;;;;;;;;;;;;;;;;;;;;;;;;

(define (left-subtree tree)
  (cadr tree))

(define (right-subtree tree)
  (caddr tree))

(define (current-node tree)
  (car tree))

(define (build-node node left-tree right-tree)
  (list node left-tree right-tree))

;;;;    end internal definitions    ;;;;;;;;;;;;;;;;;;;;;;;;;;;;

  (build-list (build-tree lst)))    ;; body of B-SORT
```

The driver function **b-sort** defines several internal functions for each tree-related task. The body of **b-sort** consists of an application of **build-list** to the tree returned by

build-tree. Recall that **build-tree** produces a binary tree by repeated insertion of elements using **insert-tree**. In an earlier section we demonstrated that an inorder traversal of an (ordered) binary tree produces the elements in sorted order. Thus for each node visited, **build-list** appends the current element to the end of **sorted-list**.

As we discussed earlier, strict comparisons of the bubble, linear insertion, and binary tree sorts aren't appropriate because of various differences in each example, such as how we accommodate multiple data types. Nevertheless, in comparison, the bubble sort and the binary tree gave about the same performance using our system, PC Scheme, whereas the insertion sort (both versions) was much slower.

The slowness of the insertion-sort implementation is as expected, in one case, due to the frequent consing. The performance of the binary tree sort is dependent on the "unsortedness" of the data. If the data is perfectly sorted, either ascending or descending sort order, the tree (in essence) degenerates into a linear list. In this case, the number of comparison operations during insertion is high on average, and the performance can be worse than a simpler sorting technique, say, a bubble sort. You may find it interesting to make comparisons among these sort utilities, and among variations of your own design, especially one that you develop with performance, and not demonstration, in mind.

17.5 format: A Utility for Column-formatted Output

In this section we present an alternate version of the **format** utility, which we defined in an earlier chapter. The main focus in this section is extending the utility of **format** to allow column formatting. However, our program does demonstrate one technique that we haven't used so far, namely, passing a port as an argument.

Common LISP (Steele, 1984) provides a formatted output function, **format**. The complexity and power of Common LISP's **format** can only be appreciated after hours of perusal of the reference manual. In this section we will be content with extending our previous version of **format** to support simple left- and right-justified column output. (See the exercises.)

The following Scheme session illustrates our extension to **format**.

```
[1] (load "jformat.s")
OK
[2] (format "~%")                    ;same as before

[3] (format "~10a|" 12345)           ;left-justified in ten columns
12345     |
[4] (format "~10@a|" 12345)          ;right-justified in ten columns
     12345|
[5] (exit)
```

That is, in our version of **format**, an "~a" (ASCII) format directive may optionally contain column directives in the following form:

```
~<field-width><right-justify-directive>a
```

where the **<right-justify-directive>** is an at-sign (@).

Extracting the field width specification and the optional right-justification control character is the principal task that must be addressed in extending **format**. In essence, we must introduce code to perform a simple *parse*, or breakdown, of an "~a" directive.

The approach that we take here is to build a list containing two pieces of vital information:

<field-spec> ::= (<field-width-string> <justify-char>)

where **<field-width-string>** is the field width in string form and **<justify-char>** is an indicator variable for whether or not right justification is required. Let's call this simple, list data structure **<field-spec>** for convenience (the "::=" means "stands for"). **<field-spec>** can be built by the following code.

```
;;;;;;;;;;;;;;;;;;;;;;;;;;;;;;;;;;;;;;;;;;;;;;;;;;;;;;;;;;;;;
;; GET-FIELD-SPEC searches forward in the format control
;; string extracting all characters up to the "a", or the
;; "@" in the case of right justification.  A list is
;; returned of the form: (<field-width-str> <just-char>).
;;;;;;;;;;;;;;;;;;;;;;;;;;;;;;;;;;;;;;;;;;;;;;;;;;;;;;;;;;;;;

(define get-field-spec
  (lambda (first-char input-str)
    (let next-char
      ((field-width-str (make-string 1 first-char))
       (char (read-char input-str)))
      (cond
        ((char=? char #\a)
         (list field-width-str char))
        ((char=? char #\@)
         (read-char input-str)          ;; absorb the "a"
         (list field-width-str char))
        (else
         (next-char (string-append field-width-str
                                   (make-string 1 char))
                    (read-char input-str)))))))
```

Recall from our earlier implementation of **format** that the first character beyond each "~" is extracted to determine the type of formatting that will be required. Thus, for format directives containing a field width specification, it's necessary to restore the first character of **<field-width-string>**. This can be handled by calling **get-field-spec** with the first character as an argument. Other aspects of this function are discussed later.

To promote data and procedure abstraction, two access functions are established for operating on **<field-spec>**. The first function, **get-field-width**:

```
;;;;;;;;;;;;;;;;;;;;;;;;;;;;;;;;;;;;;;;;;;;;;;;;;;;;;;;;
;; GET-FIELD-WIDTH determines the width of the output
;; field.  See GET-FIELD-SPEC.
;;;;;;;;;;;;;;;;;;;;;;;;;;;;;;;;;;;;;;;;;;;;;;;;;;;;;;;;

(define get-field-width
  (lambda (field-spec)
    (str->int (car field-spec))))
```

extracts the field width from **<field-spec>** and returns the result of converting it to integer form, by calling **str->int** (which we developed in an earlier chapter).

The second function, a predicate named **right-justify?**, is used to determine whether or not right justification is required:

```
;;;;;;;;;;;;;;;;;;;;;;;;;;;;;;;;;;;;;;;;;;;;;;;;;;;;;;;;
;; RIGHT-JUSTIFY? determines if the output should be
;; right justified.  See GET-FIELD-SPEC.
;;;;;;;;;;;;;;;;;;;;;;;;;;;;;;;;;;;;;;;;;;;;;;;;;;;;;;;;

(define right-justify?
  (lambda (field-spec)
    (if (char=? (cadr field-spec) #\@)
        #t
        #f)))
```

right-justify? looks at the second element of **field-spec** to determine if it is a “@”, which indicates right justification. See **get-field-spec**.

Having looked at several of the major issues involved in parsing the field specification, let’s look at the entire, modified function, **format**.

```
;;;;    jformat.s    ;;;;;;;;;;;;;;;;;;;;;;;;;;;;;;;;;;;;;;

;;;;;;;;;;;;;;;;;;;;;;;;;;;;;;;;;;;;;;;;;;;;;;;;;;;;;;;;;;;
;; FORMAT is a subset of Common LISP's FORMAT.  There is no
;; error checking.  The "a" option may contain a minimum
;; column specification, with or without a "@" to signal
;; right justification, as in Common LISP.
;; Usage:  (format <control-str> [<arg1> <arg2> ... <argn>])
;; Returns:  nothing
;; Examples:
;;   (format "~%")                    ;output a newline
;;   (format "~10a" 12345)            ;left-justify in 10 cols.
;;   (format "~10@a" 12345)           ;right-justify in 10 cols.
```

```
;;
;; FORMAT uses the library module:  str-int.s
;;;;;;;;;;;;;;;;;;;;;;;;;;;;;;;;;;;;;;;;;;;;;;;;;;;;;;;;;;;;;;;

(define format
  (lambda (control-string . objects)

;;;;;;;;;;;;;;;;;;;;;;;;;;;;;;;;;;;;;;;;;;;;;;;;;;;;;;;;;;;;;;;
;; PARSE-COLUMN-FORMAT is called to extract a minimum column
;; specification for (a)scii output.  The numeric digits are
;; read in string form and then converted to an integer.
;; PARSE-COLUMN-FORMAT also processes the corresponding
;; argument and prints the output.
;;;;;;;;;;;;;;;;;;;;;;;;;;;;;;;;;;;;;;;;;;;;;;;;;;;;;;;;;;;;;;;

(define parse-column-format
  (lambda (first-char input-str print-item)
    (let* ((print-str (cond
                        ((char? print-item)
                         (make-string 1 print-item))
                        ((symbol? print-item)
                         (symbol->string print-item))
                        ((string? print-item)
                         print-item)
                        ((number? print-item)
                         (number->string print-item '(heur)))
                        (else ""))) ;;error--print as
                                    ;;       null string
           (prt-str-len (string-length print-str))
           (field-spec (get-field-spec first-char input-str))
           (field-width (get-field-width field-spec)))

      (if (> field-width prt-str-len)
          (if (right-justify? field-spec)
              (display (string-append
                         (make-string (- field-width prt-str-len)
                                      #\space)
                         print-str))
              (display (string-append
                         print-str
                         (make-string (- field-width prt-str-len)
                                      #\space))))
          (display print-str)))))

;;;;;;;;;;;;;;;;;;;;;;;;;;;;;;;;;;;;;;;;;;;;;;;;;;;;;;;;;;;;;;
;; GET-FIELD-SPEC searches forward in the format control
```

```
;; string extracting all characters up to the "a", or the
;; "@" in the case of right justification.  A list is
;; returned of the form: (<field-width-str> <just-char>).
;;;;;;;;;;;;;;;;;;;;;;;;;;;;;;;;;;;;;;;;;;;;;;;;;;;;;;;;;;;;

(define get-field-spec
  (lambda (first-char input-str)
    (let next-char
      ((field-width-str (make-string 1 first-char))
       (char (read-char input-str)))
      (cond
        ((char=? char #\a)
         (list field-width-str char))
        ((char=? char #\@)
         (read-char input-str)          ;; absorb the "a"
         (list field-width-str char))
        (else
         (next-char (string-append field-width-str
                                   (make-string 1 char))
                    (read-char input-str)))))))

;;;;;;;;;;;;;;;;;;;;;;;;;;;;;;;;;;;;;;;;;;;;;;;;;;;;;;;;;;
;; GET-FIELD-WIDTH determines the width of the output
;; field.  See GET-FIELD-SPEC.
;;;;;;;;;;;;;;;;;;;;;;;;;;;;;;;;;;;;;;;;;;;;;;;;;;;;;;;;;;

(define get-field-width
  (lambda (field-spec)
    (str->int (car field-spec))))

;;;;;;;;;;;;;;;;;;;;;;;;;;;;;;;;;;;;;;;;;;;;;;;;;;;;;;;;;
;; RIGHT-JUSTIFY? determines if the output should be
;; right justified.  See GET-FIELD-SPEC.
;;;;;;;;;;;;;;;;;;;;;;;;;;;;;;;;;;;;;;;;;;;;;;;;;;;;;;;;;

(define  right-justify?
  (lambda (field-spec)
    (if (char=? (cadr field-spec) #\@)
        #t
        #f)))

;;;;;;;;;;;;;;;;;;;;;;;;;;;;;;;;;;;;;;;;;;;;;;;;; main program ;;;;

    (let ((input-string (open-input-string control-string)))
      (let get-args ((c (read-char input-string)) (lst objects))
        (cond
```

```
((eof-object? c)
 (display ""))                              ;return nothing
((char=? c #\~)
 (let ((option (read-char input-string)))
   (cond
     ((char=? option #\a)
      (display (car lst))
      (get-args (read-char input-string) (cdr lst)))
     ((char=? option #\s)
      (write (car lst))
      (get-args (read-char input-string) (cdr lst)))
     ((char=? option #\c)
      (write-char (car lst))
      (get-args (read-char input-string) (cdr lst)))
     ((char=? option #\%)
      (newline)
      (get-args (read-char input-string) lst))
     ((char=? option #\~)
      (write-char #\~)
      (get-args (read-char input-string) lst))
     (else
       (parse-column-format option
                            input-string
                            (car lst))
       (get-args (read-char input-string)
                 (cdr lst))))))
(else
  (write-char c)
  (get-args (read-char input-string) lst)))))))
```

The function **parse-column-format** is the driver function for our enhancement to **format**. Much of the work in **parse-column-format** is performed via a sequential **let** (**let***). First, the argument to **format** that must be printed is converted to string form. Second, the length of the resulting string is captured in **prt-str-len** for future use. Third, using the technique described previously, all characters up to the final "a" in the ASCII directive, but excluding the optional right-justification directive, are captured as a string and stored as the first element in the list **field-spec**. The second element of **field-spec** is the indicator regarding right justification as mentioned. Fourth, **get-field-width** is used to extract the numeric field width; this value is stored in the local variable **field-width**. All of this activity is driven by the initialization phase of the **let***.

The body of the **let*** uses the information collected in the initialization phase to perform the actual printing. The printing is handled by **display**, in conjunction with conditional checks on field width for proper spacing. Note that if the output is larger than the field width specified by the user, **format** automatically extends the field width.

Lastly, note the use of **open-input-string**. The "main program" area of **format** opens the format control string as a string port. In many cases, this is preferable to using the standard string manipulation functions. Having done so, it is necessary to pass this port to **get-field-width**. In Scheme, passing ports is done exactly like passing any other variable—ports are treated as first-class data objects. Hence, in **get-field-width**, the string port goes by the name **input-str**, allowing us to pick up where we left off, namely, using **read-char** to extract characters from the format control string.

Exercises

1. Develop a variation on **g-bubble!** that requires the user to pass the ordering predicate as an argument, i.e.,

```
(g-bubble! <unsorted-vector> <ordering-predicate>)
```

For example, the user could sort a vector of strings by entering

```
(g-bubble! my-vector string<?)
```

2. Modify **g-bubble!** so that it uses a list instead of a vector.

3. Provide an association list implementation of a binary tree sort program. One way to accomplish this is by coding each sublist in the association list as a triple of the form

```
(<node> <left-node> <right-node>)
```

For example, the tree given in Figure 17.1, namely,

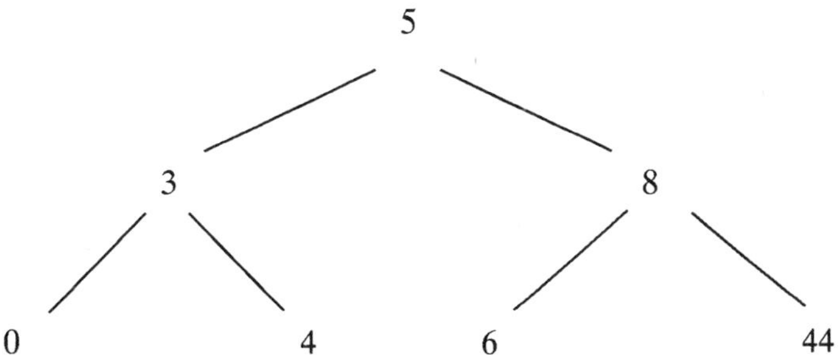

would be described by the association list

```
((5 3 8) (3 0 4) (8 6 44) (0 () ()) (4 () ()) (6 () ())
 (44 () ()))
```

Note carefully the required modification to all support routines.

4. Describe what steps would be required to implement the binary tree sort with a vector. Outline a specific approach.

5. Develop Exercise 4 as a Scheme program.

6. The quicksort algorithm is very common for sorting data. In fact, some language implementations provide it as a primitive. (Readers unfamiliar with the quicksort algorithm are referred to a data structures textbook.) Define **qsort!** as a sort utility based on the quicksort algorithm with two parameters: the vector to be sorted and the ordering predicate. That is, the call syntax would be analogous to that given in Exercise 1.

7. Study the language reference for Common LISP with regard to **format** (Steele, 1984). Develop your own version of **format** that is more extensive than the one provided in this chapter. Make your own decisions about how to extend **format**, but consider the following if you plan an extensive implementation.

format can be viewed as an interpreter in the sense that the control string, which can be quite complicated, must be, in essence, scanned and parsed in order to generate Scheme code that can be processed by your Scheme system. Thus, you may find it beneficial to develop **format** using software engineering principles and techniques that are appropriate for systems programming projects. Consider Beck (1985) for an introduction to these topics and Aho et al. (1986) for a more extensive treatment.

8. Taylor (1986a, 1986b) discusses implementation of an interpreter for the language PILOT (Starkweather, 1984). Develop your own interpreter for the core PILOT statements, as described by Taylor.

Chapter 18

A Mini-Database System

18.1 Introduction

In this chapter we present a simple database example for management of record album information. Although the term database is commonly used for the type of application developed here, our application is more appropriately called a file system; that is, there is only one file of information, not a collection of files – also, our system is tailored to this one application. (See the suggested readings for database and file system references.)

The album library system presented here is similar to, but considerably simpler than, several examples in Smith and Smith (1988). In particular, the present application uses simpler storage and retrieval techniques. However, the main focus of this section is how Scheme might be used to implement common file techniques. Scheme has features/characteristics that greatly facilitate the implementation of some aspects of the database program, and some characteristics that lead to extra programming, relative to other languages.

18.2 An Album Library System in Scheme

For our album library we maintain four items of information for each album in the library:

1. album title (the key)
2. artist
3. music type
4. price.

We refer to each collection of such information as a *database record*, even though it is not a record in the classical, computer science sense. In the general sense, each item in a record is referred to as a *field*, or an *attribute*. Attribute (1) is the *key*, that is, it serves to uniquely identify each record in the database. Attributes (2) through (4) are entirely arbitrary; a real application would typically have more attributes per database record.

The most straightforward way to represent such a record in standard Scheme is with a simple list organization:

```
("Closing Time" "Tom Waits" Rock 6.99)
```

Implementation note: Some Scheme systems may provide aggregate structures called records or structures as extensions to standard Scheme. In this case, their usage may be preferable, in terms of both performance and esthetics. Nevertheless, a simple list organization is perfectly adequate for this application.

The principal ramification of this representation is that the programmer must supply access functions to store, retrieve, modify, etc., each record. For example, with respect to coding abstraction, writing a function such as

```
(define (get-title album)
  (list-ref album 0))
```

is preferable to hard-coding **car**s, **cdr**s, etc., throughout the program code. In other words, **get-title** provides considerably more mnemonic value than: "(car album)". In the same manner, we can develop functions for all basic tasks against a record.

Having dealt with the organization of an individual record, let's consider organization of the database per se. Database and file system organization are major topics in computer science, and in general are beyond the scope of this text. However, for our purposes here, it is sufficient to pick a particular, common approach to database design, ignoring competing designs and their relative advantages and disadvantages. In particular, we implement our database system as a memory-resident hash file using a technique that is commonly called *open hashing*. (Aho et al. [1986] explains open hashing with respect to compiler symbol table design.) Open hashing and its implementation using Scheme are illustrated in Figure 18.1.

For our album library the database is implemented via a Scheme vector. Each vector element is organized as an association list and can accommodate multiple albums; hence, the term "open" hashing.

Hashing is a technique whereby a key is systematically mapped to a restricted (symbolic) address space. In the simplest applications, direct hashing can be employed. That is, key values must be compatible with address values. For example, if each item in a store inventory has a simple stock number, e.g., 1, 2, ..., these values can be directly mapped to storage addresses (vector elements). In our case, album titles are very different from vector index values, hence, an indirect hashing scheme is required. In particular, we must have an indirect translation, or mapping, of character strings

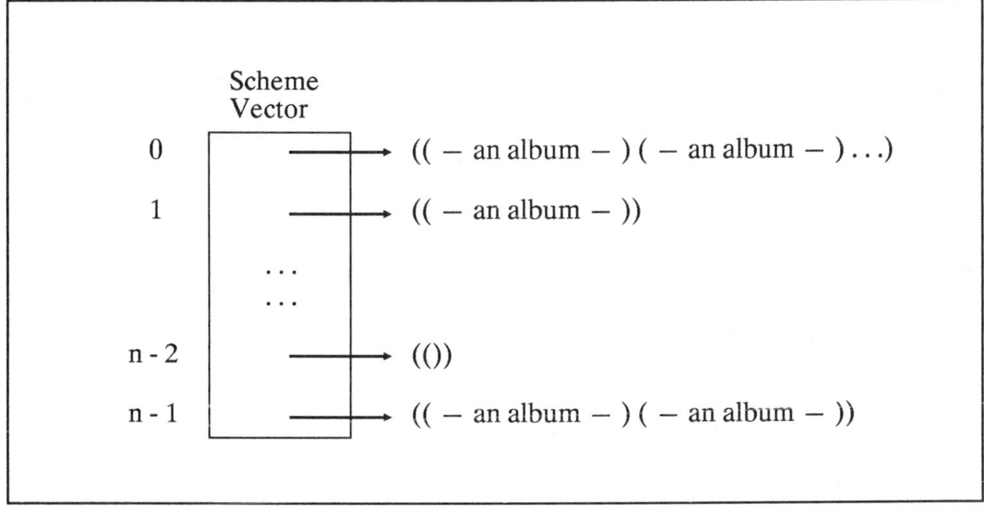

Figure 18.1 An Open Hashing Scheme

(album titles) to positions in a vector; functions that provide such a mapping are known as *hash functions*.

It's important to emphasize the reason for such a hashing scheme. First, essentially all activity against a database depends on storage and/or retrieval of individual records – in our case, database records containing album information. Thus, an efficient technique is required for storing new albums in the database, *and* for subsequent retrieval of albums for printing, updating, deleting, etc. Second, it is undesirable to add an artificial key such as album number to our database, in order to make key values and address values similar. That is, the user should be able to interact with the database in terms of the most logical attribute, album title.

Sequential storage and retrieval is inadequate for most real applications. As a result, hashing techniques have been developed that can retrieve a record in one or two disk accesses on average. Given the increasing usage of virtual storage (automatic caching of data between disk and internal memory) by hardware and software vendors, it is important to choose a reasonably efficient storage/retrieval technique.

For our application we need a hashing function that when applied to a character string generates an index value within the range of the vector used to implement the database. Again, there are many performance issues that must be considered in developing optimal hashing functions, all of which are beyond the scope of this text. Here, we use a common and intuitive hashing technique, as follows.

For our key-to-address translation there are two basic requirements:

1. converting from string to numeric data type
2. restricting numeric values to valid vector indexes.

Step (1) can be accomplished by first converting each character to an integer using **char->integer** and then summing the integers. For step (2), the **modulo** function can be applied to the resulting sum, using file (vector) size as the divisor.

Our address translation function, **hash**, is coded as follows.

```
;;;;;;;;;;;;;;;;;;;;;;;;;;;;;;;;;;;;;;;;;;;;;;;;;;;;;;;;;;
;; HASH hashes each album key by summing the ASCII
;; values for each character, modulo file size.
;;;;;;;;;;;;;;;;;;;;;;;;;;;;;;;;;;;;;;;;;;;;;;;;;;;;;;;;;;

(define (hash key)
  (let hash-it ((str-pos (- (string-length key) 1))
                (hash-value 0))
    (if (= str-pos -1)
        (modulo hash-value (file-size))
        (hash-it (- str-pos 1)
                 (+ hash-value
                    (char->integer
                      (string-ref key str-pos)))))))
```

We use a named **let** to control the iteration over each character in the string, summing the converted values into **hash-value**. When the end of the string is reached, **modulo** is applied to **hash- value** and the result of calling **file-size**, which determines the number of vector elements.

You may have noticed that this key-to-address translation scheme does not prevent what is often called record *colliding* (*collisions*). That is, two albums may hash to the same address. For example, two albums, one named "xyz" and the other named "zyx", would both hash to the same address given an arbitrary file size as a divisor. Two such albums are said to be *synonyms*. The possibility for collisions is the motivation for organizing each vector element as an association list. Thus, by using a vector implementation we achieve indexed (direct) access to a particular vector element which typically provides much better performance than, say, searching a sequential list for the key value. In the event of synonyms at a particular address space, the association list implementation provides a convenient and usually adequate method for accommodating multiple records per address.

We've chosen to implement our database in terms of a Scheme vector, and we've developed a technique for efficient storage and retrieval against the vector database. At this point, let's consider the process of transferring it to and from disk. To some extent, we would like our album library implementation to be reasonably open-ended. In particular, we want to allow for future modification of the album system at the storage structure level. That is, we don't want to write, say, an album entry routine, that is tied to secondary storage considerations. It is preferable to have a layered design, such that if it is necessary to change the method for storing the album library on disk, the effect on existing routines would be minimal.

For example, consider **album-enter**:

```
;;;;;;;;;;;;;;;;;;;;;;;;;;;;;;;;;;;;;;;;;;;;;;;;;;;;;;;;;;;;
;; ALBUM-ENTER prompts the user for album information and
;; makes an entry into the database.
;;;;;;;;;;;;;;;;;;;;;;;;;;;;;;;;;;;;;;;;;;;;;;;;;;;;;;;;;;;;

(define (album-enter)
  (let* ((album (begin
                  (format "~%~%Enter title: ")
                  (list (read-ln))))
         (album (begin
                  (format "~%~%Enter artist: ")
                  (append album (list (read-ln)))))
         (album (begin
                  (format "~%~%Enter music type: ")
                  (append album (list (read-ln)))))
         (album (begin
                  (format "~%~%Enter price (omit decimal): ")
                  (append album
                          (list (integer->$ (read-ln)))))))
    (add-album album)
    (write-database)))
```

album-enter prompts for each item of information for an album, and then calls on two separate routines to (1) add the album to the library, and (2) update the database on disk. In this manner, we are free to change the specifics of how **add-album** and **write-database** operate without having to change **album-enter**. In other words, there are no implementation-specific details of the database per se present in **album-enter**, other than the basic album structure.

(Note that we don't need **set!** in **album-enter**, even though there is interleaved prompting and reading of data for each album. In this case, **let*** is used in conjunction with **append** to prompt for and build up an album entry in a stepwise fashion. Contrast the use of **let*** with the use of **set!** for prompting in Chapter 3)

It is quite common in LISP programming to develop many small procedures in order to promote abstraction, as we did with **add-album** and **write-database**. Also, for a particular application there may be particular data structure(s) that are common to several, or even the majority, of the routines that comprise a major program. In this case, it may be acceptable to maintain these data structures in an external, or semi-external environment, so that they can be accessed without having to be passed through many levels of function calls. At the very least, this is a controversial point; global variables should never be taken lightly. Note that **let** or **let*** can be used to provide such layered variable bindings.

In general, this text does not promote the use of global variables. However, for this particular application, it may be reasonable to treat two data/file structures globally: the database and the external file. Clearly, it is possible to differentiate between these variables and other variables in the album library system. Partly for the sake of illustration, we've adopted this technique here. The advantage of this approach is that if the method of implementing the database changes at some point in the future, the (proper) global treatment of the database and the physical file can minimize the impact of the album library.

Assuming that we may want to change the physical implementation of the database or extend its capabilities at some later time, our preliminary implementation of the album library makes use of external procedures, plus the following two globals:

```
;;;;;;;;;;;;;;;;;;;;;;;;;;;;;;;;;;;;;;
;; Initialize two global variables.
;;;;;;;;;;;;;;;;;;;;;;;;;;;;;;;;;;;;;;

(define database ())
(define dos-file "")
```

dos-file represents the physical filename for the database stored on disk and **database** represents the data/file structure used in the current implementation; both are initially null.

Of course, at some point the specifics of the database's current implementation must enter the picture. Our current implementation is based on a Scheme vector and open hashing. Thus, there must be an implementation-specific procedure that establishes the database:

```
;;;;;;;;;;;;;;;;;;;;;;;;;;;;;;;;;;;;;;;;;;;;;
;; ALBUM-CREATE creates the album library.
;;;;;;;;;;;;;;;;;;;;;;;;;;;;;;;;;;;;;;;;;;;;;

(define (album-create)
  (format "
This program creates a database of album information.  Next,
you must enter a filename for the database; any existing file
by that name will be destroyed.

Enter filename: ")
    (set! dos-file (read-ln))
    (format
      "~%~%Enter file size (maximum number of records): ")
    (set! database (make-vector (str->int (read-ln)) ()))
    (write-database))
```

In this case, the size of the database is determined from applying **str->int** to the result of **read-ln**, forming the first argument to the **make-vector** primitive.

Consider the preceding use of the **format** utility, which we developed in earlier chapters. Since **format**'s first argument is a control string that contains both special formatting directives and regular characters to be printed, we can take advantage of the hidden newline characters present in each line that we enter with a standard text editor. Thus, the newline sequence that is placed after the lines ending in "Next,", "file", "destroyed.", etc. will be honored by **format** when the control string is processed. The net effect is that allowing the first argument to **format** to span multiple lines allows us to avoid the cumbersome task of coding a separate call to **format** for each line of output.

Note that our global treatment of **dos-file** and **database** leads to the use of **set!** in **album-create**. In our opinion, this is a legitimate use of **set!**, i.e., assignment operations; there is no particular advantage to using a functional style call mechanism (see the **calc** program) for establishing the physical filename, instead of a straightforward assignment.

In developing a large-scale file system, there are a number of parameters that exist for the life of the file system, and which must be accessed during normal file system activities. One such file system descriptor is file size. For example, the hashing function that we developed is dependent on file size. A common file design technique is to establish a separate database record, called a *header record*, as a repository for such information. In our current implementation a header record really isn't needed, since we can use Scheme's **vector-length** primitive to determine file size. Still, we should isolate the details of determining file size in a separate procedure:

```
;;;;;;;;;;;;;;;;;;;;;;;;;;;;;;;;;;;;;;;;;;;;;;;;
;; FILE-SIZE determines the database file size.
;;;;;;;;;;;;;;;;;;;;;;;;;;;;;;;;;;;;;;;;;;;;;;;;

(define (file-size)
  (vector-length database))
```

If our database implementation becomes more sophisticated at a later date, say, requiring a header record, the details of extracting file size from the header record can be handled by **file-size**, minimizing the overall impact on our program.

Again, let's consider the implication of using **database** globally. Normally, we don't think of the hashing process per se as being dependent on the database – the hash algorithm is applied specifically to album titles. Yet, as we've discussed, **hash** must know the database file size in order to produce a record address within the bounds of the database. If **database** were not treated globally, it would have to be passed as an argument to **hash** in order for **file-size** to do its work.

But some readers could argue (quite reasonably) that this is exactly what should take place – every item of input/data that is used by a function should be passed as an argument. By the latter argument, the black box view of a procedure, which we promoted in an earlier chapter, breaks down for any function that uses information globally. Those in favor of using "global data" could argue that it is commonplace to use procedures globally, i.e., we do not normally pass as arguments every function that is used by a particular function.

In concluding our discussion of the global variable issue, we would like to reiterate our personal dislike for global variables. Numerous introductory texts are available that point out the problems associated with global variable usage, in general. Also, we've made the argument that global variables can seriously impede procedure abstraction. Another point is that the widespread use of global variables can undermine the advantages afforded by Scheme's lexical scoping. By our previous discussion, however, we've argued that, for this particular application, it may be legitimate to treat the database globally.

Let's consider how we might write a function(s) to manage album deletions. One approach would be to use a functional programming style whereby the database would be passed as an argument to a function named **delete-one-album**. However, depending on the method of implementing the database, say, as a vector, the call-by-value philosophy of Scheme could prevent us from modifying the database "in place." In this case, a modified copy of the database could be returned by the album deletion function.

However, for more complicated implementations of the database, it may not be appropriate to return a modified copy of the database. For example, our database could be implemented as a 700 kilobyte file on secondary storage using random access I/O. In this case, modification by assignment, i.e., by causing a side effect to occur against the database, is precisely what is needed. Hence, our global treatment of **database**, specifically, making modifications to the database by side effect, facilitates the growth of our album library from a simple vector implementation to, say, a B-tree file structure implementation. (See one of the suggested readings at the end of the chapter for a discussion of file structures.)

With respect to our album library implementation based on open hashing, deleting an album from the library is a matter of removing an entry from the association list at the appropriate vector position. We can use Scheme's **vector-set!** primitive to perform this task:

```
;;;;;;;;;;;;;;;;;;;;;;;;;;;;;;;;;;;;;;;;;;;;;;;;;;;;;;;;;;;;;;;;
;; DELETE-ONE-ALBUM permanently deletes one album from
;; the album library database.
;;;;;;;;;;;;;;;;;;;;;;;;;;;;;;;;;;;;;;;;;;;;;;;;;;;;;;;;;;;;;;;;

(define (delete-one-album key)
  (let* ((pos (hash key))
         (album-list (vector-ref database pos)))
    (let delete-loop ((new-list ()) (reduced-list album-list))
      (cond
        ((null? reduced-list)
         (vector-set! database pos reduced-list))
        ((string=? (get-key (car reduced-list)) key)
         (delete-loop new-list (cdr reduced-list)))
        (else
          (delete-loop (cons (car reduced-list) new-list)
                       (cdr reduced-list)))))))
```

Here, we've established **delete-loop**, a named **let** that uses consing and cdr recursion, to delete the appropriate album from the association list.

At this point we present the entire program. We've provided a preliminary discussion of the most significant aspects of the current implementation, including introduction of some of our own biases. Much of the code requires no further explanation. However, selected aspects of the program are discussed subsequently.

```
;;;;    album.s    ;;;;;;;;;;;;;;;;;;;;;;;;;;;;;;;;;;;;;;;;;;

;;;;;;;;;;;;;;;;;;;;;;;;;;;;;;;;;;;;;;;;;;;;;;;;;;;;;;;;;;;;;;;
;; The following code manages a database of information
;; about an album library.  The database is implemented as a
;; Scheme vector.  Each vector element manages all albums
;; that hash to that location; each element is organized as
;; an association list.  Error checking for file status
;; is minimal, in order to maximize portability.  The
;; following library files are used:
;;   format.s
;;   read-ln.s
;;   str-int.s
;;;;;;;;;;;;;;;;;;;;;;;;;;;;;;;;;;;;;;;;;;;;;;;;;;;;;;;;;;;;;;;


;;;;;;;;;;;;;;;;;;;;;;;;;;;;;;;;;;;;;;;;;;;;;;;;;;;;;;;;;;;;;;
;; ALBUM is the driver program for the album library menu.
;;;;;;;;;;;;;;;;;;;;;;;;;;;;;;;;;;;;;;;;;;;;;;;;;;;;;;;;;;;;;;

(define (album)

;;;;;;;;;;;;;;;;;;;;;;;;;;;;;;;;;;;;;;;;;;;;;;;;;;;;;;
;; Initialize two global variables--global to other
;; internal routines, but still local to ALBUM.
;;;;;;;;;;;;;;;;;;;;;;;;;;;;;;;;;;;;;;;;;;;;;;;;;;;;;;

(define database ())
(define dos-file "")


;;;;;;;;;;;;;;;;;;;;;;;;;;;;;;;;;;;;;;;;;;;;;;;;;;;;;;;;;
;; PROCESS-OPTION invokes the "main" functions for each
;; option.
;;;;;;;;;;;;;;;;;;;;;;;;;;;;;;;;;;;;;;;;;;;;;;;;;;;;;;;;;

(define (process-option option)
  (case option
    (("c") (album-create))
    (("f") (album-filename))
    (("e") (album-enter))
    (("d") (album-delete))
    (("u") (album-update))
```

```
    (("p") (album-print))
    (("x") (format "~%END OF PROGRAM~%"))
    (else
      (format "~%*** invalid choice ***~%"))))


;;;;;;;;;;;;;;;;;;;;;;;;;;;;;;;;;;;;;;;;;;;;;
;; ALBUM-CREATE creates the album library.
;;;;;;;;;;;;;;;;;;;;;;;;;;;;;;;;;;;;;;;;;;;;;

(define (album-create)
  (format "
This program creates a database of album information.  Next,
you must enter a filename for the database; any existing file
by that name will be destroyed.

Enter filename: ")
    (set! dos-file (read-ln))
    (format
      "~%~%Enter file size (maximum number of records): ")
    (set! database (make-vector (str->int (read-ln)) ()))
    (write-database))


;;;;;;;;;;;;;;;;;;;;;;;;;;;;;;;;;;;;;;;;;;;;;;;;;;;;;;;;;;;;;;;;;;
;; ALBUM-ENTER prompts the user for album information and
;; makes an entry into the database.
;;;;;;;;;;;;;;;;;;;;;;;;;;;;;;;;;;;;;;;;;;;;;;;;;;;;;;;;;;;;;;;;;;

(define (album-enter)
  (let* ((album (begin
                  (format "~%~%Enter title: ")
                  (list (read-ln))))
         (album (begin
                  (format "~%~%Enter artist: ")
                  (append album (list (read-ln)))))
         (album (begin
                  (format "~%~%Enter music type: ")
                  (append album (list (read-ln)))))
         (album (begin
                  (format "~%~%Enter price: ")
                  (append album
                          (list (integer->$ (read-ln)))))))
    (add-album album)
    (write-database)))
```

```
;;;;;;;;;;;;;;;;;;;;;;;;;;;;;;;;;;;;;;;;;;;;;;;;;
;; ALBUM-DELETE prompts for an album title and
;; optionally perform the album deletion.
;;;;;;;;;;;;;;;;;;;;;;;;;;;;;;;;;;;;;;;;;;;;;;;;;

(define (album-delete)
  (let ((album (album-print)))
    (if album
        (let ((yes (begin
                     (format "~%You have chosen to delete")
                     (format " the above album.~%")
                     (query-yes))))
          (if yes
              (begin
                (delete-one-album (get-key album))
                (write-database)))))))


;;;;;;;;;;;;;;;;;;;;;;;;;;;;;;;;;;;;;;;;;;;;;;;;;;;;;;;
;; ALBUM-UPDATE manages a field update for one album.
;;;;;;;;;;;;;;;;;;;;;;;;;;;;;;;;;;;;;;;;;;;;;;;;;;;;;;;

(define (album-update)
(let ((album (album-print)))
    (if album                        ;; re-indent for true if;
                                     ;; there is no else clause
  (let ((field
          (begin
            (format
              "~%Enter field to update (a,m,p,q = quit): ")
            (read-ln))))
    (case field
      (("t")
       (format "~%~%Key field (title) cannot be updated--~%")
       (format
         "You must delete and then re-enter the album.~%"))
      (("a" "m" "p")
       (update-one-album (get-key album) field)
       (write-database)))))))


;;;;;;;;;;;;;;;;;;;;;;;;;;;;;;;;;;;;;;;;;;;;;;;;;;;;;;;;;;;;;;;;
;; ALBUM-PRINT prints an album AND returns the album.  The
;; returned value may be used or discarded.
;;;;;;;;;;;;;;;;;;;;;;;;;;;;;;;;;;;;;;;;;;;;;;;;;;;;;;;;;;;;;;;;
```

```
(define (album-print)
  (let* ((album-key (begin
                      (format "~%~%Enter album title: ")
                      (read-ln)))
         (album (get-album album-key)))
    (if album
        (print-one-album album)
        (format "~%~%*** album does not exist ***"))
    album))  ;; return the album


;;;;;;;;;;;;;;;;;;;;;;;;;;;;;;;;;;;;;;;;;;;;;;;;;;;;;;;;;
;; QUERY-YES prompts the user for a yes or no response.
;;;;;;;;;;;;;;;;;;;;;;;;;;;;;;;;;;;;;;;;;;;;;;;;;;;;;;;;;

(define (query-yes)
  (format "~%(y/n): ")
  (case (read-ln)
    (("y" "Y") #t)
    (("n" "N") #f)
    (else (format "~%~%*** invalid choice ***~%"))))


;;;;;;;;;;;;;;;;;;;;;;;;;;;;;;;;;;;;;;;;;;;;;;;;;;;;;;;;;;;
;; INTEGER->$ converts a string price to a real number.
;; If your version of Scheme doesn't implement STRING->
;; NUMBER, you'll have to substitute something else here.
;;;;;;;;;;;;;;;;;;;;;;;;;;;;;;;;;;;;;;;;;;;;;;;;;;;;;;;;;;;

(define (integer->$ str)
  (string->number str 'I 'D))


;;;;;;;;;;;;;;;;;;;;;;;;;;;;;;;;;;;;;;;;;;;;;;;;;;;;;;;
;; ALBUM-FILENAME establishes the global DOS filename
;; for the album library and reads the library.
;;;;;;;;;;;;;;;;;;;;;;;;;;;;;;;;;;;;;;;;;;;;;;;;;;;;;;;

(define (album-filename)
  (format
    "~%~%Enter the DOS filename for the album library: ")
  (set! dos-file (read-ln))
  (read-database))
```

```
;;;;;;;;;;;;;;;;;;;;;;;;;;;;;;;;;;;;;;;;;;;;;;;;;
;; READ-DATABASE reads the database from disk.
;;;;;;;;;;;;;;;;;;;;;;;;;;;;;;;;;;;;;;;;;;;;;;;;;

(define (read-database)
  (with-input-from-file dos-file (lambda ()
                                  (set! database (read)))))


;;;;;;;;;;;;;;;;;;;;;;;;;;;;;;;;;;;;;;;;;;;;;;;;;
;; WRITE-DATABASE writes the database to disk.
;;;;;;;;;;;;;;;;;;;;;;;;;;;;;;;;;;;;;;;;;;;;;;;;;

(define (write-database)
  (with-output-to-file dos-file (lambda () (write database))))


;;;;;;;;;;;;;;;;;;;;;;;;;;;;;;;;;;;;;;;;;;;;;;;;;;
;; FILE-SIZE determines the database file size.
;;;;;;;;;;;;;;;;;;;;;;;;;;;;;;;;;;;;;;;;;;;;;;;;;;

(define (file-size)
  (vector-length database))


;;;;;;;;;;;;;;;;;;;;;;;;;;;;;;;;;;;;;;;;;;;;;;;;;;;
;; GET-ALBUM returns an album from the database.
;;;;;;;;;;;;;;;;;;;;;;;;;;;;;;;;;;;;;;;;;;;;;;;;;;;

(define (get-album key)
  (assoc key (vector-ref database (hash key))))


;;;;;;;;;;;;;;;;;;;;;;;;;;;;;;;;;;;;;;;;;;;;;;;
;; ADD-ALBUM adds an album to the database.
;;;;;;;;;;;;;;;;;;;;;;;;;;;;;;;;;;;;;;;;;;;;;;;

(define (add-album album)
  (let ((pos (hash (get-key album))))
    (vector-set! database
                 pos
                 (cons album (vector-ref database pos)))))


;;;;;;;;;;;;;;;;;;;;;;;;;;;;;;;;;;;;;;;;;;;;;;
;; GET-KEY retrieves the key for an album.
```

```
;;;;;;;;;;;;;;;;;;;;;;;;;;;;;;;;;;;;;;;;;;;;;;;;;;

(define (get-key album)
  (get-title album))


;;;;;;;;;;;;;;;;;;;;;;;;;;;;;;;;;;;;;;;;;;;;;;;;;;;;;;;;;;;;;;;;;
;; PRINT-ONE-ALBUM prints to the screen the contents of
;; one album.
;;;;;;;;;;;;;;;;;;;;;;;;;;;;;;;;;;;;;;;;;;;;;;;;;;;;;;;;;;;;;;;;;

(define (print-one-album album)
  (format
    "~%~%Title: ~a~%Artist: ~a~%Music type: ~a~%Price: ~a~%"
    (get-title album)
    (get-artist album)
    (get-music album)
    (get-price album)))


;;;;;;;;;;;;;;;;;;;;;;;;;;;;;;;;;;;;;;;;;;;;;;;;;;;;;;;;;;;;;;;;
;; DELETE-ONE-ALBUM permanently deletes one album from
;; the album library database.
;;;;;;;;;;;;;;;;;;;;;;;;;;;;;;;;;;;;;;;;;;;;;;;;;;;;;;;;;;;;;;;;

(define (delete-one-album key)
  (let* ((pos (hash key))
         (album-list (vector-ref database pos)))
    (let delete-loop ((new-list ()) (reduced-list album-list))
      (cond
        ((null? reduced-list)
         (vector-set! database pos reduced-list))
        ((string=? (get-key (car reduced-list)) key)
         (delete-loop new-list (cdr reduced-list)))
        (else
          (delete-loop (cons (car reduced-list) new-list)
                       (cdr reduced-list)))))))


;;;;;;;;;;;;;;;;;;;;;;;;;;;;;;;;;;;;;;;;;;;;;;;;;;;;;;;;;;;;;;;;;
;; UPDATE-ONE-ALBUM permanently modifies one album from
;; the album library database.
;;;;;;;;;;;;;;;;;;;;;;;;;;;;;;;;;;;;;;;;;;;;;;;;;;;;;;;;;;;;;;;;;

(define (update-one-album key task)
  (let* ((pos (hash key))
```

```
         (album-list (vector-ref database pos)))
    (let update-loop ((new-list ()) (old-list album-list))
      (cond
        ((null? old-list)
         (vector-set! database pos new-list))
        ((string=? (get-key (car old-list)) key)
         (update-loop (cons (update-field (car old-list) task)
                            new-list)
                      (cdr old-list)))
        (else
          (update-loop (cons (car old-list) new-list)
                       (cdr old-list)))))))


;;;;;;;;;;;;;;;;;;;;;;;;;;;;;;;;;;;;;;;;;;;;;;;;;;;;;;;;;;;
;; UPDATE-FIELD prompts the user for album information
;; for one field and makes a modification to that field.
;;;;;;;;;;;;;;;;;;;;;;;;;;;;;;;;;;;;;;;;;;;;;;;;;;;;;;;;;;;

(define (update-field album task)
  (let ((value (begin
                 (format "~%Enter new value: ")
                 (read-ln))))
    (if (string=? task "p")
        (replace-album-field album task (integer->$ value))
        (replace-album-field album task value))))


;;;;;;;;;;;;;;;;;;;;;;;;;;;;;;;;;;;;;;;;;;;;;;;;;;;
;; HASH hashes each album key by summing the ASCII
;; values for each character, modulo file size.
;;;;;;;;;;;;;;;;;;;;;;;;;;;;;;;;;;;;;;;;;;;;;;;;;;;

(define (hash key)
  (let hash-it ((str-pos (- (string-length key) 1))
                (hash-value 0))
    (if (= str-pos -1)
        (modulo hash-value (file-size))
        (hash-it (- str-pos 1)
                 (+ hash-value
                    (char->integer
                      (string-ref key str-pos)))))))


;;;;;;;;;;;;;;;;;;;;;;;;;;;;;;;;;;;;;;;;;;;;;;;;;;;;;;;;;;;
;; REPLACE-ALBUM-FIELD replaces a particular field of an
```

```
;; album with a new value.
;;;;;;;;;;;;;;;;;;;;;;;;;;;;;;;;;;;;;;;;;;;;;;;;;;;;;;;;;;;;

(define (replace-album-field a f n)            ;; a = album
  (case f                                      ;; f = field
    (("t")                                     ;; n = new value
     (list n (get-artist a) (get-music a) (get-price a)))
    (("a")
     (list (get-title a) n (get-music a) (get-price a)))
    (("m")
     (list (get-title a) (get-artist a) n (get-price a)))
    (("p")
     (list (get-title a) (get-artist a) (get-music a) n))
    (else
      a)))  ;; error -- return the album unchanged


;;;;;;;;;;;;;;;;;;;;;;;;;;;;;;;;;;;;;;;;;;;;;;;;;;;;;;;;;;;;;;
;; The following functions retrieve each of the respective
;; fields of an album.
;;;;;;;;;;;;;;;;;;;;;;;;;;;;;;;;;;;;;;;;;;;;;;;;;;;;;;;;;;;;;;

(define (get-title album)
  (list-ref album 0))

(define (get-artist album)
  (list-ref album 1))

(define (get-music album)
  (list-ref album 2))

(define (get-price album)
  (list-ref album 3))


;;;;    end internal definitions    ;;;;;;;;;;;;;;;;;;;;;;;;;;;

(do ((option ()))
      ((equal? option "x") (display #\newline))
      (format "

*** ALBUM MENU ***

Choose option (lowercase):

c -- Create a new album library
```

```
f -- set library Filename for current session
e -- Enter a new album
d -- Delete an existing album
u -- Update an existing album
p -- Print info for an album
x -- eXit

")
      (set! option (read-ln))
      (if database
          (process-option option)
          (case option
            (("e" "d" "u" "p")
             (format
        "~%*** You must first establish a database. ***~%"))
            (else
              (process-option option))))))
```

The preceding program was developed with top-level, external procedures – each function coded separately to facilitate debugging. However, depending on the environment in which a program is used, it is often prudent to make a final recoding in terms of a **letrec**, or with internal **define**s, as we did in a couple of our earlier programs; e.g., **math-menu** used a **let-rec**.

Encapsulating all functions and global variables inside a driver function reduces the possibility of inadvertent interaction among identifiers associated with **album** and other top-level identifiers. In those cases where either **define** or **letrec** is appropriate for encapsulating functions, we personally prefer internal, independent, procedure definitions using **define**. This approach allows the programmer to move procedures back and forth, as needed, between a position internal to the driver function and the top-level REP loop with a minimal number of editor keystrokes.

At the expense of conciseness of code, we have avoided any special features provided by PC Scheme that would make **album** non-portable with respect to other Scheme systems. In particular, we have avoided potential interactions between **read-char**, **read**, and **read-ln** by using our **read-ln** function for all user input. Of course, programmers often have particular preferences with respect to input functions; however, in our opinion, there are advantages to using a single, basic input function, especially in terms of code readability.

In order to update the database on disk, **write-database** must be invoked. **write-database** uses **with-output-to-file** in conjunction with **write** to perform the disk write operation. That is, each modification of the album library database first occurs in memory to the Scheme vector, **database**. Subsequently, **with-output-to-file** (in **write-database**) redirects standard output to the disk file named by **dos-file**, allowing the use of a standard **write** to write the database to disk. In a complementary fashion **read-database** uses **with-input-from-file** to **read** the database into memory, i.e., for database initialization.

Next consider the way we've used **format** in **album** to present the menu. Although there may be some problems with this approach on some Scheme systems, we feel that the convenience afforded by allowing the output string to span multiple lines is preferable to multiple **formats**. Thus, the programmer can type the menu into the editor directly as it should appear on the screen; then upon execution, newline sequences between double quotes generate new lines at the screen. This is particularly convenient in comparison to the formatted output facilities in more traditional computer languages.

The remaining code is straightforward and left for the reader's perusal. Lastly, we would like to reemphasize the importance and utility of Scheme's vector and association list data structures. For example, a similar program in Smith and Smith (1988), written in Pascal, requires more than twice as much code. The conciseness of the Scheme code is primarily the result of the automatic provision of list processing facilities, unavailable in traditional computer languages, e.g., Pascal, PL/I, and COBOL. This serves to emphasize the opinion raised earlier that Scheme is a very good language for programming of all types, not just AI programming.

Exercises

1. There are many ways to extend the database application provided in this chapter—many AI programs make use of such a memory-resident database. Extend and/or modify the album library program with respect to an application in your area of interest. Applications include: a dog database, a cat database, a horse database, an automobile database, and so on.

2. Extend the mini-database application to support listing (displaying) individual albums, or all albums, at the console and to support printing of individual albums, or all albums, to the printer. In the case of displaying multiple albums at the console, your program should pause each time it displays an arbitrary number of albums, probably either two or three albums, allowing the user to view the console. A prompt should be provided to tell the user how to continue the display operation.

3. The mini-database application in this chapter has no provision for accessing information via fields other than album title. In the beginning of the chapter we called album title the *key*. More specifically, the album title field is called the *primary key*, since it uniquely identifies each database record. A *secondary key* is a field in a record that provides an alternate method for accessing records; typically, the secondary key field does not uniquely identify records.

For example, in an album library system it could be quite useful to impose an alternate organization on the database, namely, organization by type of music. In particular, it would be useful to be able to *retrieve* records by music type, e.g., printing a listing of all rock albums. (Albums should still be *stored* in the database based on the primary key, album title.)

For this exercise, build a supplemental data structure that serves as a secondary key *index*; that is, a structure that indexes the albums by music type. A reasonable structure for implementing the secondary key index would be a vector, where each vector element contains an association list of the albums for a particular music type:

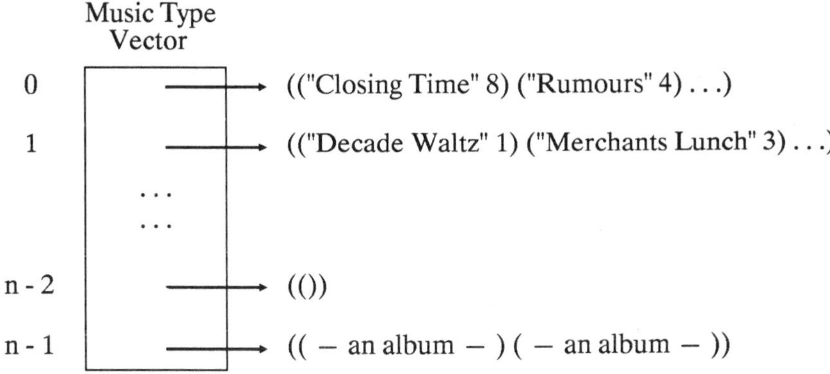

In this example, rock albums are referenced by the 0th element of the index (vector) and bluegrass albums are referenced by the 1st element of the index, and so on, for however many music types you plan to accommodate. (You may want to set a fixed limit, say, five, music types—at least in your initial implementation.)

In this example, the numbers in the association lists represent the positions in the database (vector implementation) where each album is stored. For example, according to our index, the first two rock albums (ordered alphabetically by album title) are stored in the database vector in elements 8 and 4, respectively. Note that the provision of a secondary key index implies that the index must be updated each time an album is added to or deleted from the database.

The final exercise is designed for readers with a background in file processing.

4. A Scheme vector provided the physical implementation for the database in this chapter. If your Scheme system supports direct (random) access I/O, e.g., PC Scheme 3.0, modify the preceding database system so that each album's information is stored in a file record. (You may need to review the discussion in Chapter 9 regarding standard Scheme I/O ports.)

There are two major issues that must be addressed in this exercise:

1. hashing and collision resolution
2. file-level record management.

With respect to (1), note that the open hashing scheme that worked beautifully in memory (primary storage) is inappropriate for secondary storage file structures. Thus, you must develop a specific approach to collision resolution, such as open addressing (e.g., simple linear probing).

As for (2), you must supply routines for advancing forward to the *i*th record and storing or retrieving a record. This is not a trivial exercise, if your Scheme system provides byte-level, direct access of files. In this case, you will have to supply routines to impose record-level file processing on top of the byte-level file processing provided by your Scheme system.

Suggested Readings

Hashing schemes and memory management techniques are discussed in a variety of computer science subfields including data structures (Augenstein and Tenenbaum, 1979; Dale and Lilly, 1985), file structures (Smith and Barnes, 1987; Smith and Smith, 1988), compiler design (Aho et al., 1986), and database systems (Date, 1986; Korth and Silberschatz, 1986).

Answers to Selected Exercises

Chapter 1

1. In our opinion, some advantages are:

- **a.** easier for implementors to support the entire language, thus
- **b.** easier to designate a (realistic) language standard, thus
- **c.** easier to write portable code – you have the option of coding within the standard
- **d.** easier for the programmer to "know" the language.

Disadvantage: Programmers must deal with code implemented under other systems; typically, such code uses language extensions that are nonportable.

Pascal is an example of a good idea that failed miserably, in the sense that Standard Pascal failed to address two important language features adequately: (1) strings, and (2) I/O. Hence, Pascal dialects have handled both of these features in a variety of ways, making it difficult to port Pascal code to different compilers.

In our opinion, standard Scheme's lack of support for either binary I/O or random I/O will be an important issue in the future.

3. Basically, in syntax-bound languages the programmer must deal with many more issues of syntax during coding. In fact, this is one of the main reasons for advocating program design via pseudocode – don't worry about issues of syntax until the algorithm is worked out.

Chapter 2

2. a.

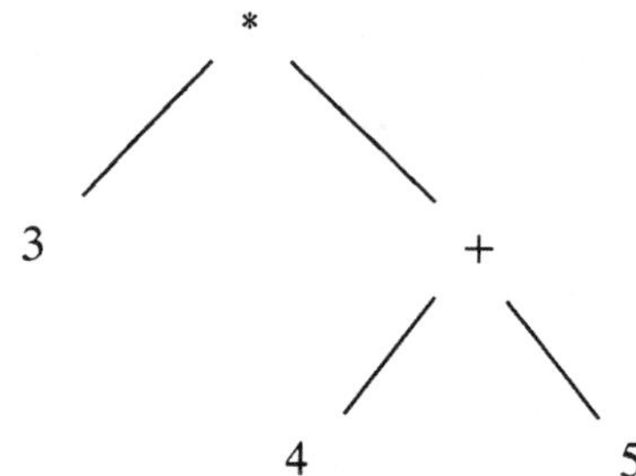

5. For example, PC Scheme 2.0 returns:

```
0.999999956014926
```

PC Scheme 3.0 returns:

```
1.
```

6. For 121332323 X 121332323 PC Scheme returns:

```
14721532604576329
```

For 45! PC Scheme returns:

```
119622220865480194561963161495657715064383733760000000000
```

Chapter 3

2.

```
;;;;     greeting.s     ;;;;;;;;;;;;;;;;;;;;;;;;;;;;;;;;;;;;;;;;;

;;;;;;;;;;;;;;;;;;;;;;;;;;;;;;;;;;;;;;;;;;;;;;;;;;;;;;;;;;;;;;;;
;; GENERAL-GREETING prints the message "Hello world!"
;;;;;;;;;;;;;;;;;;;;;;;;;;;;;;;;;;;;;;;;;;;;;;;;;;;;;;;;;;;;;;;;

(define (general-greeting)
  (display "Hello world!"))
```

3.

```
;;;;    temper.s    ;;;;;;;;;;;;;;;;;;;;;;;;;;;;;;;;;;;;;;;;;

;;;;;;;;;;;;;;;;;;;;;;;;;;;;;;;;;;;;;;;;;;;;;;;;;;;;;
;; F->C converts Fahrenheit temperatures to Celsius.
;;;;;;;;;;;;;;;;;;;;;;;;;;;;;;;;;;;;;;;;;;;;;;;;;;;;;;

(define (f->c f)
  (/ (* 5 (- f 32)) 9))


;;;;;;;;;;;;;;;;;;;;;;;;;;;;;;;;;;;;;;;;;;;;;;;;;;;;;;
;; C->F converts Celsius temperatures to Fahrenheit.
;;;;;;;;;;;;;;;;;;;;;;;;;;;;;;;;;;;;;;;;;;;;;;;;;;;;;;

(define (c->f c)
  (+ 32 (/ (* 9 c) 5)))
```

4.

```
;;;;    circle.s    ;;;;;;;;;;;;;;;;;;;;;;;;;;;;;;;;;;;;;;;;;

;;;;;;;;;;;;;;;;;;;;;;;;;;;;;;;;;;;;;;;;;;;;;;;;;;;;;;;;;;;;
;; CIRCUMFERENCE calculates the circumference of a circle,
;; given the diameter.
;;;;;;;;;;;;;;;;;;;;;;;;;;;;;;;;;;;;;;;;;;;;;;;;;;;;;;;;;;;;

(define (circumference diameter)
  (define pi 3.14159)
  (* pi diameter))
```

5.

```
;;;;    power.s    ;;;;;;;;;;;;;;;;;;;;;;;;;;;;;;;;;;;;;;;;;;

;;;;;;;;;;;;;;;;;;;;;;;;;;;;;;;;;;;;;;;;;;;;;;;;;;;;;
;; FOURTH-POWER calculates n^4, using an internally
;; defined function.
;;;;;;;;;;;;;;;;;;;;;;;;;;;;;;;;;;;;;;;;;;;;;;;;;;;;;

(define (fourth-power n)
  (define (square n)
    (* n n))
```

```
  (* (square n) (square n)))
```

6.

```
;;;;    circle.s    ;;;;;;;;;;;;;;;;;;;;;;;;;;;;;;;;;;;;;;;;

;;;;;;;;;;;;;;;;;;;;;;;;;;;;;;;;;;;;;;;;;;;;;;;;;;;;;;;;;;;;
;; CIRCUM-PROMPT calculates the circumference of a circle,
;; given the diameter.
;;;;;;;;;;;;;;;;;;;;;;;;;;;;;;;;;;;;;;;;;;;;;;;;;;;;;;;;;;;;

(define (circum-prompt)
  (define pi 3.14159)
  (define diameter)
  (newline)
  (display "Enter the diameter: ")
  (set! diameter (read))
  (newline)
  (display "The circumference is: ")
  (display (* pi diameter)))
```

Chapter 4

3.

```
;;;;    list.s    ;;;;;;;;;;;;;;;;;;;;;;;;;;;;;;;;;;;;;;;;;;

;;;;;;;;;;;;;;;;;;;;;;;;;;;;;;;;;;;;;;;;;;;;;;;;
;; FIRST returns the car of a list.
;;;;;;;;;;;;;;;;;;;;;;;;;;;;;;;;;;;;;;;;;;;;;;;;

(define (first lst)
  (car lst))         ;; also, (list-ref lst 0)
```

4.

```
;;;;    list.s    ;;;;;;;;;;;;;;;;;;;;;;;;;;;;;;;;;;;;;;;;;;

;;;;;;;;;;;;;;;;;;;;;;;;;;;;;;;;;;;;;;;;;
;; REST returns the cdr of a list.
;;;;;;;;;;;;;;;;;;;;;;;;;;;;;;;;;;;;;;;;;
```

```
(define (rest lst)
  (cdr lst))          ;; also, (list-tail lst 1)
```

6.

```
;;;;    stacks.s    ;;;;;;;;;;;;;;;;;;;;;;;;;;;;;;;;;;;;;;;;;;;;

;;;;;;;;;;;;;;;;;;;;;;;;;;;;;;;;;;;;;;;;;;;;;;;;;;;;
;; Access functions for a list-based stack.
;;;;;;;;;;;;;;;;;;;;;;;;;;;;;;;;;;;;;;;;;;;;;;;;;;;;

(define (pop stack)    ;; not really a "pop" since
  (car stack))         ;; it is nondestructive

(define (push element stack)  ;; not really a "push" since
  (cons element stack))       ;; it is nondestructive
```

11.

```
;;;;    stacks.s    ;;;;;;;;;;;;;;;;;;;;;;;;;;;;;;;;;;;;;;;;;;;;

(define (call-by-value-demo stack)  ;; doesn't "pop" anything
  (let* ((first (car stack))        ;; due to call-by-value
         (stack (cdr stack)))       ;; parameter is only
    first))                         ;; modified locally
```

If **stack** is passed a list, Scheme makes a *copy* of the argument. Any changes to **stack** are thus made to a different data structure than the one passed as an argument. See Exercise 12 for examples of **set-car!** and **set-cdr!**.

12.

```
;;;;    stacks.s    ;;;;;;;;;;;;;;;;;;;;;;;;;;;;;;;;;;;;;;;;;;;;

;;;;;;;;;;;;;;;;;;;;;;;;;;;;;;;;;;;;;;;;;;;;;;;;;;;;
;; Access functions for a list-based stack.
;;;;;;;;;;;;;;;;;;;;;;;;;;;;;;;;;;;;;;;;;;;;;;;;;;;;

(define (pop! stack)
  (let ((first (list-ref stack 0)))
    (set-car! stack (list-ref stack 1))
    (set-cdr! stack (list-tail stack 2))
```

```
    first))

(define (push! element stack)
  (set-cdr! stack (cons (car stack) (cdr stack)))
  (set-car! stack element)
  stack)
```

Chapter 5

3.

```
;;;;    cond.s    ;;;;;;;;;;;;;;;;;;;;;;;;;;;;;;;;;;;;;;;;;;;;;;;;;;

;;;;;;;;;;;;;;;;;;;;;;;;;;;;;;;;;
;; GE implements greater than.
;;;;;;;;;;;;;;;;;;;;;;;;;;;;;;;;;

(define (ge x y)
  (or (> x y) (= x y)))
```

6.

```
;;;;    cond.s    ;;;;;;;;;;;;;;;;;;;;;;;;;;;;;;;;;;;;;;;;;;;;;;;;;;

;;;;;;;;;;;;;;;;;;;;;;;;;;;;;;;;;;;;;;;;;;;;;;;;;;;;;;;
;; MONTH->INTEGER converts a month in symbol form
;; to an integer.
;;;;;;;;;;;;;;;;;;;;;;;;;;;;;;;;;;;;;;;;;;;;;;;;;;;;;;;

(define (month->integer month)
  (cond
    ((equal? month 'january) 1)
    ((equal? month 'february) 2)
    ((equal? month 'march) 3)
    ((equal? month 'april) 4)
    ((equal? month 'may) 5)
    ((equal? month 'june) 6)
    ((equal? month 'july) 7)
    ((equal? month 'august) 8)
    ((equal? month 'september) 9)
    ((equal? month 'october) 10)
    ((equal? month 'november) 11)
    ((equal? month 'december) 12)
```

```
    (else 0)))
```

7.

```
;;;;    cond.s    ;;;;;;;;;;;;;;;;;;;;;;;;;;;;;;;;;;;;;;;;;;;;

;;;;;;;;;;;;;;;;;;;;;;;;;;;;;;;;;;;;;;;;;;;;;;;;
;; MONTH->#DAYS returns the number of days in a
;; month; the argument must be in symbol form.
;;;;;;;;;;;;;;;;;;;;;;;;;;;;;;;;;;;;;;;;;;;;;;;;

(define (month->#days month)
  (case month
    ((september april june november)  ;; thirty days has ...
     30)
    ((january march may july august october december)
     31)
    ((february)          ;; ignore leap year
     28)
    (else
      0)))
```

9.

```
;;;;    cond.s    ;;;;;;;;;;;;;;;;;;;;;;;;;;;;;;;;;;;;;;;;;;;;

;;;;;;;;;;;;;;;;;;;;;;;;;;;;;;;;;;;;;;;;;;;;;;;;;;;;;;;;;;
;; BUY-A-VOWEL illustrates using case to filter input
;; for a particular class of values.
;;;;;;;;;;;;;;;;;;;;;;;;;;;;;;;;;;;;;;;;;;;;;;;;;;;;;;;;;;

(define (buy-a-vowel)
  (display "I'd like to buy a vowel... ")
  (newline)
  (display "OK, which vowel?...")
  (newline)
  (case (read-char)
    ((#\a #\e #\i #\o #\u)
     (display "OK, good choice!"))
    (else
      (display "That's not a vowel--go back to school."))))
```

Chapter 6

1.

```
;;;;    rep.s    ;;;;;;;;;;;;;;;;;;;;;;;;;;;;;;;;;;;;;;;;;;;;;

;;;;;;;;;;;;;;;;;;;;;;;;;;;;;;;;;;;;;;;;;;;;;;;;;;;;;;;;;
;; LIST-OF-ELEMENT forms a list of <count> <element>s.
;;;;;;;;;;;;;;;;;;;;;;;;;;;;;;;;;;;;;;;;;;;;;;;;;;;;;;;;;

(define (list-of-element element count)
  (do ((lst () (cons element lst))
       (count count (- count 1)))
      ((<= count 0) lst)))
```

2.

```
;;;;    rep.s    ;;;;;;;;;;;;;;;;;;;;;;;;;;;;;;;;;;;;;;;;;;;;;

;;;;;;;;;;;;;;;;;;;;;;;;;;;;;;;;;;;;;;;;;;;;;;;;;;;;;;;;;;;;
;; ROSE? demonstrates repetition of output to the screen.
;;;;;;;;;;;;;;;;;;;;;;;;;;;;;;;;;;;;;;;;;;;;;;;;;;;;;;;;;;;;

(define (rose? anything)
  (display "A rose")
  (do ((clause " is a rose")
       (i 1 (+ i 1)))
      ((= i 4) (display "."))
      (display clause)))
```

4.

```
;;;;    rep.s    ;;;;;;;;;;;;;;;;;;;;;;;;;;;;;;;;;;;;;;;;;;;;;

;;;;;;;;;;;;;;;;;;;;;;;;;;;;;;;;;;;;
;; I-LAUNCH illustrates the Scheme
;; looping/repetition structure.
;;;;;;;;;;;;;;;;;;;;;;;;;;;;;;;;;;;;

(define (i-launch n)
  (do ((count n (- count 1)))
      ((< count 0)
       (display 'B-L-A-S-T-O-F-F))
```

```
      (display count)
      (newline)))
```

5.

```
;;;;    rep.s    ;;;;;;;;;;;;;;;;;;;;;;;;;;;;;;;;;;;;;;;;;;;;

;;;;;;;;;;;;;;;;;;;;;;;;;;;;;;;;;;;;;;;;;;;;;;;;;;;;;;;;;;
;; LIST-OF-ELEMENT-R forms a list of <count> <element>s.
;;;;;;;;;;;;;;;;;;;;;;;;;;;;;;;;;;;;;;;;;;;;;;;;;;;;;;;;;;

(define (list-of-element-r element count)
  (define (build-list lst count)
    (if (<= count 0)
        lst
        (build-list (cons element lst) (- count 1))))

  (build-list () count))
```

7.

```
;;;;    list.s    ;;;;;;;;;;;;;;;;;;;;;;;;;;;;;;;;;;;;;;;;;;;

;;;;;;;;;;;;;;;;;;;;;;;;;;;;;;;;;;;;;;;;;;;;;;;;
;; LIST? determines if its argument is a list,
;; either proper or improper.
;;;;;;;;;;;;;;;;;;;;;;;;;;;;;;;;;;;;;;;;;;;;;;;;

(define (list? lst)
  (cond
    ((null? lst) #t)
    ((pair? lst) #t)
    (else #f)))
```

8.

```
;;;;    list.s    ;;;;;;;;;;;;;;;;;;;;;;;;;;;;;;;;;;;;;;;;;;;

;;;;;;;;;;;;;;;;;;;;;;;;;;;;;;;;;;;;;;;;;;;;;;;;;;;;;;;;;
;; P-LIST? determines if its argument is a proper list.
;;;;;;;;;;;;;;;;;;;;;;;;;;;;;;;;;;;;;;;;;;;;;;;;;;;;;;;;;

(define (p-list? lst)
```

```
  (cond
    ((null? lst) #t)
    ((pair? lst) (p-list? (cdr lst)))
    (else #f)))
```

9.

```
;;;;    rep.s    ;;;;;;;;;;;;;;;;;;;;;;;;;;;;;;;;;;;;;;;;;;;;;

;;;;;;;;;;;;;;;;;;;;;;;;;;;;
;; Euclid's GCD algorithm.
;;;;;;;;;;;;;;;;;;;;;;;;;;;;

(define (gcd i j)
  (if (zero? j)
      i
      (gcd j (remainder i j))))
```

11.

```
;;;;    read-ch.s    ;;;;;;;;;;;;;;;;;;;;;;;;;;;;;;;;;;;;;;;;;

;;;;;;;;;;;;;;;;;;;;;;;;;;;;;;;;;;;;;;;;;;;;;;;;;;;;;;;;;;;;
;; READ-CH reads and displays a single character from the
;; console.  There is no error checking.
;;;;;;;;;;;;;;;;;;;;;;;;;;;;;;;;;;;;;;;;;;;;;;;;;;;;;;;;;;;;

(define (read-ch)
  (define ch (read-char))
  (display ch)
  ch)                       ;return the character
```

Chapter 7

1.

```
;;;;    circle.s    ;;;;;;;;;;;;;;;;;;;;;;;;;;;;;;;;;;;;;;;;;

;;;;;;;;;;;;;;;;;;;;;;;;;;;;;;;;;;;;;;;;;;;;;;;;;;;;;;;;;;;;;;
;; CIRCUMFERENCE calculates the circumference of a circle,
;; given the diameter.
;;;;;;;;;;;;;;;;;;;;;;;;;;;;;;;;;;;;;;;;;;;;;;;;;;;;;;;;;;;;;;
```

```
(define (circumference diameter)
  (let ((pi 3.14159))
    (* pi diameter)))
```

2.

```
;;;;    tri.s    ;;;;;;;;;;;;;;;;;;;;;;;;;;;;;;;;;;;;;;;;;;;;

;;;;;;;;;;;;;;;;;;;;;;;;;;;;;;;;;;;;;;;;;;;;;;;;
;; TRI-AREA determines the area of a triangle.
;;;;;;;;;;;;;;;;;;;;;;;;;;;;;;;;;;;;;;;;;;;;;;;;

(define (tri-area base height)
  (let ((one-half 0.5))
    (* one-half base height)))
```

3.

```
;;;;    list.s   ;;;;;;;;;;;;;;;;;;;;;;;;;;;;;;;;;;;;;;;;;;;

;;;;;;;;;;;;;;;;;;;;;;;;;;;;;;;;;;;;;;;;;;;;;;;;;;;;;;;;;;;
;; AVERAGE returns the average of the elements in a list.
;; This version is not very efficient, but it illustrates
;; that the returned value from a let may be useful.
;;;;;;;;;;;;;;;;;;;;;;;;;;;;;;;;;;;;;;;;;;;;;;;;;;;;;;;;;;;

(define (average lst)
(if (null? lst)
      #f
      (/ (let sum-loop ((sum 0) (lst lst))
           (if (null? lst)
               sum
               (sum-loop (+ sum (car lst)) (cdr lst))))
         (length lst))))
```

5.

```
;;;;    addtwo.s    ;;;;;;;;;;;;;;;;;;;;;;;;;;;;;;;;;;;;;;;;;

;;;;;;;;;;;;;;;;;;;;;;;;;;;;;;;;;;;;;;;;;;;;;;;;;;;;
;; ADD-TWO adds two numbers and prints their sum.
;; User prompts are sequenced with begin and let*.
```

```
;;;;;;;;;;;;;;;;;;;;;;;;;;;;;;;;;;;;;;;;;;;;;;;;;;;;

(define (add-two)
  (let* ((first (begin
                  (display "Enter first number: ")
                  (read)))
         (second (begin
                   (display "Enter second number: ")
                   (read)))
         (sum (+ first second)))
    (newline)
    (display "The sum of ")
    (display first)
    (display " and ")
    (display second)
    (display " is ")
    (display sum)
    (display ".")))
```

6.

```
;;;;    list-sum.s    ;;;;;;;;;;;;;;;;;;;;;;;;;;;;;;;;;;;;;;

;;;;;;;;;;;;;;;;;;;;;;;;;;;;;;;;;;;;;;;;;;;;;;;;;;;;;;;;;;;;;;
;; LIST-SUM sums the elements of a list.  It uses car-cdr
;; recursion to process sublists.  A named let is used.
;;;;;;;;;;;;;;;;;;;;;;;;;;;;;;;;;;;;;;;;;;;;;;;;;;;;;;;;;;;;;;

(define (list-sum lst)
  (let sum-loop ((lst lst))
    (cond
      ((null? lst)
       0)
      ((pair? (car lst))
       (+ (sum-loop (car lst)) (sum-loop (cdr lst))))
      (else
        (+ (car lst) (sum-loop (cdr lst)))))))
```

7.

```
;;;;    square.s    ;;;;;;;;;;;;;;;;;;;;;;;;;;;;;;;;;;;;;;;;;;

;;;;;;;;;;;;;;;;;;;;;;;;;;;;;;;;;;;;;;;;;;;;;;;;;;;;;;;;;;;;;;;;
;; SQUARE-TABLE prints a table of integers and their squares.
```

```
;;;;;;;;;;;;;;;;;;;;;;;;;;;;;;;;;;;;;;;;;;;;;;;;;;;;;;;;;;;;;

(define (square-table small large)
  (let ((border "================="))
    (display border)
    (newline)
    (let print-loop ((i small))
      (if (> i large)
          (display border)
          (begin
            (display i)
            (display "   ")
            (display (* i i))
            (newline)
            (print-loop (+ i 1)))))))
```

Chapter 8

1.

```
;;;;    strings.s    ;;;;;;;;;;;;;;;;;;;;;;;;;;;;;;;;;;;;;;;;

;;;;;;;;;;;;;;;;;;;;;;;;;;;;;;;;;;;;;;;;;;;;;;;;;;
;; CHAR->STR converts a printable character to a
;; one-character string.
;;;;;;;;;;;;;;;;;;;;;;;;;;;;;;;;;;;;;;;;;;;;;;;;;;

(define (char->str char)
  (cond
    ((< (char->integer char) 32)
     #f)
    ((> (char->integer char) 126)
     #f)
    (else
      (make-string 1 char))))
```

2.

```
;;;;    strings.s    ;;;;;;;;;;;;;;;;;;;;;;;;;;;;;;;;;;;;;;;;

;;;;;;;;;;;;;;;;;;;;;;;;;;;;;;;;;;;;;;;;;;;;;;;;;;;;;
;; SUBSTR returns a substring of a string using the
;; following (zero-based) call syntax:
```

```
;;
;; (substr <string> <start-pos> <length>)
;;
;; If a substring is requested of length greater
;; than that remaining, the rest of the string is
;; returned.
;;;;;;;;;;;;;;;;;;;;;;;;;;;;;;;;;;;;;;;;;;;;;;;;;;;;;;

(define (substr str start-pos str-len)
  (if (< start-pos 0)
      ""
      (let extract-loop ((pos start-pos)
                         (len 0)
                         (sub-string ""))
        (cond
          ((>= pos (string-length str))
           sub-string)
          ((= len str-len)
           sub-string)
          (else
            (extract-loop (+ pos 1)
                          (+ len 1)
                          (string-append
                            sub-string
                            (substring str pos (+ pos 1)))))))))

;;;;;;;;;;;;;;;;;;;;;;;;;;;;;;;;;;;;;;;;;;;;;;;;;;;;;;
;; A simpler approach--without error checking.
;;;;;;;;;;;;;;;;;;;;;;;;;;;;;;;;;;;;;;;;;;;;;;;;;;;;;;
;;
;; (define (substr str start-pos str-len)
;;   (substring
;;     str
;;     start-pos
;;     (+ start-pos str-len)))
```

5.

```
;;;;    strings.s    ;;;;;;;;;;;;;;;;;;;;;;;;;;;;;;;;;;;;;;;;

;;;;;;;;;;;;;;;;;;;;;;;;;;;;;;;;;;;;;;;;;;;;;;;;;;;;;;;;;;;;;;
;; STRING-INDEX searches for a character in a string, retur-
;; ning its position -- zero-based.
;; Example usage:  (string-index "string" #\i) ==> 3
;;;;;;;;;;;;;;;;;;;;;;;;;;;;;;;;;;;;;;;;;;;;;;;;;;;;;;;;;;;;;;
```

```
(define (str-index str search-char)
  (do ((pos 0 (+ pos 1)))
      ((cond                                 ;; test condition
         ((= pos (string-length str))
          #t)
         ((char=? (string-ref str pos) search-char)
          #t)
         (else
           #f))
       (if (= pos (string-length str))       ;; return value
           #f
           pos))))
```

6.

```
;;;;    strings.s    ;;;;;;;;;;;;;;;;;;;;;;;;;;;;;;;;;;;;;;;;;;;;

;;;;;;;;;;;;;;;;;;;;;;;;;;;;;;;;;;;;;;;;;;;;;;;;;;;;;;;;;;;;;;
;; STRING-UPCASE returns a string converted to uppercase.
;;;;;;;;;;;;;;;;;;;;;;;;;;;;;;;;;;;;;;;;;;;;;;;;;;;;;;;;;;;;;;

(define (string-upcase lower-str)
  (let ((str-len (string-length lower-str)))
    (let next-char ((position 0)
                    (upper-str ""))
      (if (= position str-len)
          upper-str
          (next-char (+ position 1)
                     (string-append
                       upper-str
                       (make-string
                         1
                         (char-upcase (string-ref
                                        lower-str
                                        position)))))))))
```

Chapter 9

WARNING: Due to inherent differences among computing systems with respect to I/O, some of the following code may require modification for proper operation. Compare the two versions of **fcopy** in Exercise 10.

1.

```
;;;;    read-ch.s    ;;;;;;;;;;;;;;;;;;;;;;;;;;;;;;;;;;;;;;;;;

;;;;;;;;;;;;;;;;;;;;;;;;;;;;;;;;;;;;;;;;;;;;;;;;;;;;;;;;;;;;
;; READ-CH reads and displays a single character from the
;; console.  There is no error checking.
;;;;;;;;;;;;;;;;;;;;;;;;;;;;;;;;;;;;;;;;;;;;;;;;;;;;;;;;;;;;

(define (read-ch-2)
  (let ((ch (read-char)))
    (display ch)
    ch))                     ;return the character
```

2.

```
;;;;    read-ch.s    ;;;;;;;;;;;;;;;;;;;;;;;;;;;;;;;;;;;;;;;;;

;;;;;;;;;;;;;;;;;;;;;;;;;;;;;;;;;;;;;;;;;;;;;;;;;;;;;;;;;;;;
;; READ-CH reads and displays a single character from the
;; console.  There is no error checking.
;;;;;;;;;;;;;;;;;;;;;;;;;;;;;;;;;;;;;;;;;;;;;;;;;;;;;;;;;;;;

(define (read-ch-3)
  (display (read-char)))
```

5.

```
;;;;    f-list.s    ;;;;;;;;;;;;;;;;;;;;;;;;;;;;;;;;;;;;;;;;;;

;;;;;;;;;;;;;;;;;;;;;;;;;;;;;;;;;;;;;;;;
;; F-LIST lists a file at the console.
;;;;;;;;;;;;;;;;;;;;;;;;;;;;;;;;;;;;;;;;

(define (f-list in-file)
  (with-input-from-file in-file
    (lambda ()
      (display "=================================")
      (display " start of file ")
      (display "==================================")
      (newline)
      (do ((char (read-char) (read-char)))
          ((eof-object? char))
          (if (char=? char #\newline) ;;strip newline
```

```
              (display "")              ;;sequences--PC Scheme
              (display char)))
      (display "===================================")
      (display " end of file ")
      (display "=====================================")))))
```

6.

```
;;;;    f-list.s    ;;;;;;;;;;;;;;;;;;;;;;;;;;;;;;;;;;;;;;;;;

;;;;;;;;;;;;;;;;;;;;;;;;;;;;;;;;;;;;;;;;;
;; P-LIST lists a file at the console,
;; pausing after each screen of output.
;;;;;;;;;;;;;;;;;;;;;;;;;;;;;;;;;;;;;;;;;

(define (p-list in-file)
  (let ((screen-size 22))
    (call-with-input-file in-file
      (lambda (in-port)
        (display "===================================")
        (display " start of file ")
        (display "===================================")
        (let next-char ((char (read-char in-port)) (lcount 1))
          (cond
            ((eof-object? char))       ;;terminate read loop
            ((char=? char #\newline)   ;;must strip newlines
                                       ;;in PC Scheme <= 3.0
             (cond
               ((= lcount screen-size)
                (display "=========================")
                (display "=========================")
                (display " Enter <return> to continue...")
                (read-char)
                (newline)
                (next-char (read-char in-port) 1))
               (else
                 (next-char (read-char in-port) (+ lcount 1)))))
            (else
              (display char)
              (next-char (read-char in-port) lcount))))
        (display "===================================")
        (display " end of file ")
        (display "===================================")))))
```

7.

```
;;;;    f-list.s    ;;;;;;;;;;;;;;;;;;;;;;;;;;;;;;;;;;;;;;;;;;

;;;;;;;;;;;;;;;;;;;;;;;;;;;;;;;;;;;;;;;;;;;;;;;;;;;;;;;;;;;;;;;;
;; SPRINT (Scheme PRINT) prints a file to logical
;; device PRN, which is implementation specific.
;;;;;;;;;;;;;;;;;;;;;;;;;;;;;;;;;;;;;;;;;;;;;;;;;;;;;;;;;;;;;;;;

(define (sprint in-file)
  (let ((line-printer "prn"))          ;;device specific
    (with-input-from-file in-file
      (lambda ()
        (with-output-to-file line-printer
          (lambda ()
            (do ((char (read-char) (read-char)))
                ((eof-object? char))
                (if (char=? char #\newline) ;;strip newline se-
                    (display "")            ;;quences--PC Scheme
                    (display char)))
            (display #\page)))))))          ;;PC Scheme specific
```

8.

```
;;;;    f-list.s    ;;;;;;;;;;;;;;;;;;;;;;;;;;;;;;;;;;;;;;;;;;

;;;;;;;;;;;;;;;;;;;;;;;;;;;;;;;;;;;;;;;;;;;;;;;;;;;;;;;;;
;; FORMFEED sends a formfeed to the printer.
;; PRN is implementation specific.
;;;;;
;; PC Scheme specific:  uses #\page.
;;;;;;;;;;;;;;;;;;;;;;;;;;;;;;;;;;;;;;;;;;;;;;;;;;;;;;;;;

(define (formfeed)
  (let ((line-printer "prn"))        ;;device specific
    (with-output-to-file line-printer
      (lambda ()
        (write-char #\page)))))      ;;PC Scheme specific
```

9.

```
;;;;    strings.s    ;;;;;;;;;;;;;;;;;;;;;;;;;;;;;;;;;;;;;;;;;

;;;;;;;;;;;;;;;;;;;;;;;;;;;;;;;;;;;;;;;;;;;;;;;;;;;;;;;;;;;;;;;;;;
```

```
;; STRING-DOWNCASE returns a string converted to lowercase.
;;;;;;;;;;;;;;;;;;;;;;;;;;;;;;;;;;;;;;;;;;;;;;;;;;;;;;;;;;;;

(define (str-downcase string)
  (let ((upper-str (open-input-string string)))
    (let next-char ((char (read-char upper-str))
                    (lower-str "")
                    (position 0))
      (if (eof-object? char)
          lower-str
          (next-char (read-char upper-str)
                     (string-append lower-str
                                    (make-string
                                      1
                                      (char-downcase char)))
                     (+ position 1))))))
```

10.

```
;;;;    fcopy.s    ;;;;;;;;;;;;;;;;;;;;;;;;;;;;;;;;;;;;;;;;;

;;;;;;;;;;;;;;;;;;;;;;;;;;;;;;;;;;;;;;;;;;;;;;;
;; FCOPY copies files--character by character.
;;;;;;;;;;;;;;;;;;;;;;;;;;;;;;;;;;;;;;;;;;;;;;;

(define (fcopy old-file new-file)
  (with-input-from-file old-file
    (lambda ()
      (with-output-to-file new-file
        (lambda ()
          (do ((char (read-char) (read-char))
              ((eof-object? char))
              (write-char char))))))
  (display (string-append old-file " copied to " new-file)))


;;;;    f-list.s    ;;;;;;;;;;;;;;;;;;;;;;;;;;;;;;;;;;;;;;;;

;;;;;;;;;;;;;;;;;;;;;;;;
;; F-COPY copies files.
;; PC Scheme version.
;;;;;;;;;;;;;;;;;;;;;;;;

(define (f-copy old-file new-file)
  (with-input-from-file old-file
```

```
    (lambda ()
      (with-output-to-file new-file
        (lambda ()
          (do ((char (read-char) (read-char)))
              ((eof-object? char))
              (if (char=? char #\newline) ;;strip newline se-
                  (write-char "")         ;;quences--PC Scheme
                  (write-char char))))))))
```

Chapter 11

1.

```
;;;;    strings.s    ;;;;;;;;;;;;;;;;;;;;;;;;;;;;;;;;;;;;;;;;;;;;;;

;;;;;;;;;;;;;;;;;;;;;;;;;;;;;;;;;;;;;;;;;;;;;;;;;;;;;;;;;;
;; MAKE-STR builds a string of n characters.  Its call
;; syntax is
;;
;; (make-str <n> [<char>])
;;
;; If no <char> is specified, #\space is used.
;;;;;;;;;;;;;;;;;;;;;;;;;;;;;;;;;;;;;;;;;;;;;;;;;;;;;;;;;;;

(define make-str
  (lambda (len . char)
    (let ((char (if (null? char)
                    #\space
                    (car char))))
      (make-string len char))))
```

2.

```
;;;;    strings.s    ;;;;;;;;;;;;;;;;;;;;;;;;;;;;;;;;;;;;;;;;;;;;;;

;;;;;;;;;;;;;;;;;;;;;;;;;;;;;;;;;;;;;;;;;;;;;;;;;;;;;;;;;;
;; SUBSTRG returns a substring of a string using the
;; following (zero-based) call syntax:
;;
;; (substrg <string> <start-pos> [<end-pos>])
;;
;; If called without the third argument, the rest
;; of the string is returned.
```

```
;;;;;;;;;;;;;;;;;;;;;;;;;;;;;;;;;;;;;;;;;;;;;;;;;;;;;;;;;;;;;;

(define substrg
  (lambda (str start-pos . end-pos)
    (let ((end-pos (if (null? end-pos)
                       (string-length str)
                       (+ (car end-pos) 1))))
      (substring str start-pos end-pos))))
```

8.

```
;;;;    read-ln.s      ;;;;;;;;;;;;;;;;;;;;;;;;;;;;;;;;;;;;;;;;

;;;;;;;;;;;;;;;;;;;;;;;;;;;;;;;;;;;;;;;;;;;;;;;;;;;;;;;;;;;;;;
;; READ-LN reads a line of input from the keyboard.
;; A port may be specified, but is optional.  This
;; routine may need considerable modification for
;; your Scheme system.
;;
;; Usage:  (read-ln [<port>])
;; Returns:  a string containing the typed input
;; PC Scheme:  Cntl-<bs> erases the entire line.
;;;;;;;;;;;;;;;;;;;;;;;;;;;;;;;;;;;;;;;;;;;;;;;;;;;;;;;;;;;;;;

(define (read-ln . in-port)
  (let ((port (if (null? in-port)
                  (current-input-port) ;default here
                  (car in-port)))
        (backspace #\backspace)        ;system dependent
        (line-reset-char #\rubout)     ;system dependent
        (end-of-line-char #\return))   ;system dependent

    (let next-char ((in-char (read-char port))
                    (input-string ""))
      (cond
        ((char=? in-char end-of-line-char)
         input-string)
        ((char=? in-char line-reset-char)
         (if (output-port? port)
             (do ((i (string-length input-string) (- i 1)))
                 ((zero? i))
                 (display backspace)))
         (next-char (read-char port) ""))
        ((char=? in-char backspace)
         (if (output-port? port)
```

```
              (display backspace))
          (cond
            ((zero? (string-length input-string))
             (next-char (read-char port) input-string))
            (else
              (next-char
                (read-char port)
                (substring input-string
                           0
                           (- (string-length input-string)
                              1))))))
        (else
          (if (output-port? port)
              (display in-char port))
          (next-char
            (read-char port)
            (string-append input-string
                           (make-string 1 in-char))))))))
```

11.

```
;;;;     calc-win.s      ;;;;;;;;;;;;;;;;;;;;;;;;;;;;;;;;;;;;;;;;;;;

;;;;;;;;;;;;;;;;;;;;;;;;;;;;;;;;;;;;;;;;;;;;;;;;;;;;;;;;;;;;;;;;;;;;
;; CALC performs simple, four-function calculations.
;; This version does windows.  If the first operand
;; is missing, the previous result is used.  E.g.,
;; ===> 3 * 5
;; ===> 15
;; ===> + 3
;; ===> 18              [A null line terminates CALC.]
;;
;; CALC uses the library module:  str-int.s
;;;;;;;;;;;;;;;;;;;;;;;;;;;;;;;;;;;;;;;;;;;;;;;;;;;;;;;;;;;;;;;;;;;;

;; window definitions -- PC Scheme ;;;;;;;;;;;;;;;;
;;
(define logo (make-window "" #t))                   ;;
(define input (make-window " expression " #t))      ;;
(define output (make-window " evaluation " #t))     ;;
;;
;;;;;;;;;;;;;;;;;;;;;;;;;;;;;;;;;;;;;;;;;;;;;;;;;;;;;;;;;;;;;;;;;

(define (calc)
  (window-clear 'console)          ;clear the background first
```

```
  (set-up-window logo 1 1 3 40)
  (set-up-window input 7 1 15 40)
  (set-up-window output 7 46 1 32)
  (initial-logo)
  (newline input)
  (display "===> " input)

  (let calc-loop ((op-list (parse-input)) (result 1))
    (cond
      ((null? (car op-list))
       (window-delete input)
       (window-delete output)
       (window-delete logo)
       (window-clear 'console)
       (display "END CALC"))
      (else
        (window-clear output)
        (display (eval-string-list op-list result) output)
        (newline input)
        (display "===> " input)
        (calc-loop (parse-input)
                   (eval-string-list op-list result))))))


(define (set-up-window
          window start-row start-col no-rows no-cols)
  (window-set-position! window start-row start-col)
  (window-set-size! window no-rows no-cols)
  (window-clear window))

(define (initial-logo)
  (display "    CALC -- FOUR FUNCTION CALCULATOR" logo)
  (newline logo) (newline logo)
  (display "[Enter a null line to terminate program]" logo))

 ...
 ...

 [PARSE-INPUT, etc., same as with previous version of CALC]
 ...

;;;;;;;;;;;;;;;;;;;;;;;;;;;;;;;;;;;;;;;;;;;;;;;;;;;;;;;;;;
;; READ-LN reads a line of input from the keyboard.
;; A window may be specified, but is optional.
;; Usage:  (read-ln [<window>])
;; Returns:  a string containing the typed input
```

```
;; PC Scheme:  Cntl-<bs> erases the entire line.
;;             Uses PC Scheme windowing functions.
;;;;;;;;;;;;;;;;;;;;;;;;;;;;;;;;;;;;;;;;;;;;;;;;;;;;;;

(define (read-ln . wind-oh)
  (let ((window (if (null? wind-oh)
                    'console             ;console is default
                    (car wind-oh)))
        (backspace #\backspace)          ;system dependent
        (line-reset-char #\rubout)       ;system dependent
        (end-of-line-char #\return))     ;system dependent

    (let next-char ((in-char (read-char window))
                    (input-string ""))
      (cond
        ((char=? in-char end-of-line-char)
         input-string)
        ((char=? in-char line-reset-char)
         (do ((i (string-length input-string) (- i 1)))
             ((zero? i))
             (display backspace window))
         (next-char (read-char window) ""))
        ((char=? in-char backspace)
         (display backspace window)
         (cond
           ((zero? (string-length input-string))
            (next-char (read-char window) input-string))
           (else
             (next-char
               (read-char window)
               (substring input-string
                          0
                          (- (string-length input-string)
                             1))))))
        (else
          (display in-char window)
          (next-char
            (read-char window)
            (string-append input-string
                           (make-string 1 in-char))))))))
```

Chapter 12

1.

```
;;;;    map.s    ;;;;;;;;;;;;;;;;;;;;;;;;;;;;;;;;;;;;;;;;;;;

;;;;;;;;;;;;;;;;;;;;;;;;;;;;;;;;;;;;;;;;;;;;;;;;;;;;;
;; FOR-EACH-2 implements a version of for-each that
;; only allows two parameters:
;;
;; (for-each-2 <proc> <lst>)
;;;;;;;;;;;;;;;;;;;;;;;;;;;;;;;;;;;;;;;;;;;;;;;;;;;;;

(define (for-each-2 function lst)
  (let next-element ((element-list lst))
    (cond
      ((null? element-list)
       '())
      (else
        (function (car element-list))
        (next-element (cdr element-list))))))
```

4.

```
;;;;    sums.s    ;;;;;;;;;;;;;;;;;;;;;;;;;;;;;;;;;;;;;;;;;;

;;;;;;;;;;;;;;;;;;;;;;;;;;;;;;;;;;;;;;;;;;;;;;;;;;;;;;;;;;;;
;; SUMMATION sums values over an interval, after applying
;; a formula to each integer in the interval.  The default
;; formula is f(x) = x^2.
;;;;;;;;;;;;;;;;;;;;;;;;;;;;;;;;;;;;;;;;;;;;;;;;;;;;;;;;;;;;

(define summation (lambda lst
  (let* ((list-len (length lst))
         (formula (if (= list-len 2)
                      (lambda (x) (* x x))  ;; default
                      (list-ref lst 0)))
         (start (if (= list-len 2)
                    (list-ref lst 0)
                    (list-ref lst 1)))
         (stop (if (= list-len 2)
                   (list-ref lst 1)
                   (list-ref lst 2))))
  (do ((i start (+ i 1))
```

```
        (sum 0 (+ (formula i) sum)))
       ((> i stop) sum)))))
```

6.

```
;;;;    fact.s    ;;;;;;;;;;;;;;;;;;;;;;;;;;;;;;;;;;;;;;;;;;;;;;

;;;;;;;;;;;;;;;;;;;;;;;;;;;;;;;;;;;;;;;;;;;;
;; FACT is a tail recursive version of the
;; factorial function.
;;;;;;;;;;;;;;;;;;;;;;;;;;;;;;;;;;;;;;;;;;;;

(define (fact n)
  (let ((tr-fact (lambda (result n)          ;; define a helper
                   (if (zero? n)             ;; function
                       result
                       (tr-fact (* result n) (- n 1))))))

    (tr-fact 1 n)))                          ;; invoke the helper
```

Chapter 13

1. d.

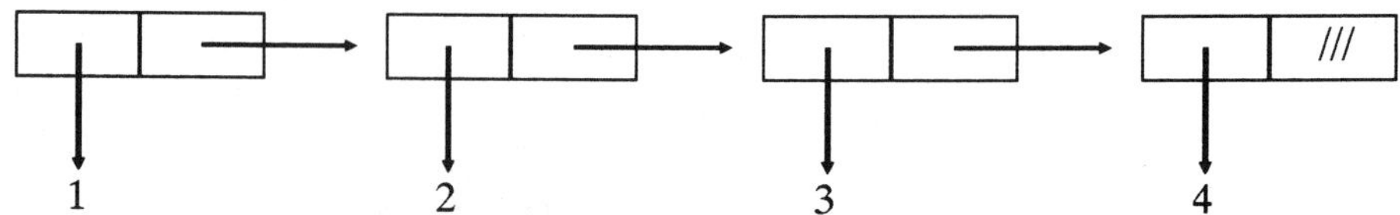

Chapter 14

5. Advantages: Vectors provide direct (indexed) access to elements. Direct access capabilities facilitate the use of standard computer science storage and retrieval techniques, e.g., hashing. Theoretically, vector processing should be more efficient than list processing when the number of elements is large and when a small percentage of the elements is accessed. Whether or not vector processing is more efficient than list processing depends on the implementation.

Disadvantages: The main disadvantage of vectors in comparison to lists is that there are fewer vector processing functions. For example, with vectors there is no analog to car-cdr recursion as there is with lists. In a sense this isn't a disadvantage; vectors are simply a more specialized data structure, i.e., used for specific purposes, whereas the list is the basic data structure in Scheme. Another characteristic of vectors, possibly a disadvantage, is that vectors are fixed length, whereas lists can be any length initially and subsequently expanded to handle additional elements. Of course, the fixed length nature of vectors facilitates indexed processing.

6. No. There is no equivalent of **cdr** for vector processing.

8.

```
;;;;     bubble.s     ;;;;;;;;;;;;;;;;;;;;;;;;;;;;;;;;;;;;;;;;

;;;;;;;;;;;;;;;;;;;;;;;;;;;;;;;;;;;;;;;;;;;;;;;;;;;;;;;;;;
;; BUBBLE! sorts a vector of numbers using a bubble
;; sorting technique, where the sorting process
;; is terminated after the first cycle for which no
;; exchange is required.  The sorting is done destruc-
;; tively.
;;;;;;;;;;;;;;;;;;;;;;;;;;;;;;;;;;;;;;;;;;;;;;;;;;;;;;;;;;

(define (bubble! vec)
  (let ((temp ())
        (last-pos (- (vector-length vec) 1)))
    (do ((i 0 (+ i 1))
         (no-element-exchange? #f))
        ((or no-element-exchange?
             (= i last-pos)) vec)
        (display i) (newline)
        (do ((j 0 (+ j 1)))
            ((= j (- last-pos i)) "")    ;nothing to return
            (set! no-element-exchange? #t)
            (if (> (vector-ref vec j) (vector-ref vec (+ j 1)))
                (begin
                  (set! no-element-exchange? #f)
                  (set! temp (vector-ref vec j))
                  (vector-set! vec j (vector-ref vec (+ j 1)))
                  (vector-set! vec (+ j 1) temp)))))))
```

Chapter 15

3. In theory, macros (a macro call) should be used anywhere the programmer expects there to be very frequent requests to perform some function, since the substitution of macro code for the macro call results in executable code containing in-line code instead of a function call; i.e., executing the macro code is more efficient than passing values to a function, due to overhead associated with a function call.

Also, macros offer an advantage in situations where the programmer doesn't want arguments to be evaluated until after they are passed to the macro code. For example, a macro implementation allows the user to enter

```
(dog-attr size newfoundland)
```

whereas a function implementation requires quoting of the symbol **size**:

```
(dog-char 'size newfoundland)
```

4. b.

```
;;;;    macros.s    ;;;;;;;;;;;;;;;;;;;;;;;;;;;;;;;;;;;;;;;;;;;;

;;;;;;;;;;;;;;;;;;;;;;;;;;;;;;;;;;;;;;;;;;;;;;;;;;;;;;;;;;;;;;;;
;; RECIPROCAL is a macro for taking the reciprocal
;; of a number.
;;;;;;;;;;;;;;;;;;;;;;;;;;;;;;;;;;;;;;;;;;;;;;;;;;;;;;;;;;;;;;;;

(macro reciprocal
  (lambda (exp)
    '(if (number? ,(cadr exp))
         (if (not (= ,(cadr exp) 0))
             (/ 1 ,(cadr exp))))))
```

5. a.

```
;;;;    macros.s    ;;;;;;;;;;;;;;;;;;;;;;;;;;;;;;;;;;;;;;;;;;;;

;;;;;;;;;;;;;;;;;;;;;;;;;;;;;;;;;;;;;;;;;;;;;;;;;;;;;;;;;;;;;;;;;;;;;
;; STRING-INDEX searches for a char. in a string, returning
;; its position -- zero-based.  STRING-INDEX is implemented
;; PC Scheme macros.
;; Example usage:  (string-index "string" #\i) ==> 3
;;;;;;;;;;;;;;;;;;;;;;;;;;;;;;;;;;;;;;;;;;;;;;;;;;;;;;;;;;;;;;;;;;;;;

(macro string-index
  (lambda (exp)
    '(let find-it ((str ,(cadr exp)) (pos 0))
       (cond
         ((= pos (string-length str))      ;; not found
          ())                              ;; return empty list
         ((char=? (string-ref str pos) ,(caddr exp))
```

```
          pos)
         (else
           (find-it str (+ pos 1)))))))
```

Chapter 16

2.

```
;;;;    list-sum.s    ;;;;;;;;;;;;;;;;;;;;;;;;;;;;;;;;;;;;;;;

;;;;;;;;;;;;;;;;;;;;;;;;;;;;;;;;;;;;;;;;;;;;;;;;;;;;;;;;;;;;;;
;; LIST-SUM sums the elements of a list.  It uses car-cdr
;; recursion to process sublists.  A named let is used.
;; The evaluation is terminated if an element is not numeric.
;;;;;;;;;;;;;;;;;;;;;;;;;;;;;;;;;;;;;;;;;;;;;;;;;;;;;;;;;;;;;;

(define (list-sum lst)
  (call/cc (lambda (exit)
    (let sum-loop ((lst lst))
      (cond
        ((null? lst)
         0)
        ((pair? (car lst))
         (+ (sum-loop (car lst)) (sum-loop (cdr lst))))
        ((not (number? (car lst)))
         (exit #f))
        (else
          (+ (car lst) (sum-loop (cdr lst)))))))))
```

6.

```
;;;;    autold-2.s    ;;;;;;;;;;;;;;;;;;;;;;;;;;;;;;;;;;;;;;;

;;;;;;;;;;;;;;;;;;;;;;;;;;;;;;;;;;;;;;;;;;;;;;;;;;;;;;;;;;;;
;; A simple illustration of the use of delay and force
;; to implement lazy evaluation and "memorizing."
;;;;;;
;; PARTITION-1 is a memory partition in a virtual machine
;; implemented as a Scheme vector.
;;;;;;;;;;;;;;;;;;;;;;;;;;;;;;;;;;;;;;;;;;;;;;;;;;;;;;;;;;;;

(define partition-1                             ;; initially,
  (delay (set! partition-1 (make-vector 10))))  ;; a promise
```

```
(define autoload
  (lambda (id)
    (if (delayed-object? (eval id)) ;; reincarnate as varia-
        (eval (force (eval id)))    ;; ble before returning it
        (eval id))))                ;; just return it
```

7.

```
;;;;    stream.s    ;;;;;;;;;;;;;;;;;;;;;;;;;;;;;;;;;;;;;;;;;;

;;;;;;;;;;;;;;;;;;;;;;;;;;;;;;;;;;;;;;;;;;;;;;;;;;;;;;;;;
;; ONE-TO-N uses a stream data structure to produce
;; the integers from 1..n.
;;;;;;;;;;;;;;;;;;;;;;;;;;;;;;;;;;;;;;;;;;;;;;;;;;;;;;;;;

(define one-to-n
  (lambda (n)
    (let print-loop ((stream positive-integer-stream))
      (cond
        ((> (head stream) n) (display #\newline))
        (else
          (display (head stream))
          (newline)
          (print-loop (tail stream)))))))
```

Chapter 17

1.

```
;;;;    bubble.s    ;;;;;;;;;;;;;;;;;;;;;;;;;;;;;;;;;;;;;;;;;;

;;;;;;;;;;;;;;;;;;;;;;;;;;;;;;;;;;;;;;;;;;;;;;;;;;;;;;;;;;;;
;; G-BUBBLE! sorts a vector using a primitive
;; bubble sorting technique, i.e., it always performs
;; every cycle.  The sorting is done destructively.
;; The ordering predicate is passed as the second
;; argument:
;;
;; (g-bubble! <vector> <ordering-predicate>)
;;;;;;;;;;;;;;;;;;;;;;;;;;;;;;;;;;;;;;;;;;;;;;;;;;;;;;;;;;;;

(define (g-bubble! vec proper-order?)
```

```
(let ((temp ())
      (last-pos (- (vector-length vec) 1)))
  (do ((i 0 (+ i 1)))
      ((= i last-pos) vec)
      (do ((j 0 (+ j 1)))
          ((= j (- last-pos i)) "")   ;nothing to return
          (if (not (proper-order? (vector-ref vec j)
                                  (vector-ref vec (+ j 1))))
              (begin
                (set! temp (vector-ref vec j))
                (vector-set! vec j (vector-ref vec (+ j 1)))
                (vector-set! vec (+ j 1) temp))))))
```

References

Abelson, H., Sussman, G.J., with Sussman, J. *Structure and Interpretation of Computer Programs*. Cambridge, Ma.: MIT Press, 1985.

Aho, A. V., Sethi, R., & Ullman, J. D. *Compilers: Principles, Techniques, and Tools*. Reading, Ma.: Addison-Wesley, 1986.

Augenstein, M. J., & Tenenbaum, A. M. *Data Structures and PL/I Programming*. Englewood Cliffs, N.J.: Prentice-Hall, 1979.

Beck, L. *Systems Software: An Introduction to Systems Programming*. Reading, Ma.: Addison-Wesley, 1985.

Bobrow, D. G., & Stefik, M. J. *The LOOPS Manual*. Palo Alto, Ca.: Xerox Corporation, 1983.

Chen, P. P. S. The Entity-Relationship Model—Toward a Unified View of Data. *ACM Transactions on Database Systems*, 1 (1986), 9-36.

Dale N., & Lilly, S. C. *Pascal Plus Data Structures, Algorithms, and Advanced Programming*. Lexington, Ma.: D. C. Heath and Company, 1985.

Date, C. J. *An Introduction to Database Systems—Volume I*. Reading, Ma.: Addison-Wesley, 1986.

Dybvig, R. K. *The Scheme Programming Language*. Englewood Cliffs, N.J.: Prentice-Hall, 1987.

Goldberg, A., & Robson, D. *Smalltalk-80: The Language and Its Implementation*. Reading, Ma.: Addison-Wesley, 1983.

International Standards Organization. *Specification for the Computer Programming Language Pascal*. May, 1980.

Korth, H. F., & Silberschatz, A. *Database System Concepts*. New York: McGraw-Hill, 1986.

Rees, J. E., & Clinger W. Revised^3 Report on the Algorithmic Language Scheme. *SIGPLAN Notices*, 21, 12 (1986), 37-79.

Smith, J. D., & Smith, J. C. *File Processing with Pascal*. St. Paul, Mn.: West Publishing Company, 1988.

Smith, P. D., & Barnes, G. M. *Files and Databases: An Introduction*. Reading, Ma.: Addison-Wesley, 1987.

Starkweather, J. *A User's Guide to PILOT*. Englewood Cliffs, N.J.: Prentice-Hall, 1984.

Steele, G. L., Jr. *Common LISP Reference Manual*. Bedford, Ma.: Digital Press, 1984.

Steele, G. L., Jr., & Sussman, G. J. The Revised Report on the Algorithmic Language Scheme. *MIT Artificial Intelligence Memo*, 452, 1 (1978).

Sussman, G. J., & Steele, G. L., Jr. Scheme: An Interpreter for Extended Lambda Calculus. *MIT Artificial Intelligence Memo*, 349, 12 (1975).

Taylor, D. Interpreter Design and Construction, Part I. *Computer Language*, 3, 7 (1986), 31-37.

Taylor, D. Interpreter Design and Construction, Part II. *Computer Language*, 3, 9 (1986), 57-66.

Texas Instruments. *PC Scheme: A Simple, Modern LISP*. Austin, Tx.: Texas Instruments, Inc., 1987.

Texas Instruments. *TI Scheme Language Reference Manual*. Austin, Tx.: Texas Instruments, Inc., 1987.

Weinreb, D., Moon, D., & Stallman, R. *LISP Machine Manual*. Cambridge, Ma.: MIT, 1983.

Index

U

V

W